CW01249606

Shakespeare and Emotional Expression

Shakespeare and Emotional Expression offers an exciting new way of considering emotional transactions in Shakespearean drama. The book is significant in its scope and originality as it uses the innovative medium of colour terms and references to interrogate the early modern emotional register. By examining contextual and cultural influences, this work explores the impact these influences have on the relationship between colour and emotion and argues for the importance of considering chromatic references as a means to uncover emotional significances.

Using a broad range of documents, it offers a wider understanding of affective expression in the early modern period through a detailed examination of several dramatic works. Although colour meanings fluctuate, by paying particular attention to contextual clues and the historically specific cultural situations of Shakespeare's plays, this book uncovers emotional significances that are not always apparent to modern audiences and readers. Through its examination of the nexus between the history of emotions and the social and cultural uses of colour in early modern drama, *Shakespeare and Emotional Expression* adds to our understanding of the expressive and affective possibilities in Shakespearean drama.

Bríd Phillips is a senior lecturer at Edith Cowan University, Australia. She has a PhD in Shakespearean Studies and her research has been supported by the Australian Research Council, Centre of Excellence for The History of Emotions. Recent publications include *Hamlet and Emotions*, edited with Paul Megna and Robert White (2019) and '"Devils Will the Blackest Sins Put On": The Emotional Register of Colour' in *Matters of Engagement: Emotions, Identity, and Cultural Contact in the Premodern World* (2020).

Routledge Studies in Shakespeare

Shakespeare and Civil Unrest in Britain and the United States
Edited by Mark Bayer and Joseph Navitsky

Shakespeare's Military Spouses and Twenty-First Century Warfare
Kelsey Ridge

Dramaturgies of Love in *Romeo and Juliet*
Word, Music, and Dance
Jonas Kellermann

The Shakespeare Multiverse
Fandom as Literary Praxis
Valerie M. Fazel and Louise Geddes

Shakespeare's Returning Warriors – and Ours
Alan Warren Friedman

Shakespeare's Influence on Karl Marx
The Shakespearean Roots of Marxism
Christian A. Smith

Shakespeare and Happiness
Kathleen French

Shakespeare and Emotional Expression
Finding Feeling through Colour
Bríd Phillips

Aemilia Lanyer as Shakespeare's Co-Author
Mark Bradbeer

For more information about this series, please visit: https://www.routledge.com/Routledge-Studies-in-Shakespeare/book-series/RSS

Shakespeare and Emotional Expression
Finding Feeling through Colour

Bríd Phillips

Routledge
Taylor & Francis Group
NEW YORK AND LONDON

First published 2022
by Routledge
605 Third Avenue, New York, NY 10158

and by Routledge
4 Park Square, Milton Park, Abingdon, Oxon, OX14 4RN

Routledge is an imprint of the Taylor & Francis Group, an informa business

© 2022 Bríd Phillips

The right of Bríd Phillips to be identified as author of this work has been asserted in accordance with sections 77 and 78 of the Copyright, Designs and Patents Act 1988.

All rights reserved. No part of this book may be reprinted or reproduced or utilised in any form or by any electronic, mechanical, or other means, now known or hereafter invented, including photocopying and recording, or in any information storage or retrieval system, without permission in writing from the publishers.

Trademark notice: Product or corporate names may be trademarks or registered trademarks, and are used only for identification and explanation without intent to infringe.

Library of Congress Cataloging-in-Publication Data
A catalog record for this title has been requested

ISBN: 978-1-032-05592-3 (hbk)
ISBN: 978-1-032-05595-4 (pbk)
ISBN: 978-1-003-19824-6 (ebk)

DOI: 10.4324/9781003198246

Typeset in Sabon
by codeMantra

Printed in the United Kingdom
by Henry Ling Limited

Contents

	Acknowledgements	vii
	Introduction: The expression of emotion through systems of colour: Uncovering ways of feeling	1
1	'And weep to hear him speak': Colour, emotion, and rhetoric in *Titus Andronicus*	17
2	'For blushing cheeks by faults are bred / And fears by pale white shown': Reading the face for colour and emotion in *Love's Labour's Lost*	45
3	'There's something in his soul / O'er which his melancholy sits on brood': Senses, science, and the imagination	79
4	'Not black in my mind, though yellow in my legs': Bodies, clothes, colour, and passions in *Twelfth Night*	109
5	'O well-painted passion': Cultural commonplaces of colour and affective patterns in *Othello*	139
	Afterword	169
	Index	173

Acknowledgements

First of all, I would like to thank Andrew Lynch and Bob White for their careful and supportive advice on my research journey. I would also like to thank Makoto Harris Takao, Ciara Rawnsley, and Theresa Miller (as an honorary office member), for the shared office support where advice and encouragement were in abundant supply. I am also very grateful to Liam Semler, Indira Ghose, and Tanya Pollard for their careful and trenchant feedback on the original work leading to this volume. For their excellent mentorship, I would like to thank Susan Broomhall, Kathryn Prince, Katrina O'Loughlin, and Penelope Woods. To everyone at the Australian Research Council Centre of Excellence for the History of Emotions, many thanks for the rich experiences and intellectual stimulation. I would also like to thank the staff at the Queen Mary Centre for the History of the Emotions, London and especially Thomas Dixon for supporting me with a Visiting PhD Scholarship.

As the project took shape, the advice and unflagging support of Bob White was invaluable and motivated me to continue with the work. Thanks also to Michelle Salyga and Bryony Reece at Routledge who supported the project through to publication. The anonymous reviewers were generous and constructive in their feedback and I thank them for their comments. In the latter stages of the project, I would like to thank everyone in the School of Allied Health, The University of Western Australia who has encouraged and supported me along the way. For their academic faith in the project, I would like to thank Tanya Dalziell, Catherine Noske, and the ever generous Claire Hansen. To Kirsty Freeman, a huge thanks for the motivational words, the belief that it could be done, and the academic collegiality. To Chris Letheby, who joined me at weekly writing sessions and kept me on track, my thanks.

To Liz and Ed Willis for the belief, the hospitality, and the holidays. To Kate Phillips for the immense task of formatting which was done with a keen eye and a careful pen. However, if there are any remaining errors it will be because I changed things after her hard work! Finally but definitely in the most heartfelt way possible, I want to thank Gareth, Lizzy, Kate, and Emma who made all things possible. This book is dedicated to them.

Introduction
The expression of emotion through systems of colour: Uncovering ways of feeling

While references to colour in his plays may not have been at the forefront of Shakespeare's mind when writing, and are certainly not an exclusive consideration in understanding the plays, close analysis reveals they are in fact remarkably coherent as a register of sometimes specific, sometimes fluctuating emotional states represented in the plays. For example, in *The Merchant of Venice*, Portia is witness to Bassanio's missive from Antonio, delivering the news that Antonio has lost the ability to pay back his loan to Shylock. Bassanio's reaction is discernable through the colouration of his face:

> There are some shrewd contents in yon same paper,
> That steals the colour from Bassanio's cheek:
> Some dear friend dead; else nothing in the world
> Could turn so much the constitution
> Of any constant man.
>
> (3.2.242–6)

Portia, alerted by the changing hue of Bassiano's face, immediately supposes that the overriding emotion caused by the news is akin to mortal grief. Such is the power of colour as an indicator of feelings, genuine or otherwise. However, these significations are complex, mutable and culturally contextual. Nevertheless, colour references provide visual support when interpreting affective patterns. Some colour significances are drawn from Galenic humoral theory, others from proverbial lore, and still others from a lexicon of received moral distinctions and paradoxes. But all are firmly situated in the context and paradigms of thought current in the early modern period.

Already in this era, through the medium of fine art, colour had an emotive imperative. The art of painting was naturally presumed to incorporate seeing, imagining, and feeling; a coherence which is reflected in the words and visual cues represented in the theatre. Colour references contribute strongly to the revelation of emotion in Shakespeare's works and incidentally to ways of feeling in the early modern period. In this book, I examine how colour terms and images help to facilitate, generate, and disseminate emotional expression in Shakespeare's works. My approach to the topic is predicated on reading Shakespeare in the context of belief structures current in the early modern period. In particular, I investigate relationships between emotion and colour in his plays with reference to contemporary ideologies of rhetorical teaching; physiognomy and the face; humoral theory; the body and its material coverings; and cultural commonplaces. My exploration of these relationships allows a lively and dynamic reassessment of emotional expression in the dramatic texts of Shakespeare. I build a coherent picture of how colour functions as a vehicle for affective exchange. The intellectual, social, and cultural field in which Shakespeare operated has a significant impact on the perceptions and shared experiences that moulded both the theatre audience and the reactions of private readers.[1] Within this paradigm, to frame a methodology for examining the emotional provocation and responses provided by colour, I explore multiple intellectual frameworks and strategies that both attend to and disrupt ways of feeling. Early modern drama provides a fertile ground for my investigations, since plays themselves were considered as vehicles for eliciting emotional responses, a phenomenon understood and used by Shakespeare himself. In *Hamlet*, for example, the titular character plots to use the dramatisation of *The Mousetrap* to provoke a guilty reaction in his uncle Claudius (2.2523–33).

Discussing the subject of cultural histories and the History of Emotions, Sarah McNamer observes '[t]hat emotions have histories – varying in structure from one culture, community, or period to the next and serving diverse social functions – is one of the chief insights of contemporary and interdisciplinary scholarship' (2010, 3). McNamer's insistence on the cultural specificity and context of emotions informs such questions as: how and to what effect does Shakespeare use colour as an emotive in the expression of passions in his drama? How do education, medical teachings, and cultural norms influence the use of colour in emotional expression? Do cumulative colour patterns create dramatic tension and, specifically, emotional tension? And, most importantly, how do these ideas culminate in new ways of uncovering early modern emotions? These questions can be fruitfully explored in dramatic works because theatre is a liminal space where the ideas and expressions of emotion are displayed and examined without the censure that public displays of emotion might ordinarily receive. This attention to colour as an emotion vector develops a richer understanding of emotional transactions within the plays.

Uncovering emotions: current methodologies

Although I am situating my examination of Shakespearean emotions within an early modern contextual framework, this does not give rise to an automatic stability of meaning. This instability means that interpretation is fraught and malleable. For example, in the matter of facial colouring, pallor may connote love in some instances, and red colouring scorn and disdain in others

> If you will see a pageant truly play'd
> Between the pale complexion of true love
> And the red glow of scorn and proud disdain
> (*As You Like It*, 3.4.48–50)

Whilst on other occasions, it is anger that can be divined in a pale complexion while the blushing face indicates a fall from grace

> The colour in thy face,
> That even for anger makes the lily pale,
> And the red rose blush at her own disgrace
> (*The Rape of Lucrece*, 477–9)

A text can generate several meanings, not because the readers of the text are conflicted but because they have individuated their response to the text according to the social, cultural, and personal pressures under which they are reading it. Susan Matt suggests that 'even within a single society, at a given moment, the meaning of those words and the feelings they describe may be understood differently by different individuals' (2014, 44). The problem raised by Matt is not insignificant prompting me to pay close attention to the broader cultural context in which moments of emotional experience occur. I take the view that emotion words themselves formed part of this context for viewers and readers, in a climate where it was thought that both plays and colours could readily influence the mind. I acknowledge that in my work the terms 'emotion', 'feelings', 'passions', and 'affect' are very slippery words, and do not always stand up to rigorous scrutiny.[2] I am, however, employing 'emotion' after Barbara Rosenwein, to mean 'a constructed term that refers to affective reactions of all sorts, intensities, and durations' (2006, 4). Lyn Enterline also provides a rationale for using the term 'emotion', stating 'I try to use our own modern and familiar term, *emotion*, to designate a commonsense understanding of personal feeling, one that often presumes emotions to be (relatively) transparent indicators for interior states' (2012, 27). My aim is to uncover instances of emotional transactions. Without disregarding the work that is being undertaken to define terminology concerning these instances, my research concentrates on individual moments of emotional exchange dependent on cultural context.

When considering colour words in light of the emotional transactions they support, it is helpful to turn to the work of William Reddy. Although his discussion of 'emotional "regimes"' is more suited to political and

4 *Expression of emotion*

historical analysis, his conception of 'emotive' is apt for literary analysis of colour terms as it regards words themselves as an important part of the transaction. 'Emotives', which often take the form of words, are 'an external means of influencing activated thought material that often enhances the effectiveness of internal strategies of mental control' (Reddy 2001, 322). In this context Reddy notes that a 'number of researchers have remarked on the powerful effects which emotional utterances can have on emotions', an observation which I find relevant to the emotional power of colour words in dramatic texts (103). Emotives are a special category of words which not only describe but produce feelings. The term 'emotive', as employed by Reddy, is a valuable tool when considering colour, because, in his words, 'emotives are influenced directly by, and alter, what they "refer" to' (105). Within a fluctuating emotional register, colour terms can be seen as altering, augmenting influences. Reddy also insists that, unlike other expressions of emotion, emotives are both managerial and exploratory, and, like McNamer and Matt, he argues for the importance of context when considering the utterance of emotives. The contextual vector is an important part of my research as it allows us to have a clearer understanding of the work that early modern emotives, such as colour terms, are doing in their contemporary setting. Contextual understanding uncovers a wealth of hitherto hidden emotional transactions.

Barbara Rosenwein offers a structure that can help understand the instability of meaning in past emotional lives. She proposes that people can exist in different 'emotional communities', and move between them, having the ability to adjust their emotional displays depending on which environment they find themselves in (2002, 842). Her conclusion is valuable when considering colour, since the significance of colour terms is fluid depending on the community that engages with them. Given that each emotion word has multiple meanings, I contend that extracting an isolated emotion, for example, a pure form of 'fear' or 'love' is impossible. A person may feel fear and also be conflicted by other emotions such as love, shame, or excitement. With this in mind, in my analysis of Shakespeare's plays, I point to likely emotional instances rather than reified absolutes. Rosenwein argues that finding an emotion word is just the beginning, and that it should be examined in conjunction with its frequency of use, its context, its gendered use, and how it is expressed (forcefully, gently, with somatic accompaniments such as blushing) (Plamper 2010, 254). This advice is applied to the question of colour and emotion in drama, since the context of the colour word is accessible. Analysing the circumstances, the speaker, and the cultural moment of the utterance helps to determine if the colour term adds emotional depth or difference.

An understanding of the cultural and social context can be structured in terms of the theoretical *habitus* expounded by Pierre Bourdieu. Bourdieu believes the idea of *habitus* is essential to understanding the social and emotional functioning of individuals and communities. The *habitus* presupposes that emotions do not occur in isolation and are, in fact, shaped by the social and cultural structures which are themselves shaped over time as an unconscious feature of the lived life. The individual, even in personal moments of introspection, is subject to the features of the *habitus* that he or she occupies which resonates with Rosenwein's thinking on emotional communities. Bourdieu describes *habitus* as

> [t]he product of the work of inculcation and appropriation necessary in order for those products of collective history, the objective structures (e.g. of language, economy, etc.) to succeed in reproducing themselves more or less completely, in the form of durable dispositions, in the organisms (which one can, if one wishes, call individuals) lastingly subjected to the same conditionings, and hence placed in the same materials of existence.
>
> (1977, 84)

The *habitus*, therefore, is a dynamic and evolving state which allows personal agency to insert itself and have an impact on the trajectory of the *habitus*, both synchronically and diachronically. The *habitus* supports the use of colour terms to both indicate and disrupt emotional transactions.

The Bourdieuian *habitus* becomes a model of analytic practice for considering the embodiment and expression of emotions through the work of Monique Scheer. Scheer suggests that

> [s]ince the *habitus* does not dictate the exact course of action in practice but rather provides a 'feel' for appropriate movements, gestures, facial expressions, pitch of voice, and so on, it leaves space for behaviors not entirely or always predictable, which can also instantiate change and resistance rather than preprogrammed reproduction.
>
> (2012, 204)

In Scheer's model, emotions emerge from bodily knowledge, since the practice of emotions is equally dependent on the body and the mind in a non-Cartesian approach. She explains how her framework can be applied to historical research by saying

> [a]ccess to emotion-as-practice – the bodily act of experience and expression – in historical sources or ethnographic work is achieved through and in connection with other doings and sayings on which emotion-as-practice is dependent and intertwined such as speaking, gesturing, remembering, manipulating objects, and perceiving sounds, smells, and spaces.
>
> (2012, 209)

6 *Expression of emotion*

Her four categories of investigation and research – mobilising, naming, communicating, and regulating – allow us to explore source material without relying on assumptions, and provoke us to 'think [...] harder about what people are *doing*, and to work [...] out the specific situatedness of these doings' (217). Particular to my research is the suggestion from Scheer that 'emotions themselves can be viewed as a kind of practical engagement with the world' (193). In this way, the social and cultural environment is brought into sharp focus as a partner in revealing emotion states. The body is a cultural product and our embodied experience reflects the way our material body and our cultural education reciprocally shape each other and are formed together.

In writing about early modern emotional responses, the emotive experience of colour was shaped by use of contemporary cultural and material references. For a modern audience, Shakespeare's employment of colour images and terms is better appreciated when we understand the social and cultural constructs within which he worked and operated. His metaphoric use of language relies on conceptual structures formed within his *habitus* and that of his audience. Given the *sui generis* nature of emotions, literature often struggles with the idea that emotion words can represent disparate objects. The important conclusion is that context becomes pivotal when extracting meaning and understanding from utterances; colour, in this situation, helps as an 'organizing metaphor'. In this way, Shakespeare uses colour to help direct certain instances of emotional response. This is demonstrated when we examine the expression of emotion through familiar colour systems such as pedagogical systems privileging rhetoric.

Richard Meek notes, 'while a Shakespeare play cannot provide us with unmediated access to the actual feelings experienced in the period, it might offer an insight into the attitudes towards emotion in the Renaissance' (2012, 281). There are various literary and dramatic means to reveal these emotional connections; I argue that invocation of colour is one of them. For literature or theatrical works to provoke a strong response, it has to offer a connection to the emotional codes and patterns that an audience feels or expects to feel in a given context. Returning to my opening quotation from *The Merchant of Venice*, Portia was drawing upon shared understandings of facial patterning common in grief to direct her audience to the emotion that Bassanio might be feeling. Therefore, it is incumbent upon the researcher to consider the historically specific nature of literary texts and the cultural parameters of their reception within particular historical periods. The early modern notion of emotion is bound up with movements of the mind and body, in a way which accords with the emphasis on embodied emotions that is current in the field of emotions studies. Thomas Wilson, in 1553, outlines his views on the emotions which he names 'affections'

Because the beautie of amplifying, standeth most in apt mouing of affections: It is needfull to speake somewhat in this behalfe, that the better it may be knowen what they are, and howe it may bee vsed. Affections therefore (called Passions) are none other thing, but a stirring or forsing of the minde, either to desire, or els to detest and loth any thing, more vehemently then by nature we are commonly wont to doe.

We desire those things, we loue them, and like them earnestly, that appeare in our iudgement to be godly: wee hate and abhorre those things that seeme naught, vngodly, or harmefull vnto vs. Neither onely are wee moued with those things, which wee thinke either hurtfull, or profitable for our selues, but also we reioyce, we be sorie, or wee pittie an other mans happe.

([1553] 1969, fol. 72)[3]

In Wilson's widely held view, thinking about an emotional state could induce that state in the subject, proceeding from the mind to create an embodiment of the emotion. Writing like Wilson's suggests that a theoretical model which acknowledges the mind-body relationship in emotion production and expression is an absolute necessity when considering the emotional states of the early modern individual.

Colour as a cultural phenomenon

Using early modern discourses around colour, as evident in works such as art treatises, I aim to uncover early modern emotional states and their changing forms. For example, because colour recognition was thought to begin in the senses, and assimilation of the experience resulted in a redistribution of the humours, colour manifested itself cognitively and bodily as a passion of one sort or another. In a world where the body was understood as a physical, symbolic, and emotional vessel, the physical and symbolic properties of colour enabled a form of shorthand, allowing people to express themselves and read others emotionally in difficult situations. The body and its experiences were dependent on a confluence of both internal and external influences and, as one such stimulus, colour could be readily manipulated to share, enhance, or disrupt meanings. Within this paradigm, both the sight of physical colours and the associations of colour words have the ability to create an affective reaction not necessarily predicated on humoral teachings (Lindquist et al. 2012, 125).

When colour and emotion are used together, the perception of the colour in question is less significant than the emotional context in which it is used. According to Reddy, 'both emotions and colors have a strong subjective or experiential character; that is, it makes sense to individuals to describe the qualities and features of the perceived color or the experienced emotion, sometimes at length' (2001, 3). Even though colour has a clear physical aspect, it is apparent that it also has distinct subjective components that have changed over time. I suggest, therefore, that it is more appropriate to consider how texts use colour emotives to facilitate emotional transactions in given situations, rather than to attempt to make universal associations of colours with emotions:

> [In] literary text[s], colour terms are assigned symbolic function. Here it is no longer the hue itself that is of relevance, but how the colour terms indicate, imply or transmit to the reader meanings the author leaves unexpressed in explicit terms.
> (Wyler 1992, 164)

For my work, this is an important observation to make because I am not discussing the appearance of physical colour, but am concerned rather with commonly held associations about individual colours. Barry Maund takes a similar position, stating that 'we can and need to make a distinction between (a) colours as they are in experience and (b) colours as they are in physical objects' (1995, 2). It is the emotional response generated by the articulation of colour terms which is of interest in this book. Armelle Sabatier notes, '[w]hen investigating the dramatization or representation of colours in Shakespeare's drama and poetry, one should also bear in mind that colour was also considered to be verbal insofar as it was perceived as a rhetorical conceit in the Renaissance' (2018, 14). Nevertheless, Maund acknowledges that a commonality of perception of colour is possible in a given social context as he asserts that 'our colour language is social: one's descriptions of perceptual experiences draw upon the public language which one shares with others' (1995, 95). In line with this view, my research focuses on colour as a term that is inflected by differing emotional ideologies and rooted in specific contexts, not tied to static lexical terms (Biggam 2012, 26), or reliant for its meaning on general surveys of colour term usages (Bennett 1988).

According to Davis R. Simmons, 'one of the most obvious routes towards an association between colour and emotion is the stereotype' (2011, 408). While it is not enough to situate an expressive meaning in the stereotype, it can be a fruitful place to start. For instance, Shakespeare relies on the stereotype when evoking the Moor and blackness in a number of his works but he often disrupts this stereotype to offer complexity within the expected illustration. Another route for colour-emotion association is via memory associations. Simmons says 'colour evokes the memory, and the (genuine) emotional response is to the memory rather than the colour itself' (409). I agree that emotional responses do arise from memories related to colour, however, the word 'genuine' remains problematic when uncovering emotions and is an assumption I would be cautious about making. In a memorial approach, one can consider how the term 'blood' may have been linked explicitly to the colour 'red' and implicitly to the notion of an emotionally courageous state. Michael J. Huxtable suggests that 'the anonymous *L'Ordene de Chevalerie* defines a set of chivalric colours, meanings and values drawn from scripture in which red, black and, most of all white stand out as spiritually significant and forming integral parts of a knight's visual identity' (2011, 196). Huxtable describes the process in this poem wherein the knight is taught the significances of these colours, and in particular the meaning of red:

> Afterwards, he clad him in a red (*vermeille*) robe: "Sire, this robe gives you to understand, quite simply, that you should spill your blood in order to defend God and his holy law. This is what is meant by the red" (lines 147–57).
>
> (197)

Within the knight's education, the sight of red was meant to represent blood. Thus the mention of blood will elucidate red imagery, for the two words are closely paired. When blood is mentioned in a text it is not a bold leap to associate it with the colour red. Bartholomaeus also suggests this close connection when he describes facial colouring

> Palenesse and discoulour is a token of dread: for the heat being drawn inward to the parts of the bodye, in the face is scarcitie of bloud, and so the face is discouloured. Also sodeine rednesse in the face, is token of shame and wrath. And that is because heate commeth outward, and bloude maketh the skinne redde without: and busieth to put off shame and wronge.
>
> ([1582] 1976, cap. 8)

In this paradigm, a red or pale face is associated with the presence or absence of blood, linking, once more, the two terms in an emotional context. The emotional states implied here are anger or shame in the case of facial redness. Similarly, black is oftentimes linked to darkness and negativity, and white to fear and dread. In this way, colour can work as metonymic representations of objects and states. My analysis, therefore, has to consider terms which at first glance may not form part of a scientific chromatic spectrum, but which maintain a powerful cultural connection between colour and emotions.

In early modern England, there was a growing interest in English methods of painting prompting, Richard Haydocke to translate Lomazzo's, *Trattato dell'arte de la pitura* (1598).[4] Lomazzo's text was highly influential and, with its translation into English, now more accessible. This is the earliest treatise in English on the art of painting and it spoke to the growing interest in the creation of an English art culture. Haydocke added his own chapter containing information on colour, wall painting, and cosmetics. The English version is considered a pioneering work in the field (Holtgen 1978, 15). In turn, Haydocke encouraged the artist Nicholas Hilliard to write a treatise on the art of limning. Hilliard also suggests that accurate portrait painting relies on three things: first, a 'fair and beautiful colour'; second 'good proportion'; and third, and most importantly, 'countenance, by which the affections appear' (Hilliard [1573] 1981, 75–7).

Speaking of 'motions in pictures', Haydocke notes that these create a more pleasing and attractive effect than those which do not follow nature in this regard (1598, 1). He also takes the trouble to explain the emotions in relation to art

> *The passions of the minde are nothing else but certaine motions, proceeding from the apprehension of some thing*, Now this *apprehension* is three-folde: *Sensitiue, Rationall, and Intellectuall*. And from these three, there arise three passions in the minde. For sometimes we follow *Sensitiue apprehensions*, and then we consider good and evill, vnder the shewe of that which is *profitable or vnprofitable, pleasant or offensiue*: and these are called *Naturall affections*. Sometimes we pursue *rationall apprehensions*; considering good and evill in maner of *vertue or vice, praise or dispraise, honestie or dishonestie*; and these are *Reasonable affections*. Sometimes we imbrace *apprehensions intellectuall*, regarding good or evill as *true* and *false*, and these are *Intellectuall apprehensions*.
>
> (1598, 9)

In Haydocke's model, the passions are linked to the visual experience of an object or situation. As passions are categorised in different ways, it follows that there are many ways to understand and manipulate those passions. He firmly aligns the motions or passions with the vision of various colours, giving an overview of the function and emotional relevance of colour in artworks

> Becavse all colours haue different qualities, therefore they cavse diuerse effects in the beholders, which arise from an inwarde contrariety of their cavses (as *Aristotle* teacheth) which I purpose here so far forth to lay open. First therefore blacke light, earthie, lead-like and obscure colours, by reason of their heauy qualities, being apprehended by the eie, doe breede in the minde of the beholder tardity, musing, melancholie, &c. Blacke, greene, the colour of the Saphire, reddish, or obscure of the colour of gold and silver mixt together as yellow, yeelde a pleasurable sweetnesse. Redde fiery, flame colour violet, Purple, the colour of iron red hote, and Sanguine cause courage, providence, fiercenesse and boldness by stirring up the minde like fire. Gold colours, yellowes, light Purples, and other bright colours make a man vigilant, adding grace and sweetnesse. The Rose

colour, light greenes, and bright yellowes yield joy, mirth, delight &c. White ingendreth a kinde of simple attentiō more melancholy then otherwise. [...] And these are the qualities of colours, in the disposition whereof we must be careful, that we make no disorder or confusion in the eie of the beholder.

(1598, 112)

Haydocke suggests, in his examination of the colour black, that through classical Greece and Rome, black was the colour of 'mourning weede' and also death. He also mentions an association with unhappiness, evil, and with madness and melancholy, since fools and mad men have an abundance of black choler. He suggests '*Painters* make the Divell Blacke, because blackenes hath a certaine inclination vnto sadnesse' (1598, 113–4). While quoting Aristotle, he also says that as black is the only colour which will not take on another hue, it can signify constancy and also obstinacy.

White, according to Haydocke, often denotes simplicity, purity, elation of the mind, and chastity. To this list, he adds goodness, intelligence, joy, and sincerity, along with burial robes and faithfulness (1598, 114–5). He notes an association with blame since the Jews clothed Christ in white to signify blame and disdain. With this in mind, it is worth noting the blame which Othello ascribes to the white Desdemona as he contemplates her murder. Haydocke also puts forward that white could be seen as a sad, vile, and base colour, given the practice of arraying inexperienced and unblooded soldiers in white to denote their lack of prowess and honour.

By contrast, the colour red, in Haydocke's litany, could signify revenge, martyrdom (again related to the spilling of blood), love, charity, ardent affections, nobility (since purple did not differ much from red), and courage, and it is nearly always associated with bold emotions (1598, 117–8). He adds that cardinals wear red to show that they are always inflamed with love and charity. Yellow signifies hope, rejoicing, desire, joy, superiority, justice and an expectation of children (120). Green had a more complicated significance and could mean diversely hope, mourning, and death (121–2).[5] In his survey of colours, Haydocke ties colours to emotions and humours but also to contemporary practices. He gives an audience a template for relating to colours in emotional and social circumstances but he also gives artists a guide to both substantiate and subvert expectations of colour.

Likewise, the burgeoning genre of moralistic emblems meshed colours with emotional states. The force of moral learnings through artwork was widely accepted which the painter in *Timon of Athens* succinctly notes '[a] thousand moral paintings I can show / That shall demonstrate these quick blows of Fortune's / More pregnantly than words' (1.1.92–4). Within Geoffrey Whitney's collection of emblems, there are a number that use colour references as an aid to convey their message. They involve specific colour terms in literary representations and images that align them with particular emotions. The following emblem is a fine example of how this was presented

> On colours
> For mourners, *blacke*, for the religious, *white*
> Which is a signe, of conscience pure, and free.
> The *greene*, agrees with them in hope that liue:
> And eeke to youthe, this colour wee do giue.
> The *yelowe*, next vnto the couetous wighte.
> And vnto those, whome ielousie doth fret.
> The man refus'd in *Taunye* doth delite.
> The collour *Redde*, let martiall captaine get.
> And little boies, whome shamefastnes did grace,
> The Romaines deck'd, in *Scarlet* like their face.
> The marriners, the *Blewe* becometh well.
> (Whitney [1586] 1988, 226)

Within the excerpt above there is a consensus of representations that accords with Haydocke. The emblem was a medium that reached another audience which might not otherwise have been exposed to Haydocke's work.

Conclusion

Shakespeare's clarity of colour imagery significantly enhances the emotional register of his theatre. Like Caroline Spurgeon, I believe that Shakespeare 'is interested in colour, not chiefly for its colour value, as is an artist, but rather as it appears in some definite object, and for the emotion which it thus arouses or conveys' (1935, 57). Shakespeare used many tools and devices to express emotion, more than are immediately perspicuous to his audience. Accordingly, he found a way to use the natural world of colour around him to augment the emotionality of the moment he was creating. The emotions were understood 'to participate naturally in the fluctuations and variations characteristic of phenomenal life in general' (Paster 2004, 27). Granted that emotions are variously internal passions, outward expressions, and bodily functions, it remains necessary to acknowledge the power and functionality of words to shape and determine emotional transactions. Shakespeare, with his visionary extension and manipulation of language, contributes hugely to the understanding and shaping of emotional transactions through colour signs and waves of colour utterances, sweeping the audience towards emotional recognition of situations, characters, and events.

The model used in this book investigates the cultural, social, and cognitive-emotional response flagged, referenced, or promoted by the use of colour terms. To be culturally and socially relevant the colour terms must have a normative collective function and relevance. For example, Shakespearean drama takes into account the audience it was written for and the ways in which that audience related to the drama as it was proposed to them on stage. This view does not negate the possibility that Shakespeare has an enduring appeal which can be felt even today but maintains that some of the subtle nuances of emotions as expressed on the early modern stage cannot be transmitted easily in a modern performance. To acknowledge this fact means that some form of historical analysis must be in play to give access to specific contemporary factors in the moment of writing and performing for the early modern Shakespearean audience. Literary language is not hermetically sealed, apart from the scope of human experience and knowledge. Its discourse is linked to questions of social and cultural power and influence. This language shapes the expression of human experience and thus is in itself dependent upon questions of social and cultural power and the influence of the *habitus* itself.

Although knowledge of the original context of reading can give an added emotional effect to the play text, it remains important to acknowledge the textual presence of multiple discourses and emotion vectors. Within this process, colour references allow the eyes, the ears and the imagination to collaborate in allowing a richer, more articulate experience of the emotional complexities Shakespeare presents to us. In my exploration of the diverse ways in which this experience can be achieved, it is important to note that I am not advocating a prescriptive approach to the expression of emotions. Looking at colour and the emotional resonances that colour terms can augment will prove key to uncovering previously obscured emotional registers. I analyse examples of individual plays through various cultural lenses whilst remaining keenly aware that each of the plays examined would bear scrutiny through a multiplicity of approaches. Using culturally synchronic approaches, in Chapter 1 I explore how rhetorical teachings of the period could be associated with colour references to shape and express emotions through the example of *Titus Andronicus*. Chapter 2 investigates the varied physiognomic expressions in *Love's Labour's Lost* in relation to colour and emotions. In Chapter 3, *Hamlet* provides a case study for investigating theories concerning sight to uncover their relation to colour and emotion and the humours. With its preoccupation with clothes and the form they cover, Chapter 4 provides a framework for exploring emotional responses concerning the body and its attendant material coverings. The concluding chapter analyses *Othello* in the context of the emotional meanings of colour in contemporary visual culture and cultural commonplaces. I draw together the ideas expressed

14 *Expression of emotion*

in previous chapters to indicate patterns of colour use and their relation to emotional arcs within the play. Of course, the considerations in this final chapter are also contingent on the way articulations of race were deployed.[6] Overall, this book demonstrates that colour can be both an emotional experience and a negotiation between different early modern discourses (such as rhetoric, scientific, and moral) that produces differing results within the habit-sets of the various plays. Consequently, this book adds to our understanding of the expressive possibilities of colour in text and performance.

Notes

1 Richard Meek notes 'Shakespeare's plays were being read … by the same people who might have seen and heard the plays' earliest performances' in '"Penn'd Speech": Seeing and Not Seeing in *King Lear*' (2008, 80).
2 Indeed, Thomas Dixon quite firmly states, 'the word "emotions" is currently often used carelessly and anachronistically to refer to theories that were in fact about "passions", "affections", or "sentiments"' (2003, 12).
3 *The Arte of Rhetorique* was reprinted and revised at least five times which demonstrates its popularity and general appeal in the early modern period.
4 Richard Haydocke trans. 1598. *A Tracte Containing the Artes of Curious Paintinge, Caruinge & Buildinge* Written First in Italian by Io. Paul Lomatius, Painter of Milan and Englished by R. H., Student in Physik. By Io. Paul Lomatius. Oxford: Joseph Barnes.
5 For a further discussion on the significance of the colour green see Bruce R. Smith, *The Key of Green: Passion and Perception in Renaissance Culture* (2009).
6 For a nuanced discussion on the construction of race using black and white binaries see Farah Karim Cooper (2021).

References

Bartholomaeus Anglicus. (1582) 1976. *Batman Uppon Bartholome: His Booke De Proprietatibus Rerum*. Translated by Stephen Batman. Hildesheim; New York: Georg Olms Verlag.
Bennett, T. J. A. 1988. *Aspects of English Colour Collocations and Idioms*. Heidelberg: Winter.
Biggam, C. P. 2012. *The Semantics of Colour: A Historical Approach*. New York: Cambridge University Press.
Bourdieu, Pierre. 1977. *Outline of a Theory of Practice*. Translated by Richard Nice. Cambridge: Cambridge University Press.
Dixon, Thomas. 2003. *From Passions to Emotions: The Creation of a Secular Psychological Category*. Cambridge: Cambridge University Press.
Enterline, Lynn. 2012. *Shakespeare's Schoolroom: Rhetoric, Discipline, Emotion*. Philadelphia: University of Pennsylvania Press.
Haydocke, Richard, trans. 1598. *A Tracte Containing the Artes of Curious Paintinge, Caruinge & Buildinge*. By Io Paul Lomatius. Oxford: Joseph Barnes.

Hilliard, Nicholas. (1573) 1981. *A Treatise Concerning the Arte of Limning.* Edited by R. K. R. Thornton and T. G. S. Cain, 61–115. Ashington: Carcanet New Press.
Holtgen, Karl Josef. 1978. "Richard Haydocke: Translator, Engraver, Physician." *The Library* s5–XXXIII, no. 1: 15–32.
Huxtable, Michael J. 2011. "Aspects of Armorial Colours and Their Perception in Medieval Literature." In *New Directions in Colour Studies*, edited by Carole P. Biggam, Carole Hough, Christian Kay and David R. Simmons, 191–204. Amsterdam; Philadelphia: John Benjamins Publishing Company.
Karim-Cooper, Farah. 2021. "The Materials of Race: Staging the Black and White Binary in the Early Modern Theatre." In *The Cambridge Companion to Shakespeare and Race*, edited by Ayanna Thompson, 17–29. Cambridge: Cambridge University Press.
Lindquist, Kristen A., Tor D. Wager, Hedy Kober, Eliza Bliss-Moreau, and Lisa Feldman Barrett. 2012. "The Brain Basis of Emotion: A Meta-Analytic Review." *The Behavioral and Brain Sciences* 35, no. 3: 121–43.
Matt, Susan J. 2014. "Recovering the Invisible: Methods for the Historical Study of the Emotions." In *Doing Emotions History*, edited by Susan J. Matt and Peter N. Sterns, 41–54. Urbana, Chicago, and Springfield: University of Illinois Press.
Maund, Barry. 1995. *Colours: Their Nature and Representation.* Cambridge: Cambridge University Press.
McNamer, Sarah. 2010. *Affective Meditation and the Invention of Medieval Compassion.* Philadelphia: University of Pennsylvania Press.
Meek, Richard. 2008. "'Penn'd Speech': Seeing and Not Seeing in *King Lear*." In *Shakespeare's Book: Essays in Reading, Writing, and Reception*, edited by Richard Meek, Jane Rickard, and Richard Wilson, 79–102. Manchester: Manchester University Press.
Meek, Richard. 2012. "Introduction: Shakespeare and the Culture of Emotion." *Shakespeare* 8, no. 3: 279–85.
Paster, Gail Kern. 2004. *Humoring the Body: Emotions and the Shakespearean Stage.* Chicago, IL: The University of Chicago Press.
Plamper, Jan. 2010. "The History of Emotions: An Interview with William Reddy, Barbara Rosenwein, and Peter Stearns." *History and Theory* 49, no. 2: 237–65.
Reddy, William M. 2001. *The Navigation of Feeling: A Framework for the History of Emotions.* Cambridge: Cambridge University Press.
Rosenwein, Barbara H. 2002. "Worrying About Emotions in History." *The American Historical Review* 107, no. 3: 821–45.
Rosenwein, Barbara H. 2006. *Emotional Communities in the Early Middle Ages.* New York: Cornell University Press.
Sabatier, Armelle. 2018. *Shakespeare and Visual Culture: A Dictionary.* London; New York: Bloomsbury Arden Shakespeare.
Scheer, Monique. 2012. "Are Emotions a Kind of Practice (And Is That What Makes Them Have a History)?: A Bourdieuian Approach to Understanding History." *History and Theory* 51, no. 2: 193–220.
Shakespeare, William. (1599) 2006. *As You Like It.* Edited by Juliet Dusinberre. London; New York: Bloomsbury Arden Shakespeare.

Shakespeare, William. (1611) 2006. *Hamlet*. Edited by Ann Thompson and Neil Taylor. London; New York: Bloomsbury Arden Shakespeare.
Shakespeare, William. (1609) 2007. *Shakespeare's Poems*. Edited by Katherine Duncan-Jones and H. R. Woudhuysen. London; New York: Bloomsbury Arden Shakespeare.
Shakespeare, William. (1600) 2010. *The Merchant of Venice*. Edited by John Drakakis. London; New York: Bloomsbury Arden Shakespeare.
Shakespeare, William. (1623) 2014. *Timon of Athens*. Edited by Anthony B. Dawson and Gretchen E. Minton. London; New York: Bloomsbury Arden Shakespeare.
Simmons, David R. 2011. "Colour and Emotion." In *New Directions in Colour Studies*, edited by Carole P. Biggam, Carole A. Hough, Christian J. Kay, and David R. Simmons, 395–414. Amsterdam; Philadelphia: John Benjamins Publishing Company.
Smith, Bruce R. 2009. *The Key of Green: Passion and Perception in Renaissance Culture*. Chicago, IL: The University of Chicago Press.
Spurgeon, C. F. E. 1935. *Shakespeare's Imagery and What It Tells Us*. Cambridge: Cambridge University Press.
Whitney, Geffrey. 1586. *A Choice of Emblemes and other Devises*. Leyden: Christopher Plantyn.
Whitney, Geoffrey. (1586) 1988. "A Choice of Emblemes and Other Devises (Leydon: Plantin, 1586)." In *The English Emblem Tradition 1*, edited by Peter M. Daly and Anthony Rasp, 80–337. Toronto: University of Toronto Press.
Wilson, Thomas. (1553) 1969. *The Arte of Rhetorique*. Amsterdam; New York: Da Capo Press, Theatrum Orbis Terrarum Ltd.
Wyler, Siegfried. 1992. *Colour and Language: Colour Terms in English*. Tubingen: Gunter Narr.

1 'And weep to hear him speak'
Colour, emotion, and rhetoric in *Titus Andronicus*

The art of oratory and expression is dominated by the efforts of both mouth and voice (Christiansen 1997, 304).[1] In *Titus Andronicus*, Quintus describes Bassianus' grave in such terms and links Bassianus' demise with both colour and the unheard voice, saying

> What subtle hole is this,
> Whose mouth is covered with rude-growing briers
> Upon whose leaves are drops of new-shed blood
> As fresh as morning dew distilled on flowers?
>
> (2.2.198–201)

The speaking mouth is allegorised as the hole which is cruelly stopped with sharp briars (Carter 2011, 27).[2] With the flashes of red blood[3] on the leaves, we are directed to consider the violence which has interrupted Bassianus' previous discourse. This will soon come to represent the bloodied mouth of Lavinia defiled in another brutal interruption of discourse. The rest of this scene is peppered with references to blood. For example, Martius describes the grave as 'this unhallowed and bloodstained hole' (2.2.210) when asking Quintus to help him out, evoking a redness that is associated with violence, loss, and the associated emotion of fear. The green represented by the leaves, which throughout the play has diverse and conflicting emotional resonance, serves here as a repository for newly shed blood contrasting with the mention of flowers and innocence. The colour red is superimposed both literally and figuratively upon the green and becomes the leading image.

Quintus, suspecting that the darkness is hiding the truth, asks Martius, '[i]f it be dark how dost thou know 'tis he?' (2.2.225). The triad of red, black, and white is again repeated by Martius when he describes his identification of Bassianus

> Upon his bloody finger he doth wear
> A precious ring that lightens all this hole,
> Which like a taper in some monument

DOI: 10.4324/9781003198246-2

    Doth shine upon the dead man's earthy cheeks
    And shows the ragged entrails of this pit.
    So pale did shine the moon on Pyramus
    When he did by night lay bathed in maiden blood.
(2.2.226–32)

The contrast of light and dark is punctuated with images of red blood. The bloody finger, heralding violence, is contrasted with the light-creating jewel; the taper creates light contrasting with the earthy cheeks; and the pale moonshine is highlighted against the violence of maidenly bloodshed. The bloody loss of innocence is again countered by the darkness through the images of 'hole', 'pit', and 'night'. Saturninus is persuaded of Quintus and Martius' guilt and after tagging them with 'bloody' as an epithet, states: 'Let them not speak a word – the guilt is plain' (2.2.301). It was expected that the man using rhetoric to persuade his audience should be an upright citizen. Conversely, the villainous man should not be allowed to speak, a practice which Saturninus is facilitating in this instance.[4]

Humanism and importance of education

Reading the great classical poets was highly valued in the schoolroom as the charms of such writers have the greatest power to excite feelings. Rhetorical practices were seen as something that people did in order to have emotions (Scheer 2012, 194). While rhetorical teachings had been downgraded in the Middle Ages, humanism, once again, brought a fresh interest to these arts (Vickers 1988, 266). By analysing the relationships between the humanist educational system, emotion, and colour within the dramatic play, we can uncover connections that strengthen the emotional cues issued by colour emotives. Observing the use of colour words within a framework of rhetorical practices makes it possible to see how emotional transactions permeate the text. When colour is used in the rhetorical context, it is often an embellishment of style used to persuade the reader or listener but we can also look to the literal, metaphorical, and metonymical uses of colour as part of the rhetorical art of persuasion. Alongside rhetoric in the schoolroom, Lynn Enterline notes the importance of the dramatic arts, saying '[t]he confusions of ear and eye, the ability to impersonate characters on demand, were crucial components of school exercises in oratory' (2012, 21). These confusions involve depicting while narrating and seeing while reading. They serve to show that the physical depiction of colour and its aural representation through the text, through the power of rhetorical training, had an equally powerful effect on audiences as they stabilised these confusions into a coherent emotion. Using *Titus*

Andronicus as a dramatic example will illustrate some very fine moments of this phenomenon in the text.

It is important to explore the humanist education, as a social structure, to which we can reasonably expect Shakespeare will have been exposed. The humanist movement influenced the education that was on offer and, as Leonard Barkan puts it, 'in an early modern education such as Shakespeare's, the progression is not from language to literature but from grammar to rhetoric' (2001, 34). The main works studied in this context were those of Aristotle; the *Ad Herennium*; the oratory works of Cicero; and Quintilian's *Institutio oratoriae* (Joseph 1947, 20; Barkan 2001, 34). These texts provided students with a firm grounding in diction, speech, argument, and style. Although there is some debate on the minutiae of Shakespeare's reading list, a lot has been surmised based on his presumed attendance at the King's Free Grammar School at Stratford (Joseph 1947, 13; Murphy 1990; Plett 1995; Burrow 2004, 11; Gillespie 2016). Around this time a shift in classical education occurred when, as Grafton and Jardine note

> early humanism gave way in the early sixteenth century to an ideology of routine, order and, above all, 'method'. Early humanism[5] had shifted the emphasis from the formal and artificial disputation within the schools to the oration as a personally tailored means of persuasion, and to mastery of language as a desirable accomplishment for the urbane member of a civilised community.
>
> (1986, 123)

With this shift came tension between the older ruling aristocratic classes and the upwardly mobile educated middle classes, which is invoked by Shakespeare to create a political narrative that would resonate with his audience.[6] The use of Rome as a location in *Titus Andronicus* intertwines ideas of classical learning with political and social instability. The scholars that came from the Roman Empire were reduced to textual references after the fall of this empire. Referencing Rome and its fall is a warning to use power and learning correctly. *Titus Andronicus* can be a contradiction to modern sensibilities which cannot conceive of the violence and butchery wrought on the characters in terms of a measured and exacting rhetorical background. However, the apparent incompatibility was acceptable to an early modern audience which in itself suffered the contradictions and pressures on society that humanist teaching uncovered.

Humanist thinking allowed Tudor writers to consider fashioning, re-fashioning, and self-fashioning as viable possibilities.[7] Arthur Golding writes in his epistle to *Metamorphoses* about the need for awareness and restraint in the bid to know oneself

> that every man
> (Endevoring for too know himself as nearly as he can,
> As though he in a chariot sat well ordered) should direct
> His mynd by reason in the way of virtue, and correct
> His fierce affections with the bit of temprance.
>
> (1567, 12)

Humanist training encouraged students to participate in constructing an individual identity while using reason to control the greater excesses of emotion. Enterline (2012) suggests that humanist training in rhetoric was designed to intervene in social reproduction; to sort out the differences between bodies (male and female) and groups (aristocrats, the middling sort, and those below); and was necessary in the process of defining and producing proper 'English' gentlemen. She adds that

> when Shakespeare creates the convincing effects of character and emotion… he signals his debt to the Latin institution that granted him the cultural capital of an early modern gentleman precisely when undercutting the socially normative categories schoolmasters invoked as their educational goal.
>
> (2012, 1)

Having an interest in manipulating language added a tool to one's own self-fashioning.[8] This contemporary emphasis on fashioning individual identity also involved a concerted effort to explore the emotionality that was involved in this sense of identity. The line between rhetorical writing and developing dramatic works became open to negotiation. The art of rhetoric used tales of fiction to promote its teaching while the fictional world of drama used rhetorical principles to give force to emotional themes, which an interest in self-fashioning opened up for exploration.

Reading from the works of Cicero added to renewed interest in the importance of emotions. In *Tusculan Disputations*, Cicero began by discussing emotion as a vigorous movement away from right reason which is contrary to nature. Emotions, in Cicero's system, had two good and two evil classes. The good were desire and gladness, arising from gladness at present goods and desire for future goods; and the evil were fear of future evils and distress at present evils ([45BC] 2002, 43). Cicero noted that 'the source of all the emotions, they say, is "loss of control", which is a rebellion in the mind as a whole against right reason' ([45BC] 2002, 46). Emotions needed regulation which resonates with the framework put forward by Monique Scheer (2012, 213).

It was a key point of rhetoric to effect a change in the audience: colour references were able, both literally and figuratively, to cause such a change to take place (Plett 1995, 121). Cicero warned that what made the speech of the orator or poet jar more quickly was 'faults of overcolouring [...] detected not only by the verdict of the ears but even more by that of the mind' ([55-45BC] 1948, 81). The use of colouring, both literal and metaphorical, must be subtle, sparse, and not over-painted. If the lessons on oratory suggested colouring one's speech to improve the quality of the oratory, then it was not such a leap to expect that some writers in the early modern literary field chose to understand this exhortation as an invitation to use actual colour references in their work to do just this and attempted to use colour to improve the power of their oratory. Colour was embedded in the actual text not merely as an adjective for surface ornamentation or description of a commonplace noun, but also as an aid for moving the audience. In this schema, colour became an aide-memoire to create images that moved emotions. In *Titus Andronicus*, the explicit mention of both Cicero and sweet poetry (suggesting works by Ovid), highlighted the important role they served in the humanist tradition and, implicitly, Shakespeare's familiarity with that system. For example, Cornelia was exemplified as the model of a proper educator to the young in her care (4.1.12–14).

Rhetorical devices

Embellishment was advocated as a proper tool if used with caution. Cicero discussed the merits of embellishment in terms of colour. Cicero believed

> the embellishment of oratory is achieved in the first place by general style and by a sort of inherent colour and flavour; for that it shall be weighty and pleasing and scholarly and gentlemanly and attractive and polished, and shall possess the requisite amount of pathos, is not a matter of particular divisions of framework, but these qualities must be visible in the whole of the structure. But further, in order to embellish it with flowers of language and gems of thought, it is not necessary for this ornamentation to be spread evenly over the entire speech, but it must be so distributed that there may be brilliant jewels placed at various points as a sort of decoration.
> ([55-45BC] 1948, 77)

Cicero's influential view provides us with one explanation for how colour words in the rhetorical context, understood as brilliant jewels, became an integral part of speech patterns designed to effect a change in the audience. These words support and enhance the emotional register conveyed by the text. Cicero asserted that an injection of colour is captivating but familiar patterns of colour provide comfort in their familiarity ([55-45BC] 1948, 79), indicating that colour could support emotional moments (Vickers 1988, 276). In the sixteenth century, Thomas Wilson, in his widely used pedagogical work, *The Arte Of Rhetorique*, followed Cicero noting

> When wee haue learned apte wordes, and vsuall phrases to set foorth our meaning, and can orderly place them without offence to the Eare, wee may boldely commende and beautifie our talke with diuers goodly colours, and delitefull translations, that our speech may seeme as bright and precious, as a rich stone is faire and orient.
>
> ([1553] 1969, III fol. 81C)[9]

Rhetorical embellishment was best achieved, Quintilian argued, by following nature since 'all eloquence relates to the transactions of human life; every man refers what he hears to himself; and the mind easily admits what it recognizes as true to nature' ([95CE] 2006, 8.3.71). Many of the colour references in *Titus Andronicus* originate from a natural, organic source. Aaron uses allusions to greenery when he begins to lay plans with Chiron and Demetrius for the rape of Lavinia, saying '[t]he forest walks are wide and spacious' (1.1.614). He creates an image of airy, green woods which are pleasant for those who wish for agreeable recreation. However, he creates tension and dread by suggesting the same natural space is used for violent acts: '[f]itted by kind for rape and villainy' (1.1.616). For Aaron, the woods are also 'ruthless, dreadful, deaf and dull' (1.1.628), which now links green with these qualities. Like Aaron, Titus uses colour, especially green, to create the scene for his audience, saying

> The hunt is up, the morn is bright and grey,
> The fields are fragrant and the woods are green
>
> (2.2.1–2)

By referring to colour, Titus ensures the scene has more potency since the colours serve to enhance the underlying emotional landscape. His description uses green to indicate a pastoral scene in contrast to the violence in Aaron's green landscape. The conflicting representations of the colour green suggest the struggle for emotional positioning of the wood: the wood for hunting, walks, and recreation versus the wood that accommodates rape, murder, and destruction. Bassianus also suggests diametrically opposed readings of the green forest by pitting a chaste Diana against a Diana who abandons her religious haunts for the hunt

> Or is it Dian, habited like her,
> Who hath abandoned her holy groves
> To see the general hunting in this forest?
>
> (2.2.57–9)

Here the green forest exemplifies the abandonment of principles and becomes a site of contention where violence and fear ultimately triumph.

Quintilian highlighted the need for *enargeia*, clearness or distinctiveness, in rhetorical work using the concept of colour to help his explanation

> It is a great merit to set forth the objects of which we speak in lively colours, and so that they may as it were be seen; for our language is not sufficiently effective, and has not that absolute power which it ought to have, if it impresses only the ears.
>
> ([95CE] 2006, 8.3.62)

For example, when Martius orders Quintus to 'look down into this den, and see a fearful sight of blood and death' (2.2.215–6), Martius is indicating, through language, the behaviour, and emotion that his orders will bring. Martius is asking the onlookers to analyse the scene in front of them, where he connects the colour word 'red' through bloody representations with the emotions which he feels and expects others to feel. By naming the emotions, it lends them clarity in this context. In order to add the clarity that is vital in oratory, he describes the scene in critical detail

> Lord Bassianus lies berayed in blood
> All on a heap, like to a slaughtered lamb,
> In this detested, dark, blood-drinking pit.
>
> (2.2.222–4)

He exacts a horrified reaction by increasing the emotional register when he entangles images of red blood shed by an innocent white lamb against a background of darkness, blackness, and grief. The red representing Bassianus' life force seeps away into the dark thirsty hole. The emotionally potent red has overshadowed the white of perceived innocence.[10]

When pleading for her son's life, Tamora uses the device of *destruccion* or subversion that is outlined by Richard Rainolde in his book on rhetoric. This device encourages the user 'to caste doune by force, and strengthe of reason, the contrarie induced,' which for Tamora is the wanton revenge killing of her eldest son (Rainolde 1563, fol. xxiij.v). In her speech, she urges Titus to 'stain not thy tomb with blood' (1.1.119). The red blood links her speech to the red bleeding Marcus mentioned when trying to sway the crowd to appoint his brother as emperor. Tamora tries to link herself, through the colour reference, to the feelings that Titus had when he lost all his sons in battle. However, she does not understand Titus' rigid internal code of loyalty which puts personal griefs second to civic duty. Tamora aligns greatness with god-like mercy while, for

Titus, greatness is dependent upon his perceived duty to the state and how this can be enacted within the patriarchy of the family. Tamora's misunderstanding of Titus' emotional context thwarts her efforts to use *destruccion* to move him.

Another device, *chria,* is in Rainolde's words, a

> a rehersall in fewe wordes,
> of any ones fact, or of the saiyng of any man, vpō the
> whiche an oracion maie be made. As for example, Isocrates
> did say, that the roote of learnng was bitter, but the fruictes
> pleasaunt: and vpon this one sentence, you maie dilate a am-
> ple and great oracion.
>
> (1563, fol. xvj.v)

Demetrius attempts to use *chria* to describe Lavinia and how they are going to abuse her, saying '[f]irst thresh the corn, then after burn the straw' (2.2.123). If Demetrius had a full and proper education, he would have used oratory ethically and expounded, in a prescribed manner, praise for the author; an explanation; a comparison and a contrast; and provided a reasonable conclusion. But his limited education makes him resort to slang and colloquialisms. His description employs a bright, natural image which contrasts with the 'barren detested vale' (2.2.93). Unwittingly, Demetrius' negative associations of the golden corn accord with the problematic use of golden imagery by Aaron. Green and also gold continue to provide counterintuitive flags in the emotional register when a duplicitous letter suggests that the murderers look for their reward 'among the nettles at the elder tree' (2.2.272). There is no relief in Mother Nature's healing green as the audience is directed, through the nettles, to connect green with a stinging harmful evil. Aaron points to 'the bag of gold' (2.2.280), which is to be their reward. The gold is not associated with any glorious or noble state but is brought onstage as an illustration of the fall and wickedness of men. This was flagged by Aaron's previous references to gold. Aaron twisted the goodness of nature in previous associations of green, and, in the end, nature does not work for Aaron. The idea of extended comparisons and subtle referencing also relates to colour words as emotives, which are repeated in emotional contexts forming patterns of intertextual references such as the links between corn and its golden overtones, and other uses of golden imagery.

From the beginning of the play, colours mark, align, and misalign loyalties and families in blood, military, and emotional ties. Ambitions and loyalties are the immediate concerns that exist from the outset, distinctly foregrounded by colours. Marcus makes a speech in Titus' honour, saying that 'Five times he hath returned / Bleeding to Rome, bearing his valiant sons / In coffins from the field' (1.1.33–5). With these words, Marcus implies a red chromatic marker in the form of the 'blood' reference, connecting Titus physically and emotionally to Rome. Titus, Rome, and suffering are linked in a description that foregrounds the sacrifice that runs through the play in various forms. The method that Marcus employs directly follows Richard Rainolde's teaching with regard to device of narration. Rainolde states

> A Narracion is an exposicion, or declaracion of any thyng dooen in deede, or els a settyng forthe, forged of any thyng, but so declaimed and declared, as though it were doen. In euery Narracion, ye must obserue sixe notes.
>
> 1. Firste, the persone, or doer of the thing, whereof you intreate.
> 2. The facte doen.
> 3. The place wherein it was doen.
> 4. The tyme in the whiche it was doen.
> 5. The maner must be shewed, how it was doen.
> 6. The cause wherevpon it was doen.
>
> (1563, fol. xij.v)

The object of Marcus' speech or narration is to persuade the sparring brothers that Titus has a legitimate claim to be ruler of Rome. Whilst staying within stated rhetorical parameters, he uses the flash of colour to add appeal and emotional weight to his plea which touches on all the requirements of narration. It is interesting to note that 'blood' or 'bloody' is mentioned some 35 times in the text and is used emotively in most cases.

When creating an argument, it was important to indicate what was to come. Cicero notes

> There is another kind of argument that is taken from the mere indications of an action, for instance a weapon, blood, a cry, a stumble, change of colour, stammering, trembling, or anything else that can be perceived by the senses: also some sign of preparation or of communication with somebody, or something seen or hinted at later on.
>
> ([55-45BC] 1948, 341)

Cicero's argument here is consistent with my suggestion that colour references can be a flag warning of emotional activity, depending on the context. A change in colour references can herald the introduction of an emotion or indicate a change in the emotional atmosphere. For example, Titus' return to Rome comes with a detailed description of the funeral procession that includes 'coffins covered with black'. This entrance is in stark contrast to the previous triumphal entrances. The change in tone and colour causes a hiatus in the drama and a sudden shift in emotional tone foreshadowing upcoming events. Titus describes Rome as 'victorious in thy mourning weeds' (1.1.73). The blackness and sorrow associated with Titus is foregrounded from his first entrance onto the stage. The term 'mourning weeds' would have intensified the effect as it was a description which had gained currency in the early modern period. It designated black garments worn in token of bereavement, and was first noted c1540, but soon became a popular reference point combining the concept of black clothing and sorrow in association with bereavement.[11] Shakespeare uses the term four times in his plays, two of which are in *Titus Andronicus*.

To garner support from the senate, Titus mentions his sons' blood '[f]or all my blood in Rome's great quarrel shed' (3.1.4). He has paid a personal price for Rome by freely offering his sons as sacrificial warriors in war. Later his sacrifice appears tragically redundant when his pleas to save two of his remaining sons fall on deaf ears. The Roman authorities ignore him executing, Quintus and Martius. In reply, Titus links their deaths to the shame of Lavinia's spilt blood, drawing attention to colour by referring to 'blood' and 'blush'

> Let my tears staunch the earth's dry appetite;
> My sons' sweet blood will make it shame and blush.
>
> (3.1.14–15)

Titus' lamentations evoke colours which alert the audience to the grief, violated innocence, treachery, and violence that has enveloped Rome

> O earth …
> In winter with warm tears I'll melt the snow
> And keep eternal springtime on thy face,
> So thou refuse to drink my dear sons' blood.
>
> (3.1.16; 20–2)

Through his reference to melting snow, Titus erases the whiteness which by now has become a familiar colour trope in the play; he wants to keep springtime, which is marked by lush green, *in perpetuo*, but the audience knows that green has by now been linked to treachery which began with Aaron's discussion of the green woods. Tropes are important as they give rise to many colour representations allowing colour to be viewed both literally, and as a trope or signal for emotional meanings. Titus concludes with a return to the bloody red of violence.

Oratory and *Imitatio* in *Titus Andronicus*

Titus actively links himself to the distress and sorrow of his family in an attempt to create an emotional connection with the audience and cement his identity as a wronged citizen of Rome. His efforts follow the teachings of Quintilian who exhorted orators to 'endeavor to believe and to feel convinced that the evils of which we complain have actually happened to ourselves' ([95CE] 2006, 6.2.34). In terms of acting, Quintilian stated that it was not enough to assume a character; we must also assume the feelings of the character. Titus refers to his mobilisation of emotions as a conscious rhetorical practice: 'My tears are now prevailing orators!' (3.1.26). To implicate himself in Lavinia and Tamora's emotional and violent tangle, Titus describes Rome as 'a wilderness of tigers', and warns that '[t]igers must prey, and Rome affords no prey/ [b]ut me and mine' (3.1.54–6). At this point, no one is listening to Titus and his pleas and orations are in vain. His unheard voice is linked to Lavinia who is physically silenced, the silenced voices of his sons, and the silenced body politic of Rome.

Titus poignantly describes the loss of Lavinia's innocence

> When I did name her brothers, then fresh tears
> Stood on her cheeks, as doth the honey-dew
> Upon a gathered lily almost witherèd.
>
> (3.1.112–4)

Marcus has previously mourned the loss of her 'lily hands' and now Titus mourns the withering of her innocence using the same simile redolent of pale innocence through the metaphor of the lily.[12] Titus is fundamentally respectful as it is a personal not an abstract concept of Lavinia that he laments, despite reducing her mutilations to component pieces. He is not reductive but rather distracted as, with any person suffering from severe shock, there is a tendency to consider the particular in order to deal with the unimaginable. In this situation, Christopher Crosbie (2007) makes the case for Titus' trying to moderate between emotional and ethical extremes following an Aristotelian model of ethics, to which I would add Titus' need to react within the boundaries of normal human experience.

Marcus, without understanding, alludes to Lavinia's rape which is figured literally in her colourful wounds. However, his emotional reaction, and that of the family, is motivated by distress and grief rather than acknowledgment of the true crime. Her severed tongue is punishment by the Goths for a misuse of its abilities and her outspoken behaviour in the forest when she taunted Tamora. It is also a representation of a rape on Rome itself. The original Lavinia married Aeneas and bore Silvius, thus beginning the hereditary line which founded Rome. In another way, the lost tongue may be symbolic of the lack of a full education which has led Lavinia to use rhetoric in a fragmentary fashion. Her mutilated mouth and, allegorically, her rape are representative of a limitation of her rhetorical skills (Carter 2011, 27). As a comment on the importance of moral correctness in oratory, the metaphor is not complete until Lavinia learns to use some of the holistic tools of oratory still open to her. Through her use of Ovid, she communicates again. In her truncated state, she can use text, gesture, and writing to express herself and eventually she does this to extreme and fatal lengths. Her hands are forcefully linked to her silence as their loss is linked to a loss of communication skills.[13] Marcus laments the loss of 'those lily hands' (2.3.44), which could charm the lute as Orpheus did. As previously, the white has been replaced by red and innocence and communication has been lost, at least at this moment.[14]

Another important feature of rhetorical teaching *imitatio* (imitation) was actively encouraged in students. Indeed, Quintilian observed that the 'greater portion of art consists in imitation' ([95CE] 1987, 10.2.1). When practising *imitatio*, works should rival and vie with the original in their efforts to express similar thoughts (Dickson 2009, 384). The dramatic arts are a natural progression for Quintilian's students because he emphasised the equal importance of reading, writing, and speaking as inter-dependent and co-dependent skills, declaring 'in truth they are all so connected, so inseparably linked with one another, that if any one of them is neglected, we labor in vain in the other two' ([95CE] 1987, 10.1.1–2). Just as Quintilian urged students of his time to read the great poets, many in the early modern period were keen to obey. In the case of *Titus Andronicus*, Shakespeare drew on the poetry of Ovid as a model for *imitatio*, which he put to service in developing the emotional strengths of the play.[15] As a source of inspiration, Ovidian references are frequently made by characters who recall their education 'in the grammar long ago' (4.2.23) (Burrow 2013, 105). On many occasions in the play, the rhetorical device *imitatio* is first practised and then exceeded, the final stage in the rhetorical educational journey. Yet since this level of education and dedication is not adhered to by some characters, their emulation becomes vulgar and macabre, often with tragic consequences. Dickson notes '[a]s the characters compete to outdo available texts and each other's imitations of these texts and precedents, they weave throughout *Titus* a destructive pattern of conflicted, partial, and uncritical emulations' (2009, 379). Only when Titus incorporates both writing stories and reading myth into staging revenge does he appear to surpass his teacher and the Ovidian text that is his model (Pearson 2010, 45). The decay of Rome is paralleled by a decline in the proper use of rhetorical tools and teaching. There are minor triumphs by the old régime when rhetoric is used properly but overall the rhetoric of a new Rome formed by an alliance with the Goths holds no higher political or moral standards at heart; it is used piecemeal for nefarious gains.

Titus hints at a flash of green when he describes himself, on his return to Rome, as 'bound with laurel boughs' (1.1.77), thus practicing *imitatio*. His description recalls Ovid's *Metamorphoses*, retold by Golding, where Daphne becomes the laurel tree and nothing remains of her 'but beautie fresh and greene' ([8CE] 1567, 676). Daphne is pursued by Apollo and when she cannot love in return she begs to be transformed into a tree, the laurel, whereupon Apollo continues to express his love by kissing the tree. Daphne's metamorphosis foregrounds and becomes layered with the later fate of Lavinia who is also likened to a metaphorical tree when pursued for perverted love in the form of lust and rape. Marcus describes her mutilations in terms of a desecrated tree and when Titus discovers her fate, he offers to kiss her lips. Her lips are bloodied and a further symbol of her desecration signalling sorrow and tragedy. The green hinted at in the opening scene becomes overtly contentious later in the drama, no longer signifying pride for Titus as it did initially, but now defiled by more negative associations.

Green and gold, in tandem, vacillate in meaning as the play progresses before making way for the ultimate signifier of conflict and violence: murderous red. Tamora urges Aaron to enjoy the delightful surroundings, and, like Titus did previously, paints a colourful scene with her words using phrases like 'cheerful sun', 'green leaves', 'chequered shadow', and 'yellowing noise' of the hounds (2.2.13–20). Although 'yellowing' is referring to the bellowing of the hounds, its dual meaning adds to the colour of the scene. There is also a faint allusion to jealousy as during this period yellow was also associated with jealousy. She uses gold again, commenting on their 'golden slumber' (2.2.26). The reference to gold is heavily reliant upon the Golden age which is the first age detailed by Ovid in the declining ages of man. Gold was positive, bountiful, and pleasant until 'after Saturn had been banished to the dark land of death, [and] the silver race came in' ([8CE] 2004, II.63*ff*). The disruption to the purity of gold happens because of the behaviour of man and is directly alluded to in the text by the mention of gold, Saturn, and destructive behaviour. Aaron seeks to darken the scene with his talk of Saturn and melancholy serving to underscore the relationship to the ages of man as described by Ovid with the idea of colour and emotion. During the Iron Age, *terras Astraea reliquit* (Astraea abandoned the earth) ([8CE] 2004, I.150), a thought echoed by Titus near the end of the play when all justice appears to have left Rome and he must take matters into his own hands (4.3.4).[16] Robert S. Miola suggests, 'the matrix of ideas evolving from the commonplace notion that the world had degenerated from a golden past ruled by Saturn to a decadent iron present bereft of Astraea, goddess of justice, has special importance for *Titus Andronicus*' (1983, 62). The degeneration appears to justify the actions Aaron takes as he is a man inhabiting the barbaric Iron Age. His motive is revealed when he changes the emotional timbre of the scene expressing his need for 'blood and revenge' (2.2.39). He indicates that the day will culminate with Tamora's sons washing their hands in Bassianus' blood.

Lavinia's defilement is highlighted with numerous references to red. Marcus draws on his classical education to provide a 'paradigm in which such an atrocity can be made bearable and intelligible' (Weber 2015, 709). He first alludes to colour in his monologue when he describes the effect of Lavinia's arms, '[w]hose circling shadows Kings have sought to sleep in' (2.3.19). Grey is implicit in the shadows and acts as a presage of the tragedy described by Marcus

> Alas, a crimson river of warm blood,
> Like to a bubbling fountain stirred with wind,
> Doth rise and fall between thy rosèd lips,
> Coming and going with thy honey breath.
> But sure some Tereus hath deflowered thee
> And, lest thou shouldst detect him, cut thy tongue.
> Ah, now thou turn'st away thy face for shame,
> And notwithstanding all this loss of blood,
> As from a conduit with three issuing spouts
> Yet do thy cheeks look red as Titan's face
> Blushing to be encountered with a cloud.
>
> (2.3.22–32)[17]

The colour in this passage is integral to Lavinia's body and not merely a surface embellishment. As well as *imitatio*, it is an example of *enargeia* which seeks to make present in the inner eye of the imagination an affective image. Red is intertwined with Lavinia's internal state of violation, sorrow, and shame. Her bleeding limbs are subordinate to her state of shame; she has not turned pale from the physical assault but is marked more by her blushing and shame. Here, the colour occupies the liminal space between the internal experience of her emotion and the physical expression that emotion can be seen to have. The Ovidian text which Shakespeare imitates, while also using colour terms, indicates that Lavinia's model, Philomel, was '*pallentem trepidamque*' (pale and trembling) in the face of her rape, and later when found by her sister she '*expalluit*' (grew pale) (Ovid [8CE] 2004, 521, 602).[18] While Ovid uses colour terms, a precedent which Shakespeare follows, Shakespeare employs his own colours with, perhaps, different expressive aims in mind.[19] After cataloguing the violence that has been wreaked upon the Andronici, Marcus changes the emotional register by moving away from the bloody-red references. He notes that Lucius has been 'struck pale and bloodless' (3.1.258), while he describes himself with bleak colourless references such as 'stony', 'cold', 'numb', and 'silver' (3.1.259–61). The Andronici are about to react against the flood of violence they have suffered: 'now is a time to storm' (3.1.264). The occurrence of red references and red's indicators 'blood' and 'bloody' diminish significantly after this scene as the Andronici's calculated revenge overtakes their distress and sorrow.

Humanism and morality

The importance of colour in foreshadowing tragedy and highlighting moral issues is initially stressed when Marcus tries to persuade Titus to the role of emperor by emphasising the white purity of the office's garment: '[t]his palliment of white and spotless hue' (1.1.185). Marcus urges him to don the white and take up the office: '[b]e *candidatus* then, and put it on' (1.1.188). Titus turns down the opportunity and does not don the white. His rejection of white appears to signal the first step on an unavoidable path towards destruction, both moral and literal, for the Romans. The white garment, representing purity and integrity can, perhaps, cover the bloody colours of war and the fiery emotions of revenge and anguish that have just passed. However, Titus does not sway from the military path of destruction that has been highlighted in red thus far, and it appears that his choice makes blood-red murder and misery the path he forges for Rome. The political agenda in *Titus Andronicus* can be related to the shift in classical education from an emphasis on training the humanist individual in arts of oratory and the morally upright citizen, to the later routine application of rhetorical rules to facilitate rote learning. This constitutes a misuse of the art of oratory and has repercussions for both the individual and the state.

Bassianus also uses the purity of white to move his audience affectively. He contrasts black and white imagery to besmirch Tamora's character, using the chromatic distance between black and white to emphasise the difference between pure and evil

> Believe me, queen, your swart Cimmerian
> Doth make your honour of his body's hue,
> Spotted, detested and abominable.
> Why are you sequestered from all your train,
> Dismounted from your snow-white goodly steed,
> And wandered hither to an obscure plot,
> Accompanied but with a barbarous Moor,
> If foul desire had not conducted you?
>
> (2.2.72–9)

The white steed continues the metaphor of travelling from pure to evil in terms of colour representations of emotional and moral decisions. Tamora has moved towards darkness, evil, and black dishonour, and away from white purity of reputation. Lavinia augments her husband's insults, saying 'let us hence, / and let her joy her raven-coloured love'

(2.2.82–3). There is a tension between distancing Tamora from Aaron's dark and black coloured complexion while maintaining the idea of Tamora as evil. As Noémie Ndiaye (2021, 165) notes, this puts pressure on the meaning of whiteness. Such colour-coding returns later in the play in times of increased tension. Demetrius asks his mother why she looks so pale. Tamora repeats the word 'pale' in her reply, contrasting it with their environment which is suffused with blackness, 'never shines the sun', 'nightly owl or fatal raven', and 'dead time of the night' (2.2.96–9). The colour of Tamora's skin figures both literally and allegorically in the play and becomes aligned with various emotional references and states.

Aaron begins his description of Tamora in act two with 'pale' and 'golden' adjectives recalling Ovid's text describing dawn and Phoebus' chariot passage across the sky (Ovid [8CE] 2004, I.89–115). Aaron describes Phoebus' position high in the heavens after bathing the earth in golden sunlight, and proclaims that the description represents Tamora. However, we are reminded of the episode in *Metamorphoses*, when proud and ambitious Phaëthon also wished to drive the god's chariot of gold and light, but with fatal results. Gold is charged in this context with doom and destruction. Aaron switches to black colour references describing how he will 'mount her pitch' (1.1.513). He creates crude sexual imagery that is interwoven with blackness and dark, as the word 'mount' is sexually suggestive. Pitch as a colour can refer both to his skin but also to the black character present in the far-reaching trajectory of Tamora's evil. Aaron reinforces the stark crudeness of his sexual ambition by returning to bright and golden imagery when referring to himself: 'I will be bright, and shine in pearl and gold' (1.1.518).

At the beginning of the third scene, red blood is associated with loyalty, self-sacrifice, and bravery. Lucius points out to Titus that his 'youth can better spare my blood than you' (3.1.166). An emotional connection is created between Titus and his remaining son through an association of their shared blood and blood line, but this connection also resonates with a sense of loss and poignancy related to the physical loss of family, limbs, and Lavinia's chastity. We are directed to consider the waning of life in a philosophical context. Red blood is finite and to lose some of it and its colour means it is lost forever. Marcus asks of them both

> Which of your hands hath not defended Rome
> And reared aloft the bloody battleaxe,
> Writing destruction on the enemy's casque?
>
> (3.1.168–70)

We are brought back from the personal to the public image of war which is still flagged with the red of bloodshed. The image highlights violence while suggesting that Roman war efforts are coupled with intelligence and good moral agency marked by their literacy. It takes physical skill to wield a sword or a battle-axe, but it takes education and intelligence to use opportunities in battle and out-manoeuvre the enemy, thereby 'writing destruction' on one's opponent. The pinnacle of the scene involves Aaron chopping off Titus' hand. The deed is marked by Aaron's forcible acknowledgement his evil nature, associated with blackness

> Let fools do good, and fair men call for grace,
> Aaron will have his soul black like his face.
>
> (3.1.205–6)

Aaron, although sophisticated in his thinking, is morally and emotionally lacking. In his use of colour terms, he is shown to identify with a simplistic moral code and is complicit with his part as the 'black other'. At this point, Aaron does not perceive any tension between his character and his appearance. He embraces conventional moral markers. In the next scene, black is the only colour referenced and this is again in relation to Aaron and evil. Marcus kills a fly and calls it 'a black ill-favoured fly / Like to the Empress' Moor' (3.2.67–8). Titus reiterates that it is the 'likeness of a coal-black Moor' (3.2.79). The discussion centres on their agreement that a thing of blackness and ugliness should not be allowed to live.

In the play, characters engage with humanist educational ideals in an effort to master the struggle with their sense of identity. In act four, scene one, 'Young Lucius enters with books under his arm'. Lucius is using these books as a method of self-fashioning both figuratively and literally on stage. It is a self-conscious move that actually highlights educational deficits since Lucius cannot understand Lavinia's relationship to the texts. Noting the boy's entrance, Marcus declares

> Ah, boy, Cornelia never with more care
> Read to her sons than she hath read to thee
> Sweet poetry and Tully's Orator.
>
> (4.1.12–4)

Since Marcus also failed 'to read' Lavinia's literal and metaphorical plight it may be that Lavinia needed various media to express herself. This would be a theatrical omission rather than a theatrical awkwardness as only a single attempt to clarify her hurt is staged. Lavinia, with the book onstage, speaks through Ovid and Ovid speaks for her. One of the text's properties is to provide an expressive medium to quantify and explain the meaning and extent of affective situations. While I agree with Jonathan Bate's assessment that Lavinia's 'reading signals that the play is both a revisionary reading of the Ovidian text and an examination of the efficacy of humanist education' (1993, 104), it also, in my opinion, develops an argument against a Universalist approach to education. The play demonstrates that selective abstraction can have catastrophic consequences when not employed correctly. For example, the woods have previously been situated in Titus' mind as a *locus amoenus*, but he has neglected the *locus inamoenus* that was often also described by Ovid (Phillips 2015). After realising Lavinia's fate, Titus recognises his omission

> Patterned by that the poet here describes,
> By nature made for murders and for rapes.
>
> (4.1.57–8)

Lavinia, when encouraged by Titus, takes his staff in her mouth and writes in the sand the words, '*Stuprum*. Chiron. Demetrius' (4.1.78). As John Wesley notes, this becomes 'a record of both the loss and gain of language, of articulation wrested from the inarticulate, and of the inspiration necessary to channel the action toward a restoration of civic order in the final scene' (2015, 1290).

The moment of revelation elicits radically differing responses if one examines the colour referencing used. The emotional register around the Andronici has changed by this time and this change is reflected in a chromatic shift from red spattered, helpless outrage to a pale, cold acceptance that more violent action is now required to deal with the horror that had assailed their lives. Titus laments to the gods about their inaction whilst tacitly acknowledging that it will be his own efforts that effects some resolution. However, Marcus, on the other hand, is still showing some reluctance to seek justice. His hesitation is marked by the ongoing presence of the bloody red in his utterances which, by now, have disappeared from Titus' speech. Marcus reacts by saying

> What, what! The lustful sons of Tamora
> Performers of this heinous bloody deed?
>
> (4.1.79–80)

He is overwhelmed, horrified, and clinging to the civilities of Roman life, and his aversion to rash reaction is suggested when he says

> That we will prosecute by good advice
> Mortal revenge upon these traitorous Goths,
> And see their blood, or die with this reproach.
>
> (4.1.92–4)

It is notable that young Lucius also continues using the heightened red marker, calling Demetrius and Chiron 'bloody villains' (4.2.17), aligning his emotional state more with Marcus than with Titus.

In act four, the idea of blackness and evil is foregrounded. The nurse enters 'with a blackamoor Child' (4.2.52). The stage direction underscores the necessity of both the visually literal blackamoor and the discourse surrounding blackness that is championed by Aaron. When Aaron asks what the baby is like, he is told it is a 'devil' (4.2.66). Aaron remains wilfully obtuse replying, '[w]hy then, she is the devil's dam. / A joyful issue' (4.2.67). Of course, the nurse has no doubts about her parcel and makes the baby's situation and Tamora's wishes clear

> A joyless, dismal, black and sorrowful issue.
> Here is the babe, as loathsome as a toad
> Amongst the fair-faced breeders of our clime.
> The empress sends it thee, thy stamp, thy seal,
> And bids thee christen it with thy dagger's point.
>
> (4.2.68–72)

The nurse's disgust prompts Aaron to utter, for the first time, a defence of blackness, '[z]ounds, ye whore, is black so base a hue?' (4.2.73). He asserts the injustice of the argument which, until this point, he has harnessed as justification for his evil actions, finally acknowledging the bias of a system that condemns him for his colour and racial heritage. Race and racism are social constructs which have been deployed in the embodiment of Aaron prompting an affective response that is highly coloured and emotional when speaking of his 'flesh and blood' (4.2.86). As Farah Karim-Cooper notes, '[i]n this period, whiteness and blackness are constructed as not just colors but also entire systems of value codified to produce a dubious but enduring sense of difference' (2021, 18). His confusion about the status of his black colour appears resolved when he exclaims

> What, what, ye sanguine, shallow-hearted boys,
> Ye white-limed walls, ye alehouse painted signs!
> Coal-black is better than another hue
> In that it scorns to bear another hue;
> For all the water in the ocean
> Can never turn the swan's black legs to white.
>
> (4.2.99–104)

Previously, Aaron has championed his blackness to himself and others. Now, we are asked to feel for Aaron's experience as a black man in a pale-faced world. Aaron suggests the brothers Demetrius and Chiron, with their fair Gothic complexions, have malleable colouring which can be changed or exposed by, and to, the view of others. Demetrius confirms this suggestion by saying that their mother will be shamed by the birth of a black baby while Chiron says that he 'blush[es] to think upon this ignomy' (4.2.117).

Aaron reveals one of the reasons for his native pride

> Why, there's the privilege your beauty bears.
> Fie, treacherous hue, that will betray with blushing
> The close enacts and counsels of thy heart.
> Here's a young lad framed of another leer:
> Look how the black slave smiles upon the father,
> As who should say, 'Old lad, I am thine own'.
>
> (4.2.118–23)

It is white skin, read through its colour changes, which betrays its owner and reveals. The brothers' shame is manifestly apparent, as was Lavinia's previously, unlike Aaron's.

Aaron, ever quick-witted, has a plan to save his son by swapping him for the fair-skinned baby of a fellow Moor, Muli, who has a white wife. Again, we are drawn to acknowledge the instability of skin colour while understanding that colour is both internal and external. Francesca Royster asserts

> [t]he essence of Moorishness is not blackness of skin but an inner, 'foreign' wickedness that remains even though by some genetic accident the skin may be white. Insofar as hidden evil is more difficult to detect and combat than overt evil, a white Moor is even more threatening than a blackamoor.
>
> (2000, 453)

Aaron credits Muli with a temperament like his own when he instructs Demetrius 'His child is like to her, fair as you are. / Go pack with him [Muli], and give the mother gold' (4.2.156–8). With Aaron's use of colour, fair innocence is contrasted with the treachery of gold. This treachery points to Aaron's previous use of gold, both literally and as a signifier of treachery and deception. Tamora echoes the treachery of gold saying that she can manipulate Titus with 'golden promises' (4.4.96). Aaron's underlying attitude to blackness and his own blackness resists guilt in the person of his son but he admits the possibility that his son will grow to have a similar pride in the white negativity surrounding evil black Moorishness. Towards the end of the play, Aaron whispers to his son,

> Peace, tawny slave, half me and half thy dame!
> Did not thy hue bewray whose brat thou art,

Had nature lent thee but thy mother's look,
Villain, thou mightst have been an emperor.
But where the bull and cow are both milk-white,
They never do beget a coal-black calf.
Peace, villain, peace

(5.1.27–33)

Again, in this passage Aaron uses contrasts of black and white to state his position. He is undone both by his own colour and his hitherto unknown sense of love and loyalty for his son. Despite his paternal feelings of love, he acknowledges the inner threat of evil associated with Moorishness by referring to the baby twice by the epithet 'villain'. Lucius colludes in the myth and also the perceived reality that, as a Moor, Aaron is a black unholy being who affects those who fall under his influence calling him the 'devil incarnate' (5.1.40). In his embodied and, therefore, tangible incarnation of the devil, Aaron admits to committing 'acts of black night' (5.1.64).

When Tamora appears to Titus as Revenge, she boldly engages him in talk of 'bloody murder' and 'detested rape', vowing to work 'wreakful vengeance on all [his] foes' (5.2.37; 32). Sensing an opportunity, Titus returns to his measured and calculating self, emphasised by a switch from red to black imagery. He offers to provide Tamora with palfreys, 'black as jet' (5.2.50), while warning her of the danger of having 'miserable, mad, mistaking eyes' (5.2.66). Tamora is slow to heed the dangers of the duplicitous nature of eyes and the visions presented to them. While Titus is discussing Tamora with Tamora-as-Revenge, he manages to reference the Moor and the devil twice each without alerting Tamora to the dangers she is facing.

Once left with Chiron and Demetrius, Titus reverts to red colour coding after he holds up Lavinia's desecrated 'spotless chastity' (5.2.176) to the brothers as the pinnacle of their crimes. While Titus is venting his revenge on the brothers he mentions 'blood' or 'bloody' four times. He wants an excessive amount of revenge, as '[f]or worse than Philomel you used my daughter, / [a]nd worse than Progne I will be revenged' (5.2.194–5). He has planned a bloody banquet like that of Domitian who hosted a black feast as a warning, but Titus has gone one step further and patterned the feast with red (Dio Cassius [c.233CE] 1925, 337–9). Shame, clearly linked to red and blushing in previous episodes in the play, reaches its dreadful zenith when Titus kills Lavinia who has been stained by her rape and cannot outlive her shame. Titus, killing her, exclaims, '[d]ie, die, Lavinia, and thy shame with thee; / And, with thy shame, thy father's sorrow die!' (5.3.45–6). The carnage unleashed by Titus ends with his own death and a death sentence passed upon Aaron. Lucius places a kiss on Titus' 'pale cold lips' and tears upon his 'bloodstained face' (5.3.152; 3).

Conclusion

There is a sense in the play that the humanist approach to learning has failed. The Andronici struggle to continue acting within the moral and ethical mores which were important in the early modern educational system. Some of the failure lies outside of their control because their rhetorical and affective skills have been truncated by the atrocities they have suffered. The political lack of control felt by the Andronici also reflects the struggle that the discipline of rhetoric experiences; their attempts to persuade through the ornaments of rhetoric meet accusations of harlotry and lies (Crane 1993, 39). Titus laments to Marcus because

> Thy niece and I, poor creatures, want our hands
> And cannot passionate our tenfold grief
> With folded arms.
>
> (3.2.5–7)

The necessary oratorical gestures, which are part of the socially conditioned body located in the *habitus*, have been blocked due to their amputations.[20] By naming his grief, Titus moves towards an emotional understanding of his experience previously denied to him since the loss of his right hand had left him unable to emote adequately through gestures (Pope 2019, 328). As Titus instructs Lavinia in violent ways, Marcus alone is hesitant and tries to recall Titus to the gentler ways of teaching that hallmarked the educational treatises; '[t]each her not thus to lay / Such violent hands upon her tender life' (3.2.21–2).

When using the classics for self-expression, Titus sends a verse to Demetrius and Chiron which says in Latin, '[the man] upright of life and unstained by crime does not need the javelins or the bow of the Moor' (4.2.20–1).[21] Tamora's sons do not have the wit to understand the significance of the note. Chiron remarks, 'O, 'tis a verse in Horace, I know it well. / I read it in the grammar long ago' (4.2.22–3). Such a misunderstanding is a direct critique of some aspects of humanist teachings which relied on method rather than true understanding. Aaron replies 'Ay, just – a verse in Horace, right, you have it. / [*Aside*] Now what a thing it is to be an ass' (4.2.24–5). Francesca Royster notes that Aaron 'can mimic Roman rhetoric and knows his Virgil and his Ovid better than the young Goths do. (2000, 438) illustrating a discourse that emphasises the gap between rhetorical knowledge and moral employment of rhetoric (Roe 2011, 58). Unbeknownst to the brothers, but evident to Aaron, when Titus cites the black Moor in his Latin quotation he is referring to the present evils of the Moor within their midst. Titus has warned them of Aaron's vile influence while also revealing his knowledge of the brothers' activities.

Loomba notes '[f]or most characters in this play, but also, disturbingly, for Aaron himself, blackness is a moral quality' (2002, 79).

Aaron proudly admits his influence over Tamora's sons saying, '[i]ndeed, I was their tutor to instruct them... That bloody mind, I think, they learn'd of me' (5.1.98; 101). The time between the ages of 17 and 27 was the most dangerous for a man and evil could only be avoided with careful teaching (Ascham [1570] 1967, 40). It can be assumed that Aaron had influence over the boys during at least a portion of this timeframe. Aaron parodies the humanist way of life which espouses civilising boys through their studies. Civic virtue breaks down when the texts are studied too selectively or if one learns by experience rather than schooling. Roger Ascham states that '[l]earning teacheth more in one year than experience in twenty' ([1570] 1967, 50). These factors helped to create the violent and naïve sons of Tamora. Ascham also supposed that the daily use of writing 'is the only thing that breedeth deep root, both in the wit for good understanding and in the memory for sure keeping of all that is learned' ([1570] 1967, 83). Three people are shown to write in the play: Aaron, Titus, and Lavinia. All of their writings prove to be pivotal moments in the text. However, it is a misappropriation of the tools of writing that has disastrous consequences in the play. Aaron's appropriation of a humanist education is representative of the tension between the pagan origins of humanism and the need for Christians to adapt the classical works to suit their own agenda as his character enacts the 'other' whilst clearly having an educated mind. Aaron admits using letter writing to incriminate Andronicus' sons, in another betrayal of the principles of humanism. We are reminded of the treachery of gold as he triumphantly relates how he 'hid the gold within that letter mentioned' (5.1.107). Meg F. Pearson notes, '[t]he execution of his [Aaron's] plan relies on the literal written word, and his capacity to read, interpret, and rewrite the actions of others that helps him to maintain his dominance' (2010, 35). Similarly, once the Andronici master writing properly and use it well, they break Aaron and Tamora's dominance. Aaron acknowledges his perversion of the humanistic tradition when he admits with pride to a string of heinous crimes, including his mockery of teaching. His lack of shame is marked by his inability to blush. He is asked, 'canst thou say all this and never blush?' (5.1.121), to which he replies 'like a black dog as the saying is' (5.1.122). Reddening of the skin is undetectable in his black complexion, suggesting that without the colour marker the emotion of shame cannot be properly felt. The colour and the physical appearance of the emotion are inextricably linked to its reality. He is positioned as an invocation of the prejudices which 'legitimize[s] particular structures of power in which some people are deprived of their social, material, sexual, and intellectual rights' (Loomba 2002, 39).

The physicality of colour and emotion, apparent in the act of writing, is promoted by the humanistic tradition and executed by Titus. Titus exclaims, 'See here, in bloody lines I have set down; / And what is written shall be executed' (5.2.14–5). As Meg F. Pearson (2010) suggests, just as staining a letter with tears increases its emotional effect, so bloodying a letter inserts some of the author into the inscription. Titus makes a permanent record of his violent and bloody plan while suffused with feelings of revenge. Titus acknowledges the shortcomings of rhetoric for his purposes. When he cannot refine his oratory because of both his physical and his ideological shortcomings, he says, '[h]ow can I grace my talk, / Wanting a hand to give it action?' (5.2.17–8). The hand is closely connected with oratory and emotional expression. Colour flags the excesses that are spawned through revenge motivations, even though, through the act of writing, Titus tenuously relies on humanistic rhetoric to legitimise the bloody outcomes.

In the Ovidian model, human characters are transformed into objects, such as birds and trees. The Shakespearean model remains firmly focused on the human element maintaining a close emotional connection between the characters on stage who are deeply changed but exist as humans. The *imitatio* surpasses the original in emotional scope and depth because of Shakespeare's unwillingness to objectify his characters to ameliorate the sheer extent of the tragedy. Throughout the play, Shakespeare's reference to humanist ideology extends and develops the emotional register associated with the fashioning of identity in the period. Through noting the influence of rhetorical teaching, the power of colour as a necessary embellishment of speech and as a means to heighten affect becomes clear. Colour works to create a connection between the speaker and the audience by means of exhibition and illustration through the medium of rhetoric. In a dramatic work, the visual and the aural become a direct transaction between a character and his audience, there is no anonymous description or narrator to interfere with that transaction. Shakespeare repeatedly harnesses the potential of colour within a rhetorical framework and uses it as a metaphor, as an expression of emotion, and as a physical entity to enhance the affective potential of his play. He eschews a superficial representation and through the dramatic mobilisation of colour and rhetoric promotes a deeper engagement with the social, cultural, and scientific wisdom that permeated contemporary thought through treatises, literary works, and social discourse. This accords with Scheer's emphasis on 'the mutual embeddedness of minds, bodies, and social relations in order to historicize the body and its contributions to the learned experience of emotion' (2012, 199). Shakespeare also uses colour to engage with anxieties around identity and social mobility, thereby imbuing colour with metonymical significance. Moving the passions through speech was central to Renaissance rhetorical teaching, but moving the passions was also bound up integrally with both the mind and the body, and in some instances with colour.

Notes

1 Nancy L. Christiansen argues the importance of oral performance as part of the early modern engagement with the rhetorical arts: 'Thomas Wilson's *The Arte of Rhetorique*, does treat delivery and goes through eight editions, more than any other sixteenth-century English handbook. Delivery, otherwise called "Pronunciation," "Utterance," or "Action," is the branch of rhetoric imparting instruction in voice and gesture—the two elements of oral performance, ordered according to principles of decorum' (1997, 304).
2 There is, of course, a dual analogy at play with the bloodied hole also representative of Lavinia's sexual injuries.
3 See the Introduction for a discussion on blood as metonym for the adjective red.
4 There are conflicting ideas about how practising the art of rhetoric was linked to good moral behaviour. There was a school of thought that believed in this argument in the early modern period (Christiansen 1997). Henry Peacham in his dedicatory preface notes that the pursuit of rhetorical skill is 'to obtayne Wysedome, and Eloquence, the onelye Ornamentes, whereby mannes lyfe is bewtifyed, and a prayse most precyous purchased' ([1577] 1971, Aij).
5 Mary Thomas Crane defines 'humanism' as 'a program of educational reform that sought to replace the existing scholastic and professional training with a curriculum based on the rhetorical study of classical authors and designed to teach its students to speak fluent, classical Latin' (1993, 6).
6 For a further discussion on the socially-mobile Elizabethan see Frank Whigham (1984).
7 Discussed in the introduction to Kinney (1986).
8 See Stephen Greenblatt (1980) for a landmark discussion on self-fashioning in early modern England.
9 This text went through eight editions between 1553 and 1585. Skinner notes that this treatise was 'by far the most popular vernacular rhetoric of the second half of the sixteenth century' (2014, 39).
10 Heinrich Plett (2012) gives a full exposition of enargeia in Shakespeare in chapter three of *Enargeia in Classical Antiquity and the Early Modern Age: The Aesthetics of Evidence*.
11 See OED Online, 'mourning'.
12 She has also lost social value through the loss of her hands. See Farah Karim-Cooper (2016).
13 Katherine A. Rowe (1994) discusses the dismembered hand in particular and the agent it possesses.
14 From the fourteenth century the lily was 'applied to persons or things of exceptional whiteness, fairness, or purity'. See OED Online, 'lily'.
15 There is also substantial evidence for allusions to Seneca, Virgil, Livy, and Horace but I am concentrating for illustrative purposes on Ovidian intertextuality. Kahn (1997) also notes a body of research devoted to identifying classical sources in the play; Liz Oakley-Brown notes that 'Ovid's poem was an integral part of the humanist programme of education' (2006, 3).
16 Chaudhuri (2014) makes the case for a connection between George Peele's *Descensus Astraeae* and this quotation despite the Ovidian context which does not underscore the possibility of a second golden age which the Virgilian eclogue advocates.
17 Italics are my own to denote red references.
18 Interestingly, Golding (1567) also uses pale in this instance not red or blushing.
19 Robert Joseph Edgeworth states that 'Ovid uses colour terms abundantly and displayed a fondness for using colours even where his primary model used no colours at all' (1992, 15).

20 For more on the subject of hand gestures in oratory and in particular in relation to Shakespeare, see Farah Karim-Cooper (2016).
21 Translated from Latin to English in the notes to 4.2.20-1 (Shakespeare [1594] 2006, 219).

References

Ascham, Roger. (1570) 1967. *The Schoolmaster*. Edited by Lawrence V. Ryan. Ithaca, NY: Cornell University Press.
Barkan, Leonard. 2001. "What Did Shakespeare Read?" In *The Cambridge Companion to Shakespeare*, edited by Margreta de Grazia and Stanley Wells, 31–48. Cambridge: Cambridge University Press.
Bate, Johnathan. 1993. *Shakespeare and Ovid*. Oxford: Clarendon Press.
Burrow, Colin. 2004. "Shakespeare and Humanistic Culture." In *Shakespeare and the Classics*, edited by Charles Martindale and A. B. Taylor, 9–27. Cambridge: Cambridge University Press.
Burrow, Colin. 2013. *Shakespeare & Classical Antiquity*. Oxford: Oxford University Press.
Carter, Sarah. 2011. *Ovidian Myth and Sexual Deviance in Early Modern English Literature*. New York: Palgrave Macmillan.
Chaudhuri, Pramit. 2014. "Classical Quotation in *Titus Andronicus*." *English Literary History* 81, no. 3: 787–810.
Christiansen, Nancy L. 1997. "Rhetoric as Character-Fashioning: The Implications of Delivery's 'Places' in the British Renaissance Paideia." *Rhetorica: A Journal of the History of Rhetoric* 15, no. 3: 297–334.
Cicero, Marcus Tullius. (55-45BC) 1948. *De Oratore III, De Fato, Paradoxa Stoicorum, De Partitione Oratoria*. Translated by H. Rackham. Cambridge, MA: Harvard University Press.
Cicero, Marcus Tullius. (45BC) 2002. *Cicero on the Emotions: Tusculan Disputations 3 and 4*. Translated by Margaret Graver. Chicago, IL; London: University of Chicago Press.
Crane, Mary Thomas. 1993. *Framing Authority: Sayings, Self, and Society in Sixteenth-Century England*. Princeton, NJ: Princeton University Press.
Crosbie, Christopher. 2007. "Fixing Moderation: '*Titus Andronicus*' and the Aristotelian Determination of Value." *Shakespeare Quarterly* 58, no. 2: 147–73.
Dickson, Vernon Guy. 2009. "'A Pattern, Precedent, and Lively Warrant': Emulation, Rhetoric, and Cruel Propriety in *Titus Andronicus*." *Renaissance Quarterly* 62, no. 2: 376–409.
Dio Cassius. (c.233CE) 1925. *Roman History, Volume VIII, Books 61–70*. Translated by Earnest Cary and Herbert B. Foster. Cambridge, MA: Harvard University Press.
Edgeworth, Robert Joseph. 1992. *The Colors of the Aeneid*. New York: Peter Lang.
Enterline, Lynn. 2012. *Shakespeare's Schoolroom: Rhetoric, Discipline, Emotion*. Philadelphia: University of Pennsylvania Press.
Gillespie, Stuart. 2016. *Shakespeare's Books: A Dictionary of Shakespeare Sources*. London; New York: Bloomsbury Arden Shakespeare.

Golding, Arthur, trans. 1567. *The XV Bookes of P. Ouidius Naso, Translated Oute of Latin into English Meeter*. London: Willyam Seres.
Grafton, Anthony and Lisa Jardine. 1986. *From Humanism to the Humanities: Education and the Liberal Arts in Fifteenth- and Sixteenth-Century Europe*. London: Duckworth & Company Ltd.
Greenblatt, Stephen. 1980. *Renaissance Self-Fashioning from More to Shakespeare*. Chicago, IL: University of Chicago Press.
Joseph, Sister Miriam. 1947. *Shakespeare's Use of the Arts of Language*. Philadelphia, PA: Paul Dry Books Inc.
Kahn, Coppélia. 1997. *Roman Shakespeare: Warriors Wounds and Women*. London; New York: Routledge.
Karim-Cooper, Farah. 2016. *The Hand on the Shakespearean Stage: Gesture, Touch and the Spectacle of Dismemberment*. London: Bloomsbury Arden Shakespeare.
Karim-Cooper, Farah. 2021. "The Materials of Race: Staging the Black and White Binary in the Early Modern Theatre." In *The Cambridge Companion to Shakespeare and Race*, edited by Ayanna Thompson, 17–29. Cambridge: Cambridge University Press.
Kinney, Arthur. 1986. *Humanist Poetics: Thought, Rhetoric, and Fiction in Sixteenth-Century England*. Amherst: University of Massachusetts Press.
Loomba, Ania. 2002. *Shakespeare, Race, and Colonialism*. Oxford: Oxford University Press.
Miola, Robert S. 1983. *Shakespeare's Rome*. Cambridge: Cambridge University Press.
Murphy, James J., ed. 1990. *A Short History of Writing Instruction: From Ancient Greece to Twentieth-Century America*. Davis, CA: Hermagoras Press.
Ndiaye, Noémie. 2021. "Shakespeare, Race, and Globalization." In *The Cambridge Companion to Shakespeare and Race*, edited by Ayanna Thompson, 158–74. Cambridge: Cambridge University Press.
Oakley-Brown, Liz. 2006. *Ovid and the Cultural Politics of Translation in Early Modern England*. Aldershot, Hampshire: Ashgate Publishing Ltd.
Ovid. (8CE). 2004. *Metamorphoses: Books I-VII*. Translated by Frank Justus Miller. Cambridge, MA: Harvard University Press.
Oxford University Press. n.d. "Oxford English Dictionary Online." Accessed August, 2021. https://www.oed.com/
Peacham, Henry. (1577) 1971. *The Garden of Eloquence 1577*. Menston: The Scholar Press Limited.
Pearson, Meg F. 2010. "'That Bloody Mind I Think They Learned of Me': Aaron as Tutor in *Titus Andronicus*." *Shakespeare* 6, no. 1: 34–51.
Plett, Heinrich. 1995. *English Renaissance Rhetoric and Poetics: A Systematic Bibliography of Primary and Secondary Sources*. New York; Leiden: Brill.
Plett, Heinrich. 2012. *Enargeia in Classical Antiquity and the Early Modern Age: The Aesthetics of Evidence*. Leiden: Brill.
Pope, Stephanie L. 2019. "Gestures and the Classical Past in Shakespeare's *Titus Andronicus*." *Shakespeare* 15, no. 4: 326–34.
Quintilian. (95CE) 1987. *Quintilian: On the Teaching of Speaking and Writing*. Translated by Reverend John Selby Watson. Edited by James J. Murphy. Carbondale and Edwardville: Southern Illinois University Press.

Quintilian. (95CE) 2006. *Institutes of Oratory*. Translated by Reverend John Selby Watson. Edited by Lee Honeycutt. http://rhetoric.eserver.org/quintilian/.

Rainolde, Richard. 1563. *A Booke Called the Foundacion of Rhetorike*. London: Ihon Kingston.

Roe, John. 2011. "Shakespeare: What Rhetoric Accomplishes." In *Shakespeare and Renaissance Literary Theories: Anglo-Italian Transactions*, edited by Michele Marrapodi Farnham, 73–90. Surrey: Ashgate Publishing Ltd.

Rowe, Katherine A. 1994. "Dismembering and Forgetting in *Titus Andronicus*." *Shakespeare Quarterly* 45, no. 3: 279–303.

Royster, Francesca. 2000. "White-Limed Walls: Whiteness and Gothic Extremism in Shakespeare's Titus Andronicus." *Shakespeare Quarterly* 51, no. 4: 432–55.

Scheer, Monique. 2012. "Are Emotions a Kind of Practice (And Is That What Makes Them Have a History)?: A Bourdieuian Approach to Understanding History." *History and Theory* 51, no. 2: 193–220.

Shakespeare, William. (1594) 2006. *Titus Andronicus*. Edited by Jonathan Bate. London; New York: Bloomsbury Arden Shakespeare.

Skinner, Quentin. 2014. *Forensic Shakespeare*. Oxford: Oxford University Press.

Vickers, Brian. 1988. *In Defence of Rhetoric*. Oxford: Clarendon Press.

Weber, William W. 2015. "'Worse than Philomel': Violence, Revenge, and Meta-Allusion in *Titus Andronicus*." *Studies in Philology* 112, no. 4: 698–717.

Wesley, John. 2015. "Rhetorical Delivery for Renaissance English: Voice, Gesture, Emotion, and the Sixteenth-Century Vernacular Turn." *Renaissance Quarterly* 68, no. 4: 1265–96.

Whigham, Frank. 1984. *Ambition and Privilege: The Social Tropes of Elizabethan Courtesy Theory*. Berkeley: University of California Press.

Wilson, Thomas (1553) 1969. *The Arte of Rhetorique*. New York: Da Capo Press.

2 'For blushing cheeks by faults are bred / And fears by pale white shown'
Reading the face for colour and emotion in *Love's Labour's Lost*

In the early modern period, emotional disruptions were thought to directly influence physiological processes and their chromatic signifiers, particularly those visible in the face. For example, Nicholas Coeffeteau, a Dominican philosopher, describes blushing as a signifier of shame, saying

> Shame… is a kinde of feare, which ariseth, for that man doubts some blame and some censure of his actions. As Feare then retires the blood, and makes it descend about the heart, how comes it that Shame should cause the blood to ascend unto the countenance, and make the face to blush?
>
> (1621, 496)

Thomas Wright also comments on the apparent double reality of blushing, saying

> we may also perceive the cause of blushing, for those that have committed a fault … or at least imagine they are thought to have committed it … they blush, because nature being afraid, lest in the face the fault be discovered, sendeth the pure blood, to be a defence and succor, the which effect, commonly, is judged to proceed from a good and virtuous nature, because no man can but allow, that is good to be ashamed of a fault.
>
> ([1624] 1986, 1.7.106–16)

That expression of shame comes under scrutiny from Shakespeare in the play *Much Ado About Nothing*, where Friar Francis is convinced that Hero blushes due to her chastity and shame

> I have marked
> A thousand blushing apparitions
> To start into her face, a thousand innocent shames
> In angel whiteness beat away those blushes,

DOI: 10.4324/9781003198246-3

> To burn the errors that these princes hold
> Against her maiden truth.
>
> (4.1.157–63)

However, other characters see Hero's blush as an indicator of guilt. The discrepancy between the reception of one moment of blushing undermines its reliability as a sign.[1] Armado, in *Love's Labour's Lost*, notes he betrays his own reality of affections through blushing, however, such blushing cannot be trusted in the face of females (1.2.118).[2] The ephemeral nature of blushing seems to be part of the fascination it holds, particularly since it cannot be artificially produced.

In this chapter, I explore various ways facial colour influenced emotional responses. Key to my discussion is the fact that a change or a heightening of facial colour, natural or artificial, is widely discussed in early modern philosophical works, tracts on art, religious texts, and pamphlets on the theatre. The complexities of facial colouring, as articulated in *Love's Labour's Lost* and mediated through contemporary writings, show how various representations of the face function both to collude with and strain against emotional transparency. To ground early modern theories, I look to classical precedents: the idea of physical beauty, humours and the complexion, and attitudes towards cosmetics and disguise, all of which are demonstrable through differing hues of the face. Racial difference is examined with regards to 'a staging of racial and sexual difference which scrutinizes the construction of cultural desirability' (Chedgzoy 1998, 109). This so-called staging is important as race itself 'is social constructed' (Akhimie 2021, 52). It is important to note that race and racial difference were not fixed concepts, since ideas about racial differences were still being negotiated through cultural, social, and physical means.

My consideration of the face in *Love's Labour's Lost* rests on Shakespeare's heavy reliance on the word 'face'. Shakespeare mentions the word 'face' 25 times, more than in any other play he wrote, suggesting in this instance a fascination with the face as a site of emotional expression.[3] 'Complexion', another word suggesting facial colouring, is mentioned five times. It is discussed with regard to humours, green sickness and the disease of virgins, the desired colours of white and red, and racial differences, all the while reflecting a complex register of emotions. The powerful persistence in *Love's Labour's Lost* of themes such as surface and interior, artifice and nature, appearance and truth make up an emotional drama of colour-in-complexion. The play also deals with the ambiguities that arise from misreadings of faces, masks, and disguises. The play both privileges and applies pressure to the face as a gendered site that needs to be regulated to maintain social and cultural boundaries.

Emotional susceptibility

Coeffeteau notes in *A Table of Humane Passions* that 'the Eyes are only employed to judge of the difference of colours' (1621, 14). It is the processing of the visual image that causes disturbance. The image presented to us is processed according to the subjectivity of the beholder. If the beholder is concurrently moved by desire, then the image is able to move more potent passions. The colours and other images we see which can bring us pleasure and pleasant emotions are complicated by the presence of desire and excess. Coeffeteau suggests that this is because 'there are pleasures of the eyes, which pollute by the excesse of our cupidites, and by the disorder of our desires: as when our eyes not content to behold the beauty of a woman, conceive an unchaste desire' (1621, 235). This belief can be applied to the four men in *Love's Labour's Lost* who all are moved by desire on seeing the ladies when they arrive to court. Coeffeteau maintains that

> Desire differs from Loue, and Plasure, for that Loue is the first motion, and the first Passion we haue of any good thing, without respect whether it be present or absent; Desire is a Passion for a good that is absent, and pleasure a contentment wee haue to enjoy when wee haue gotten it.
>
> (218)

When the object that we desire is absent because we cannot possess it or it is removed from our reach, passions become excessive and they cloud our judgement towards that object. Coeffeteau warns people to moderate their desire because an excess engenders other excessive passions which have the ability to become destructive

> the excess of our Desire doth Blemish the pursuit. As for example, Pictures, Images, Statues, Porphyrie, Marble, Amber, Crystal, Ivory, Flowers, Tapistries, Diamonds, Rubies & all other things, where the eye discouers the wonders of nature and the Art of man, are the objects of an innocent pleasure if we could use them moderately. But wee suffer ourselves to bee transported with so furious a Desire, and we seeke them with such an inraged heate, as it is rather a madnesse then a Desire.
>
> (233)

Desire, along with love and shame, is explored in *Love's Labour's Lost* through the complicated relationships between King Ferdinand of Navarre and three of his lords, and the Princess of France and three of her ladies. The King's opening speech to his lords indicates the play's preoccupation with passion and desire

> Therefore, brave conquerors – for so you are,
> That war against your own affections
> And the huge army of the world's desires –
> Our late edict shall strongly stand in force.
>
> (1.1.8–11)

The King suggests that the men need courage and self-control to avoid succumbing to passionate excess. While the King sets out the struggle against passion as central to the aims of the academy, Berowne describes the pain, suffering, and ultimately the folly attached to the course of study proposed by the King. In doing so, Berowne reiterates the importance of the eye in this emotional transaction

> Light seeking light doth light of light beguile;
> So, ere you find where light in darkness lies,
> Your light grows dark by losing of your eyes.
> Study me how to please the eye indeed
> By fixing it upon a fairer eye,
> Who dazzling so, that eye shall be his heed,
> And give him light that it was blinded by.
>
> (1.1.77–83)

In tension with the King's plan, Berowne suggests that books and words will never provide adequate learning by themselves because the eye will become weary and dimmed without the stimulation of pleasing sights in the shape of a woman's face to gaze upon. Farah Karim-Cooper notes, '[t]he imagery of light and darkness anticipates the thematic importance of dark beauty and its defence as a rhetorical exercise in the play' (2006, 143). Berowne is, with the skill of an experienced rhetorician, advocating against the embargo on women. It is implied that restricted access to women leaves the men without the necessary skills to read the emotional nuances in women's faces, words, and gestures. Vision, knowledge, and a variety of sights are key and are foreshadowed as necessary tools when reading emotional responses.

Berowne continues by suggesting that the lack of interaction with women in the academy will stunt the men's growth and development: '[t]he spring is near when green geese are a-breeding' (1.1.97). He gestures towards a verdant green spring with callow youth needing to mate, while also hinting at lust and prostitution, since 'geese' could refer to prostitutes. In his view, while their little coterie is too old for the student life, they are not averse to female temptations, much like younger students who are similarly distracted. Already the audience is prepared for the men's failure; they will prove 'green' emotionally and socially. When Berowne reluctantly agrees to the edict, the King replies '[h]ow well this yielding rescues thee from shame!' (1.1.118). The King's assertion is linked to the performance of shame in early modern courtly and chivalric practice. Naming the emotion of shame is, of course, a form of emotional practice and partly a way to experience it. Stephanie Trigg identifies a stoic discourse of resistance to passion which deploys 'shame' as a mechanism of social regulation (2007, 84). While I agree that in *Love's Labour's Lost* the performance of shame is embedded in public reputation, I would argue that there is a strong sense of psychological inwardness present as well – a personal internal struggle against desire is set as central to the discourse. Maintaining self-control becomes an easy test to fail. Inability to control the passions becomes shameful, both privately and publicly, intensified by the King's public proclamations concerning interactions with women.

The King associates desire and the passions with shame, a stance which will come to haunt him as the play progresses. Indeed, almost immediately Berowne points out that the proclamation banning women will have to be contravened because the King is about to receive a royal visit from the French King's daughter. The immediate suspension of the decree underlines its untenable nature, which unravels further as the play progresses. Berowne notes, 'Necessity will make us all forsworn / Three thousand times within this three years' space' (1.1.147–8). Eternal shame, Berowne comments, will be the result of transgression. It also will have political consequences since the social element of shame will be performed in the public forum. The King will be marked as a monarch who breaks his oaths. With the edict already under scrutiny, the King mentions a missive which comes from Armado. While trying to recuperate from melancholy, Armado happens upon Costard and Jacquenetta *in flagrante delicto*. He describes the shameful event in terms of black and white, foreshadowing royal sins

> I did encounter
> that obscene and most preposterous event that draweth from
> my snow-white pen the ebon-coloured ink, which here thou
> viewest, beholdest, surveyest, or seest.
>
> (1.1.234–7)

The black/white contrast creates a stark image of black sins pouring from the pure white pen. Vision is privileged, though in absurd fashion, as the conduit of truthful information.

Colour and complexion

The use of the word complexion grew in the Middle Ages when, in physiological and natural philosophy, 'complexion' meant the 'combination of supposed qualities ... determining the nature of a body...[or] humours of the body... [or] temperament' (OED Online, 'complexion'). Stephen Batman's sixteenth-century translation of Bartholomaeus' thirteenth-century book, *De proprietatibus rerum*, uses 'complection' to describe the colours that appear in various temperaments directly connecting the chromatic and the affective. The Oxford English Dictionary notes in 1569 the first use of a secondary meaning of 'the natural colour, texture, and appearance of the skin, esp. of the face' (OED Online, 'complexion').

Indeed, Shakespeare is listed as one of a vanguard of writers to coin the word 'complexion' to mean 'colour, visible aspect, look, appearance'. This semantic shift opened the word up to a duality of meaning that combined the previous idea of temperament with ideas concerning facial colouring. The shift possibly arose as there was a coincidental need to note the possible relationship between facial colouring and interiority of feeling, with the face being probed as a vehicle for accessing a person's interior. Such a relationship is mooted by Lemnius when he notes

> not only in the inward mynd of man, do these ornaments and giftes of nature appeare & expressly shew out themselves but even in the outward shew, shape and behauyour of the body there is evidently descryed and perceyued a comly grace and portly dignitye. For in the countenaunce, which is the image of the mynde, in the eyes, which are the bewrayers and tokentellers of the inward conceiptes: in the colour, lineaments: proportion and feacture of the whole body, ther appeareth a kind of heroicall grace.
>
> (1581, 36)

Lemnius is pointing out that the workings of the mind can be 'read' through the outward features and colouring of an individual's body, with the face being the most prominent part of that body on view.[4] The semantic shift associated with the word 'complexion' gains currency as the emotional discourse of the face and its attendant staining become a subject of inquiry.

It is useful to look at the complexities surrounding a 'wan' colour since such an example illustrates the multivalent emotional meanings attached to colour. A wan colour is occasionally used in relation to the complexion but it is to be examined with caution, as it is capable of conflicting meanings. Shakespeare uses this colour on several occasions in his work in connection with the complexion, including: 'pale and wan' in both *Comedy of Errors* (4.4.103), and *Titus Andronicus* (2.3.90); while in *Henry IV, Part 1*, he uses the phrase 'wan with care' (1.1.1). However, Bartholomaeus describes an alternate meaning to the word 'wan' in the following passage

> Wan coulour is euill in men and in beasts, for it betokeneth masterie of cold, which quencheth kindly heat: or els it betokeneth superfluitye of melancholye bloud, which defileth all the skin without: or els it betokeneth anguish & passion of the heart, which draweth inward the heate of bloud, as it fareth in those persons, that bee envious or wrathfull.
>
> ([1582] 1976, cap. 21)

Here the term, which is derived from Old English, means dark, gloomy, or black. It is also linked to lacking light or lustre (OED Online, 'wan').

Although the term 'wan' does not occur in *Love's Labour's Lost*, the conflict and complexity of deciphering the meaning behind this particular colour term strikes a cautionary note regarding all colour references. The context of the chromatic descriptor needs to be carefully examined to avoid misreading emotional situations. Interestingly, Bartholomaeus considers paleness as a colour title in its own right, close to white but with less coldness. He also connects paleness with various emotional states, positioning it as an emotional reference

> Then paleness is a mene colour: it beginneth from white, & passeth out of kind toward blacke. Also pale gendred, & commeth of dread of right great businesse, & of great travaile, and of other causes, by the which bloud is drawn inward, and then the bodye is pale and discoulored without... Palleat omnis amans, hic est color aptus amanti. This verse meaneth, that every louer is pale, and pale coulour is couenable to the louer.
>
> ([1582] 1976, cap. 13)

Again such diverse explanations for a pale visage point to the importance of context. The expected association must be tempered with a logical assessment of both the text and cultural context.

For example, Armado is confounded by Moth, his page, when discussing the discourse of love and desire – 'the humour of affection' – Armado asks '[w]ho was Samson's / love, my dear Moth?', and '[o]f what complexion?' (1.2.73–4; 76). Armado has in mind the balance of bodily humours – blood, phlegm, melancholy, and choler. Moth's answer, that Delilah was 'sea-water green' (1.2.80), gestures instead towards skin colouring, indicating the unstable contemporary meaning of 'complexion'. Delilah, Moth implies, was either immature, of small childish intelligence, or afflicted by chlorosis. Green was commonly associated with youth and immaturity but also the maiden's illness: green sickness visible in the face was commonly associated with pubescent girls. As Ursula Potter remarks

> the dramatic representation of puberty as a crisis period in young girls is largely consistent with prevailing 17th century medical texts on the topic. This indicates a fairly informed level of popular knowledge among theatre audiences of the condition of green sickness and of the precipitating factors which caused it.
>
> (2009, 383)

Helen King suggests an even earlier public awareness of green sickness: '[s]omewhere between 1547 and Jane Kitson's illness in 1558, green sickness became a condition in its own right, rather than a form of jaundice, and – in the process – it became associated with young women' (2004, 25).

In 1581, Lemnius noted the condition of lusty maids and virgins who remain unmarried

> For besyde their unruly motions of tickeling lust, besyde theyr secrete flames and burning affections, they be ill coloured, and nothing pleasauntly complexioned, their myndes unstedy and out of quiet frame, by meanes of a naughty vapour that ascendeth upward and disturbeth their brayne.
>
> (106)

The implied reference to chlorosis has relevance to the desires and perceptions of the men in the play since female sexuality can be seen as an illness requiring a male cure. As the 'disease of virgins', green sickness has its cure incorporated in its title.[5] The idea is also found in *Romeo and Juliet* when Romeo describes Juliet, saying: 'Her vestal livery is but sick and green' (2.1.50). Many have noted that according to Hippocrates the cure for women suffering from this malady is marriage and in particular pregnancy (Starobinski 1981; Schleiner 2009). If women actively tried to achieve this pale (and, on occasion, greenish) colour through diet and other artificial means then they risked their lives (Caries 1583, 40).

Green has a long and varied association in the early modern period with both young women, as described above, and lovers. Armado notes

> Green indeed is the colour of lovers. But to
> have a love of that colour, methinks Samson had small
> reason for it. He surely affected her for her wit.
>
> (1.2.83–5)

Lovers were considered to be suffering from a sickness in varying degrees, and the imbalance in their humours is evident in the green or sickly colour they display (Fleissner 1961, 48).

Armado uses chromatic references to signify a change in the emotional register. He identifies his feelings as 'love', declaring '[m]y love is most immaculate white and red' (1.2.87). White and red identify both the lover and the beloved in the arrangement defined by Armado, but Moth immediately rebuts, playing on the word 'immaculate', saying, '[m]ost maculate thoughts, master, are masked / under such colours' (1.2.88–9). The purity expressed by Armado, idealised in terms of white complexion, is sullied. We are reminded of the duplicity of colours and complexion, now viewed as superficial appearances rather than true signs of an inner mental and emotional state.[6] Annette Drew-Bear notes that '[f]ace-blackening and face-spotting are thus used to symbolically transform the face to indicate sin... The etymology of 'immaculate' (without spots and without sin) suggests this as conversely "maculate" means both spotted and sinful' (1994, 38). Whoredom and religious impiety are thus associated within the character of Jacquenetta.

Armado and Moth's exchange offers the audience the play's first disruptive suggestion that the values assigned to colours in complexion are duplicitous. Moth expands on his analysis by way of a traditional rhyme

> If she be made[7] of white and red,
> Her faults will ne'er be known,
> For blushing cheeks by faults are bred,
> And fears by pale white shown.
> Then if she fear or be to blame,
> By this you shall not know,
> For still her cheeks possess the same
> Which native she doth owe.
> A dangerous rhyme, master, against the reason of white and red.
>
> (1.2.94–103)

Moth warns of the dangers that lie in the interpretation of blushing. The meaning of blushing depends both upon the viewer and the context, and may be further complicated by the use of a cosmetic mask. If the lady has fabricated her colour by using cosmetics, the onlooker will not be able to discern her true complexion, let alone her true feelings. Almost immediately Armado illustrates the vagaries of facial staining when he spies his love object Jacquenetta, and whispers, 'I do betray myself with blushing' (1.2.126). Armado is stained publicly with evidence of his love. His face remains under public scrutiny when he offers to tell Jacquenetta of wonders. She replies, '[w]ith that face?' (1.2.134), suggesting shortcomings in Armado's physiognomic repertoire. She suggests, perhaps, that the public should be able to judge a story from the teller's face but that with a face like his, the truth of such a story could not be trusted.

Historically, humoral states were implicated in facial colouring. The humours could influence the passions and consequently influence chromatic manifestations of the face. While humours and passions could act together, they also could work independently of each other. Bartholomaeus explains in detail how colour of the skin could arise in two ways:

> [s]ometimes of humours inward, and sometimes of passions of the soule. Also chaunging of coulour in the skin commeth of inner things: sometime by hot humours, and sometime by cold ... and according thereunto the coulour in the skinne is wont to varie, for when the colde houmoures ware hotte, white colour turneth into citrine or into red. And when hot humours doth coole, then red coulour doth chaunge to white or pale, and so of other it is to be understood. Also chaunging in the skin commeth of passions of the

soule. The red wareth pale for anguish or dreade, for in dread the heart closet, and heate that is in the otter partes draweth inward, and therefore the otter partes ware pale. Also the pale wareth red for wrath, for in wrath the heart openeth and desireth wreake, and the heat passeth sodeinly from the inner parts to the otter parts, and so the bloud heateth, and is betweene the skin and the flesh, and so red colour is sodeinly gendered.

([1582] 1976, cap. 10)

This passage is useful as it points to the discrepancies in understanding why the face has changed colour and clearly nominates the passions for involvement alongside the humours. Lemnius also points to the relationship of the humours to facial colouring when he describes humoral disturbances experienced by the body. He suggests that the colours visible in the complexion – be they pale, yellow, tawny, brown, or dusky – indicate the humours within. A very white look indicates a phlegmatic excess, while a pale or yellowish colouring is perhaps melancholic, and choleric is associated with the presence of fresh red blood. A blackish appearance suggests adust choler (1581, 90). If great 'affectes and passions' intoxicate and perplex the mind, the humours will sometimes manifest themselves in the skin. This assertion means that sometimes men who appear affected by great heat are not affected by sickness 'but of the motion and stirring of the humours: againe them that be affrighted and in mynd amazed, to be pale' (90). In treatises, there is often a cyclical argument that suggests an affinity between the humours and the passions with a disturbance in facial colouring as the outward sign.

Facial perfection

As well as considerations regarding passions and humours, there was also a societal consensus on the perfect or expected form of colouring the face should take. Lemnius notes that, in its perfect form, 'the colour [is] freshe, sweete and pleasaunte. The cheekes and the balles therof steined, and died in perfecte hewe of whyte and red, and that naturally, specially in the lusty yeares of Adolesency' (1581, 36). Tensions arise between societal expectations of facial perfection and the reality of the individual's features. With a prescriptive ideal of facial colouring and the established link to external displays of passions it was not long before opinions and practice around cosmetic use were discussed in treatises, pamphlets, and other publications. Patricia Phillippy notes that '[u]nderlying the advice of instructional manuals is a consensus on ideals of feminine beauty – blonde hair, black eyes, white skin, red cheeks and lips – culled from and promulgated by the Petrarchan tradition and its transmission across Europe' (2006, 6).

Again, there are classical precedents for the negativity surrounding the use of artificial face colouring which can be read in Quintilian's work

> [b]ut let the embellishment of our style (for I will repeat what I said) be manly, noble, and chaste; let it not affect effeminate delicacy, or a complexion counterfeited by paint but let it glow with genuine health and vigor.
> ([95CE] 2006, 8.3.6)

While he draws an analogy between rhetorical styles (see Chapter 1) and natural/painted faces rather than a literal comment on faces, it does indicate an accepted opinion on the painted faces. The duplicity produced by painting the face with cosmetics may not evince the best response from the audience.

Writers in the early modern period continued the classical argument against the evils of cosmetic use. In 1583, Philip Stubbes wrote *The Anatomy of Abuses* which proved a popular text (reprinted in 1583, 1585, and 1595). His main focus was the immoral behaviour of those who were associated with the stage but also of those who were influenced by the stage to indulge in elaborate displays of clothing, hats, games, dancing, and more. Stubbes, in particular, wrote on the shortcomings of make-up-wearing women

> The Women of Ailgna[8] (many of them) use to colour their faces with certain oyles, liquors, unguents and waters made to that end, whereby they think their beautie is greatly decored: but who seethe not that their soules are thereby deformed, and they brought deeper into the displeasure and indignation of the Almighty... Do they think thus to adulterate the Lord his workmanship, and to be without offence...Thinketh thou that thou canst make thy self fairer then God who made us all? These must needs be their inuentions, or els they would never go about to colour their faces with such fibbersawces... Those which paint or colour themselues in this worlde otherwise then God hath made them, let them feare least when the day of iudgement commeth, the Lorde wil not know them for his Creatures... And what are they els then the Deuils inuentions to intangle poore soules in the nets of perdition?'
> (1583, under 'A particulare Discription of the Abuses of Womens apparell in Ailgna')

Stubbes has Christianised the classical argument by insisting that not only does wearing make-up cover the natural health and vigour displayed on the face but it also consists of a sin against God and his creation of the individual's face. As Tanya Pollard notes, the idea of cosmetics 'offered moralists a forceful way to articulate links between face-paints and less tangible forms of transgression and contamination' (2005, 88). Stephen Gosson held similar views in his work, *A Glasse, to view the Pride of Vainglorious Women*, where he claims that the women who paint their faces are worse than the painters with cunning skill and players on the stage, as they allow men of 'lore and wit' to consider them to be more fit than they actually are as partners (1595, A₃). The women are likened to whores who deceive gentlemen into loving a prostitute. Cosmetics are considered evil and the work of the devil.

Kimberly Poitevin notes 'for English writers such as Tuke, Stubbes, and Rich, cosmetics inhibited men's abilities to properly distinguish ladies from laundresses, white from black, good from evil, and natural beauty from artifice' (2011, 82). In all these cases, the male judgement rests on the visual image they are presented with, and their conclusions are not tempered with reason or with any other evaluation of the woman's character. Shakespeare, in *Hamlet*, uses this idea that women deceive men by using make-up. Hamlet rails at Ophelia, damning her and all women, 'God hath given you one face and you make yourselves another' (3.1.142–3). Shirley Nelson Garner states that 'for him [Hamlet], woman's *painted* body *is* her body, and the image carries with it fallen sexuality, seduction and betrayal, the art of the courtesan… So linked with women was the custom of wearing makeup that "painting" might be a synecdoche for woman' (1989, 126).[9]

However, wearing make-up allowed women the opportunity to fulfil beauty ideals. The ideal complexion appears in Chaucer's description of Beaute in the *Romaunt of the Rose* in the fourteenth century

> Hir chere was symple as byrde in bour,
> As whyt as lylye or rose in rys (twig).
>
> ([c1372] 2008, 1014)

Chaucer continues by saying that Beaute had no need of a painted brow or made up face.[10] Poitevin observes an inconsistency here: 'references to cosmetics were wide-spread in sonnets and lyric poetry, which denigrated "painted faces" even as they idealized the red and white complexions that women who used cosmetics tried to imitate' (2011, 61). Shakespeare's 'Rose-cheeked' Adonis is

> More white and red than doves or roses are –
> …
> Twixt crimson shame and anger ashy-pale.
> Being red, she loves him best; and being white,
> Her best is bettered with a more delight.
>
> (10; 76–8)

Here, Shakespeare subverts orthodoxies of complexion by applying the female beauty blazon to the male Adonis in a poem that more generally reverses gender roles as part of its design.[11] It is a subversion that is expanded upon in *Love's Labour's Lost*. By using make-up, some women were attempting to attain the ideal and correct a complexion that was prone to change, thus masking the myriad of emotional readings that onlookers could make. Lublin notes

> [i]f a woman failed to live up to the ideal of beauty, she would have been marked by her natural, visible flaws as immoral, and if she had attempted to hide those flaws with cosmetics, she would have been marked as immoral by her painting.
>
> (2011, 30)

This impossible position led to tensions around the appearance of the female face and added moral and emotional weight to comments on the face.

The use of cosmetics also led to anxieties about interracial movement since it was thought that the skin was an unstable boundary of the body, linked to the porosity of the body in general. Gail Kern Paster argues, 'besides being open and fungible in its internal workings, the humoral body was also porous and thus able to be influenced by the immediate environment' (1993, 9).[12] Cosmetics could be highly corrosive leading to permanent blackening of the skin and compounding fears about racial contamination, because the black colour could then leech into the body beneath. The use of cosmetics was also thought to prematurely age the wearer in a confounding reversal of intent (Haydocke 1598, 130). Make-up was a costly imported product, leading to further anxieties about race. It also privileged superficial beauty at the expense of care of the soul and so posed a danger to the moral health of the wearer. Those who opposed its use felt that the wearers were 'counterfeiters who challenge the cosmic and social order by redefining their own value' (Dolan 1993, 229). It was well known that the emotions could be disturbed by diverse means; those women who challenged the stability of the social order by wearing make-up could also upset the delicate balance of the emotions, especially in anxious males. The use of cosmetics in one way consolidated the superiority of whiteness and Englishness, mostly driven by women's use of lightening materials to achieve this perfection. Still, since 'cosmetics could be so easily applied and removed ... women who made up also revealed color to be an unreliable marker of race, class, or moral truth, exposing the notion of race itself as artificial, a charade' (Poitevin 2011, 62). Farah Karim-Cooper notes, 'racial categories during the early modern period were more often than not distinguishable through the external features, colour being the most predominant' (2007, 140). Part of the anti-make-up campaign sought to reinstate natural – meaning unadorned – skin complexion as the standard racial marker. The face was an unstable text, but physical beauty, as expressed by appropriate and natural facial colouring, was thought to be indicative of inner beauty of character and thoughts; facial cosmetics, by contrast, were duplicitous, bringing about the movements of passions by false means.[13]

In *Love's Labour's Lost*, with the face foregrounded as an important, if unreliable, text that can and should be read, the Princess of France appears. Within a few lines, she makes reference to her own face suggesting that it is not the most important aspect of her strengths, however, but in doing so she draws attention to its beauty. As if continuing earlier conversations, the Princess emphasises her natural complexion to an audience already aware of the pitfalls of a duplicitous visage, stating

> Good Lord Boyet, my beauty, though but mean,
> Needs not the painted flourish of your praise.
> Beauty is bought by judgement of the eye,
> Not uttered by base sale of chapmen's tongues.
>
> (2.1.13–6)

The Princess, like Berowne previously, privileges sight over words, despite the accepted wisdom that sight should be tempered with reason. The Princess talks of her beauty not needing 'painted flourish', in response to Boyet's effusive praise and his skill as a rhetorician, but also to her disdain of applying make-up to enhance her appeal. Here, again, rhetoric and facial colouring are conflated. Her disdain can be attributed to two reasons: first, she feels that her pure and worthy character should be visible in her unadorned face; second, she wants to be seen as commanding despite her gender. A woman who does not engage in face-painting does not bring the male gaze so intensely upon her activities. Of course, the Princess *is* 'painting' her own beauty in the language of decorum by dispraising it. The Princess proclaims her skin's immutability in a time when the skin was considered an unstable boundary, linked to the porosity of the body in general. By stating that the eye of the beholder should be able to discern the true beauty of a visage without the need for artifice, the Princess sets up a further conversation on the truth of beauty. This is in opposition to the complaint that cosmetics 'sinned against truth' (Pollard 2005, 88). According to Lublin, 'cosmetics serve to cover up the signs of venereal diseases and that red and white paint serve as brands or signs of sin and lust' (2011, 29). In *Love's Labour's Lost*, the understanding around the use of cosmetics is subverted to some extent: women themselves discuss the implications of cosmetics when the men inadvertently suggest that they paint their faces.

Vision and visage

The Princess continues to reference her face as she urges Boyet to consult with Navarre on her behalf, while she waits outside the gates, '[h]aste, signify so much, while we attend, Like *humble-visaged suitors*, his high will' (2.1.33–4, my italics). In three words, she conveys the idea that the emotional state of lovers is marked by the humility of their facial appearance. At the same time, although using a self-reflexive description, she manages to describe the future emotional state of the King and his men. The men will succumb to desire and become suitors, shaming themselves in the process. The theme of desire and shame is resumed when she remarks later

> God bless my ladies! Are they all in love,
> That every one her own hath garnished
> With such bedecking ornaments of praise?
>
> (2.1.77–9)

She associates the emotions of being in love – which are accompanied by both flourishes of speech and bodily ornamentation – with a further suggestion that the praises are overdone and thus in some ways unnatural and potentially shameful. Wordplay on terms of colour increases. Rosaline then links Berowne with 'brown', in a play on colour terms

> Berowne they call him, but a merrier man,
> Within the limit of becoming mirth,
> I have never spent an hour's talk withal.
>
> (2.1.66–8)

Brown is associated with sombreness and melancholy, as in a 'brown study', (OED Online, 'brown study'), but Rosaline is foreshadowing the subversion of colour referencing which Berowne will later undertake in his ekphrastic praise of Rosaline herself.

After a witty exchange between Berowne and Rosaline, in which Rosaline proves the quicker, they take their leave of each other

> BEROWNE: Now fair befall your mask.
> ROSALINE: Fair fall the face it covers.
> BEROWNE: And send you many lovers.
> ROSALINE: Amen, so you be none.
> BEROWNE: Nay, then will I be gone.
>
> (2.1.123–7)

Berowne wishes Rosaline's mask good luck, while Rosaline replies by wishing the face underneath good luck. The lovers that Berowne wishes on Rosaline will have to contend with the face and its mask of coloured feelings should they wish to succeed and win her hand. The discourse of masks foreshadows the masked scene later in the play where the 'masking provides a symbolic visual barrier that mocks both the artificiality of the wooing and the superficiality of wooing surface appearances' (Drew-Bear 1994, 105).

The King's conduct and behaviour, affected by feelings of love and desire, is concentrated in his gaze and therefore hyper-sensitive to visual influences.[14] Boyet describes this phenomenon, saying

> Why, all his behaviours did make their retire
> To the court of his eye, peeping thorough desire.
> His heart, like an agate with your print impressed,
> Proud with his form, in his eye pride expressed.
> His tongue, all impatient to speak and not see,
> Did stumble with haste in his eyesight to be.
> All senses to that sense did make their repair,
> To feel only looking on fairest of fair.
> Methought all his senses were locked in his eye,
> As jewels in crystal, for some prince to buy.
>
> (2.1.233–42)

Boyet insists on drawing our attention to the King's eye which is the focal point and motivator of this desire. Vision is privileged and claims ascendency over the other senses and the faculty of reasoning. However, the audience is no doubt aware of the precarious nature of vision and of the danger in allowing sight to rule the mind. The King is allowing his eye to rule his reason. The 'court of his eye' points to the ineffectual court of learning proposed by the King and already compromised. The groundwork has been laid for the play's later emphasis on the uncertain judgement of true emotions by the vision of facial appearances.

In act three, Berowne soliloquises on his enslavement to love with particular and pertinent colour, referencing

> And I to be a corporal of his field
> And wear his colours like a tumbler's hoop!
> ...
> And among three to love the worst of all,
> A whitely wanton with a velvet brow,
> With two pitch-balls stuck in her face for eyes.
>
> (3.1.182–3; 190–2)

Berowne figures his love and his enslavement to love in terms of colour, suggesting that his inward condition will be made evident by his facial complexion, as if by military insignia. Passions will make a battleground of his heart and make him tumble and roll emotionally. He describes Rosaline as 'a whitely wanton', dispraising what is normally the ideal complexion in a female love interest, and further suspecting her whiteness of unchastity (Goldstein 1974, 345). The dark elements of Rosaline's face – 'pitch-ball' eyes and thick eyebrows – mean Berowne can hardly justify being passionate about such a woman in conventional terms. Indeed, the use of the word pitch semantically links Rosaline's face to Berowne's emotional turmoil. He notes the physical reality of Rosaline's appearance and concludes, despite the conventional requirements of beauty, that her reality is still attractive to him, contributing to tensions around the face.

Dark and fair faces

The expression of emotion through discourses of the face continues in act four. Each of the various characters is preoccupied with the appearance of their face and what it betrays to onlookers. The forester invites the Princess to stand on the edge of a coppice so that she 'may make the fairest shoot' (4.1.10). 'Fair' has no consistent definition in the play: it is used to denote both beauty and honesty, and can signify respect, eloquence, nobility, and favourable circumstances (OED Online, 'fair'). The Princess puns on his use of 'fairest' and gently chides the forester for a perceived slight to her beauty and her appearance. The Princess insists, as before, that her beauty should be seen as natural, once again conflating rhetoric and facial description. She confidently asserts her natural beauty, saying

> Nay, never paint me now.
> Where fair is not, praise cannot mend the brow.
> Here, good my glass, take this for telling true:
> Fair payment for foul words is more than due.
> …
> See, see, my beauty will be saved by merit!
> O heresy in fair, fit for these days!
> A giving hand, though foul, shall have fair praise.
> (4.1.16–19; 21–3)

The princess uses 'fair' to describe both her face and the compliments it commands in a way that confuses and embarrasses the forester. The exchange wakes a consciousness that the perfectly natural 'fair' look could be very fleeting, if it existed at all for the individual woman. On this note, Karim-Cooper discusses the significant tension which occurs when a virtuous woman strives to achieve a lustrous complexion (2014, 187). Hence, the Princess wants to assert that her 'fairness' is not compromised by the duplicitous and artificial means that some other virtuous ladies may use.

Directly, Boyet continues the emphasis on 'fair' when reading from the letter written by Armado to Jacquenetta

> By heaven, that thou art fair, is most
> infallible; true that thou art beauteous; truth itself that
> thou art lovely. More fairer than fair, beautiful than
> beauteous, truer than truth itself, have commiseration on
> thy heroical vassal.
> ...
> Thus, expecting thy reply, I
> profane my lips on thy foot, my eyes on thy picture and my
> heart on thy every part.
>
> (4.1.61–5; 82–4)

One of the messages in Armado's love professions is that Jacquenetta's beauty is redolent of a truth which can be discerned from an external look at her visage. And yet by using the verb 'profane' he is suggesting that her external appearance has the ability to sully or defile him. His eyes will be defiled looking upon her 'picture' or face, an idea that also links back to fear of a painted complexion. Holofernes' later utterance, 'I do fear colourable colours' (4.2.147–8), suggests a similar unease. He may mean that he fears specious arguments, or he could be referring to the proverb that truth needs no colours. In any case, his turn of phrase closely aligns with the play's tense contrast between the truthful complexion and the 'painted' or 'coloured' face. Indeed James A. Knapp notes that 'Shakespeare's seemingly contradictory attitude toward the ability to find the truth of character or emotional disposition in the face echoes contemporary debates over the validity of physiognomy as either a valuable skill for interpreting intentions and predilections or as a charlatan's ruse aimed at gulling the naïve' (2015, 5).

Berowne, whose desire for Rosaline continues to increase, enters with a paper, and says 'I am toiling in a pitch, pitch that defiles. / Defile, a foul word' (4.3.2–3). The blackness of the pitch and its filthy nature are intertwined with the features of Rosaline's face, Rosaline's eyes being the two 'pitch-balls' (3.1.192). The love that these dark features have aroused in Berowne echoes the foulness first mentioned by Armado. Love and desire are now associated with the baser emotions of shame and self-loathing. At this point, Berowne is melancholic from love, heralded by 'black' references, and sorrowful at his plight, driven to writing sonnets. In fact, he reinforces the gender roles that prevailed in lovesickness, as Dawson explains 'whereas male lovesickness is classified as a form of melancholy – a malady associated with creativity, interiority, and intellect – the female version is considered a disorder of the womb' (2008, 4). Berowne stands aside as the King enters and reads his own love sonnet aloud

> So sweet a kiss the golden sun gives not
> To those fresh morning drops upon the rose,
> As thy eye-beams when their fresh rays have smote
> The night of dew that on my cheeks down flows.
> Nor shines the silver moon one half so bright
> Through the transparent bosom of the deep
> As doth thy face, through tears of mine, give light.
> …
> How shall she know my griefs? I'll drop the paper.
> Sweet leaves shade folly.
>
> (4.3.23–9; 38–9)

The King begins his love sonnet with an array of colours composed to convey subtle emotional cues: his love's gaze is compared to the golden sun as it lands its rays upon the rose; the rose conjures up the ideal rosy hues of a perfectly coloured cheek; the silver moon recalls chaste Diana. Yet the emotional exchange also contains a hint of violence: a gaze that smites introduces the audience to the violence of emotions that occurs when love is unrequited. The King's grief becomes part of the emotions involved in loving the Princess and, by naming his emotions, he gives weight to them. The description of his love object links both the golden sun and the fresh rose favourably with the Princess, but the silver moon suggests Diana and the lovehunt as a violent necessity of love. Karim-Cooper argues that 'the moon represented chastity, but it was also an image that many satirists and poets used to mock cosmetic vanity, since the very source of the moon's shine or glow was thought to be borrowed light' (2014, 189). Karim-Cooper's comment points to the central theme of the face and its many guises. The King asks that the leaves hide the folly of his love. The leaves may suggest a broad reference to the colour 'green'. Because of the oath he made with his lords, he and the rest of the male lovers have made experiencing love shameful. Here, the King's love is to be hidden by greenery, linking it with the more lustful, intemperate loves associated with 'green', and not with the worthy love that he wishes to proclaim. The associations with shame are strengthened when the King calls Longaville '[i]n love, I hope. Sweet fellowship in shame' (4.3.46); sharing the shame might be less of a burden.

Listening to Longaville, Berowne comments, aside

> This is the liver-vein, which makes flesh a deity,
> A green goose a goddess. Pure, pure idolatry.
> God amend us, God amend! We are much out o' th' way.
>
> (4.3.71–3)

The liver was the organ 'in which bodily humours arose which influenced the passions to a wide extent'.[15] The green goose refers both to a silly young girl and a new whore; linked in the same line with 'idolatry' it becomes a duplicitous thing. Love has made all flesh godly and the wayward maid a goddess. The eyes cannot be trusted when influenced by strong emotions since the 'truth' of visual cues seems totally subjective. James L. Calderwood notes that 'the scholars have all become lyric poets singing the praises of their malady, not for the benefit of an audience, but purely for their own wonder and delight' (1965, 327). Indeed, it appears that the men's emotions are divorced from the reality of the women. This supposition gains currency when, with the women disguised, the men make love to the women wearing the gifted favour rather than the actual women they love. The women manipulate these situations to show the men that their love is not publicly endorsed, and is reliant on ostentatious rhetoric rather than viable communication (Calderwood 1965, 328). Not only does the male eye prove unreliable but male speech appears as 'painted rhetoric'.

When shame has been collectively acknowledged amongst the men, they openly discuss their love interests. While Berowne justifies his love for Rosaline, the King states that Rosaline cannot shine in the presence of the Princess. Ania Loomba notes

> the praise of black beauty in Renaissance literature and art serves to emphasize the power of the artist, or the lover. Precisely because blackness was so powerfully equated with ugliness and fairness with beauty, to 'prove' through powerfully poetic language that a black lady was fair is, in literary terms, to achieve the impossible and to wash the Ethiope white. Moreover, the conventional meanings of 'fair' and 'dark' are reinforced precisely by being momentarily displaced: the black beauty is more 'fair' than the fair woman who is actually 'dark' because false.
>
> (2002, 60)

Berowne, precisely in the vein Loomba describes, struggles to convince his friends that a dark beauty has merit. Rosaline's dark complexion cannot be described as 'fair' nor naturally 'glisten'. Berowne is quick to defend Rosaline's physiognomic 'otherness' to make his love and her appearance an emotional match. Sibylle Baumbach notes that 'Shakespeare's deviance from common norms presupposes an audience that is deeply familiar with the basic principles of physiognomy' (2008, 78). Berowne uses a contrast between day and night, and implicitly fair and dark, to compliment Rosaline

> O, but for my love, day would turn to night!
> Of all complexions the culled sovereignty

> Do meet as at a fair in her fair cheek,
> ...
> Lend me the flourish of all gentle tongues—
> Fie, painted rhetoric! O, she needs it not.
>
> (4.3.229–31; 234–5)

Her presence, despite a dark complexion, heralds the brightness of day. Berowne also insists that she is so beautiful that she does not need 'painted rhetoric' of ornamental and effusive descriptions. The Princess also made a similar case when she denounced 'painted flourish' (2.1.14). This phrase also gestures towards cosmetic use implying that she does not require a false made-up face. The King replies to Berowne's praise by saying, '[b]y heaven, thy love is black as ebony!' (4.3.243). After such an open attack on Rosaline's complexion, Berowne makes his case for a dark complexion being the most beautiful

> Is ebony like her? O wood divine!
> A wife of such wood were felicity.
> ...
> No face is fair that is not full so black.
>
> (4.3.244–5; 249)

Contrary to the usual orthodoxy, Berowne insists that black is the new fair. Shakespeare subverted the Petrarchan ideal in other works, for example, in Sonnet 127

> In the old age black was not counted fair,
> Or if it were, it bore not beauty's name;
> But now is black beauty's successive heir,
> And Beauty slandered with a bastard shame;
> For since each hand hath put on nature's power,
> Fairing the foul with art's false borrowed face.
>
> (1–6)

The King struggles to understand how judgements can be made if we cannot depend on the colour coding of a black complexion consistent with acts and persons of devilish intent, saying 'O paradox! Black is the badge of hell, / The hue of dungeons and the school of night' (4.3.250–2). This sentiment echoes many treatises of the day.

Berowne makes his case for Rosaline's complexion in a diatribe against face-painting women

> O, if in black my lady's brows be decked,
> It mourns that painting and usurping hair
> Should ravish doters with a false aspect;

>And therefore is she born to make black fair.
>Her favour turns the fashion of the days,
>For native blood is counted painting now;
>And therefore red, that would avoid dispraise,
>Paints itself black, to imitate her brow.
>
>(4.3.254–61)

Berowne points out that Rosaline is now in fashion: her natural and honest beauty is copied by means of artifice. These tricks, Berowne insists, lead lovers astray with a false exterior. Rosaline was born to champion the acceptability of a dark complexion. Through Berowne's reasoning, 'blackness' provides a reliable register for truth and beauty. The King and his lords respond by criticising Rosaline in terms that reinforce her unorthodox colour, using phrases such as: '[t]o look like her are chimney-sweepers black'; '[a]nd since her time are colliers counted bright'; '[a]nd Ethiops of their sweet complexion crack'; and '[d]ark needs no candles now, for dark is light' (4.3.262–5). While these exchanges are made in a humorous vein, it denotes the extent to which casual racism was stock in trade for early modern comedies.[16] The emphasis on her 'blackness' underlines her unknowable character for the detractors, while Berowne wishes to praise her natural purity. The argument posited by the King and his courtiers against sanctioning a dark complexion only serves to emphasise its inalterability against the unstable light complexion which can be altered with cosmetics. Both Berowne and the King avoid touching on the contemporary argument which suggested that 'black Ethiopians and tawny Indians were thought to be unable to blush and therefore to experience shame' (Iyengar 2005, 107). Berowne sees an opening to make a comment on the face-painting of the other ladies, saying '[y]our mistresses dare never come in rain, / For fear their colours should be washed away' (4.3.266–7). His comment reinforces the tensions surrounding the complexion, and particularly a fair complexion, as an emotional indicator. Berowne argues that he will 'prove her fair, or talk till doomsday here' (4.3.270). However, the insults continue to come: the King notes that she is more frightening than the devil, while Dumaine says, 'I never knew man hold vile stuff so dear' (4.3.272). Longaville then compares his shoe to Rosaline's face!

Despite these negative accusations, Berowne attempts to make sense of the predicament which all four men have found themselves in by justifying the lover's position as necessary in youth

>For when would you, my liege, or you, or you,
>In leaded contemplation have found out
>Such fiery numbers as the prompting eyes

Of beauty's tutors have enriched you with?
...
But love, first learned in a lady's eyes,
Lives not alone immured in the brain
But with the motion of all elements
Courses as swift as thought in every power
And gives to every power a double power,
Above their functions and their offices.

(4.3.294–7; 301–6)

Berowne is suggesting that the beauty of a woman's face is necessary for educational stimulation as expounded through neo-Platonic ideals and moderated by self-motivation. As the most vocal opponent of eschewing of ladies' charms, Berowne plucks at the early modern argument around beauty and learning popularised by Ficino in the fifteenth century.[17]

The discussion of love continues in an exchange between Rosaline and Katherine. Developing the discourse on beauty begun by Berowne, they align light and dark with internal emotional states:

KATHERINE: He made her [Katherine's sister] *melancholy*,
   sad and *heavy*;
And so she died. Had she been *light*, like you,
Of such a *merry*, nimble, stirring spirit,
She might ha' been a grandam ere she died.
And so may you, for a *light* heart lives long.
ROSALINE: What's your dark meaning, mouse, of this *light*
   word?
KATHERINE: A *light* condition in a beauty dark.
ROSALINE: We need more *light* to find your meaning out.
KATHERINE: You'll mar the *light* by taking it in snuff;
   Therefore I'll *darkly* end the argument.
ROSALINE: Look what you do, you do it still i' th' *dark*.
KATHERINE: So do not you, for you are a *light* wench.
ROSALINE: Indeed I weigh not you, and therefore *light*.

(5.2.14–26, my italics)

Katherine emphasises the 'light' that accompanies Rosaline despite her dark complexion, but in 'light' there is also the suggestion that she may be loose in her morals and lascivious in nature. Katherine implies that Rosaline, with her dark complexion, hides misdeeds and remains light-hearted though guilty. The audience is left with the suggestion that a light nature may conceal dark deeds. Despite their apparent light-heartedness there is an undercurrent of gravity beneath the interplay of light and dark aligning dark colours with melancholy and sadness. The descriptions they use for Rosaline seem to rely heavily on the fact that her complexion must be in some way dark. Rosaline, stung by the comments, retorts to Katherine

> 'Ware pencils, ho! Let me not die your debtor,
> My red dominical, my golden letter.
> O, that your face were not so full of O's!
>
> (5.2.43–5)

The 'pencil' originally referred to the paintbrushes that were used for fine detailing but also for applying cosmetics (OED Online, 'pencil'). Since a pencil could also be used for writing we are reminded that 'the concept of "text" in early modern culture is closely linked to the concept of physiognomy, which points to a multi-layered and complex notion of "reading"' which includes reading emotion in the face' (Baumbach 2010, 595). Both faces and texts could be read. Rosaline manages to reference both the cosmetics used by Katherine to achieve her complexion and also the reason for them; pockmarks that made face paint necessary in an age where many suffered the effects of smallpox.

Emotionally unmasked: love and shame

In the early modern period, love is conventionally thought of as a disease. The men use this commonplace to defend their emotional states: Dumaine says to Berowne that 'I would forget her; but a fever she / Reigns in my blood and will remembered be' (4.3.92–3). Berowne's reply indicates that the medical remedy for Dumaine's illness would be blood-letting, '[a] fever in your blood? Why, then incision / Would let her out in saucers. Sweet misprision!' (4.3.94–5).[18] Dumaine also turns to other conventions symptomatic of his lovesick state. His sonnet references love, the month of May, wanton air, and velvet leaves (4.3.98–107). He finishes his sonnet lamenting '[t]hou for whom Jove would swear / Juno but an Ethiop were' (4.3.114–5). The importance of colour within the emotional register is apparent. Love is aligned with the idea of spring and renewal, and synonymous with the month of May. Yet, while green is subtly hinted at through the mention of the 'velvet leaves', the image is complicated by the description of the 'wanton air'. Although 'wanton' could indeed mean playful it was also used at this time in conjunction with lasciviousness and lust. Within the allusion to Jove and Juno who represent the power (and the waywardness) of love, there is a tension: Dumaine foreshadows Berowne's discourse on the acceptability of a dark complexioned lover whose colouring does not reflect the white, pale ideal.

The shame of the male lover features as a major theme. Dumaine echoes the King's wish that others be complicit in his shame and struggles with the temptations of love.

> O, would the King, Berowne and Longaville
> Were lovers too! Ill, to example ill,
> Would from my forehead wipe a perjured note,
> For none offend where all alike do dote.
>
> (4.3.120–3)

It is important that shame be shared to remove some of the transgressor's social isolation. Accordingly, when the lovers are uncovered one by one, the complexion of shame is the main focus of attention. Longaville first unmasks Dumaine

> Dumaine, thy love is far from charity,
> That in love's grief desirest society.
> You may look pale, but I should blush, I know,
> To be o'erheard and taken napping so.
>
> (4.3.124–7)

Longaville accuses Dumaine of experiencing an unchristian love, compounded by the fact that he is pale and not blushing with the shame that he should be feeling under the circumstances. Here as in *Much Ado About Nothing*, Shakespeare is 'directing [us] to interpret the blush in multiple ways' (Dunne 2016, 239). Shame is a social practice that reinforces the boundaries of acceptable and unacceptable behaviour, but Longaville is the last lover to declare his feelings and has no idea that the others are also harbouring similar feelings towards the ladies. With no awareness of a public audience, he does not display his shame by blushing. As Lesel Dawson notes, '[f]eelings of shame are most frequently triggered by the sensation of being looked at' (2020, 238). Rather, in his ignorance, he keeps the pale complexion of a lover. The King is not long in berating both Dumaine and Longaville

> Come, sir, you blush. As his your case is such.
> You chide at him, offending twice as much.
> You do not love Maria? Longaville
> Did never sonnet for her sake compile,
> Nor never lay his wreathed arms athwart
> His loving bosom to keep down his heart.
> I have been closely shrouded in this bush,
> And marked you both, and for you both did blush.
> I heard your guilty rhymes, observed your fashion,
> Saw sighs reek from you, noted well your passion.

'Ay me!' says one, 'O Jove!' the other cries.
One, her hairs were gold; crystal the other's eyes.

(4.3.128–39)

In this parody of a lover's discourse, noting all the evidence of the Petrarchan lover's plight, blushing takes on great significance and is mentioned several times, underlining its centrality as an emotional marker. To the King, both men blush because public knowledge of their guilt for being in love has caused them shame.

However, George Sandys observed the duplicity of blushing in the early modern period

> [b]lushing is a resort of the blood to the face; which, in the passion of shame, labours most in that part, and is seen in the breast as it ascendeth: but most apparent in those that are young; in regard of their greater heat, and tender complexions ... The ensigne of natiue Modesty, & the colour of virtue.
>
> (1632, 361)

Sandys contradictorily ascribes blushing both to shame and modesty. Berowne again mentions shame, this time with regard to his love letter, but he uses the opportunity to accuse Costard of bringing shame on Berowne by exposing Berowne's letter, reinforcing the idea that shame relies on an audience. He admits his own love by implicating the others which ensures that the social shame felt is lessened. Their blushes and their lovesickness have a sense of inevitability as their youth and susceptibility to passion cannot be modified by a decree that relies on the faculty of reason.

Boyet then enters to warn the ladies that the men afflicted by love are planning a ruse, '[l]ove doth approach disguised' (5.2.83). The men will appear disguised by clothing and masks, again referencing appearances and emotions as duplicitous. They have elected to wear masks and appear in the guise of Muscovites – a metatheatrical performance in which the men believe they are performing a script written by themselves. Being forewarned gives the Princess the upper hand and allows her to control this performance. She decides that the women will match the men by disguising themselves as well:

> For, ladies, we will every one be masked,
> And not a man of them shall have the grace,
> Despite of suit, to see a lady's face.
>
> (5.2.127–9)

Physical masks, as opposed to cosmetic ones, will now hide the ladies' faces, in an effort to test the true emotional worth of the lords' love. By wearing each other's favours, they will trick the men. The ladies perform a role reversal here, since tradition dictates that they should be unmasked in such a scenario. The unfolding drama mimics the amorous masking common in Tudor times where a young male is masked and can flirt without commitment with a lady (Twycross and Carpenter 2002, 161–3; 171*ff.*). By masking up, the ladies maintain control of the men with the Princess saying

> Their several counsels they unbosom shall
> To loves mistook, and so be mocked withal
> Upon the next occasion that we meet,
> With visages displayed to talk and greet.
>
> (5.2.141–4)

It is an interesting use of the word 'displayed', given the debate around the sincere appearance of feeling and the need to regulate or control the appearance of feeling. The real faces of the women will shame the men. 'Displayed' connotes an 'opened up' or 'exposed' countenance; the women's real faces and the false pretensions of the men will both be put on show (OED Online, 'display'). The men will be shamed for their emotional outpourings on love and for attempting to trick the ladies, and more importantly for breaking their oaths. Their trickery and deception correspond to, and exceed, the deceptions of female complexion that have been underlined in the play's obsession with duplicity, part of a contemporary societal anxiety about the relationship between appearances and reality. It is clear that the onstage drama requires complexions and masks to be highlighted. For Berowne, it is supposedly enough to be able to worship the ladies' faces, but in fact this is exactly what is being denied to them and they woo the wrong women. After the men leave, Boyet warns that the lords will return, noting that the performance of 'love' will cause the lords to 'leap for joy' (5.2.291). The ladies are urged to '[b]low like sweet roses' (5.2.293) with reference to the traditional beauty of reddened cheeks. Boyet suggests the mask hides what might be a perfect complexion while they might appear as overblown roses in the flesh

> Fair ladies masked are roses in their bud;
> Dismasked, their damask sweet commixture shown,
> Are angels vailing clouds, or roses blown.
>
> (5.2.295–7)

The damask rose reference plays nicely into both the hue of the rose and phonetically into the idea of masking and concealment of the true complexion, or commixture, and in this case the identity of the ladies. There is also a reference to loss of virginity and pregnancy in their 'dismasked', 'blown' state.

When the men are exposed, Rosaline demands of Berowne, '[w]hich of the visors was it that you wore?' (5.2.385). Berowne pretends to be nonplussed and Rosaline continues, '[t]here, then, that visor: that superfluous case / That hid the worse and showed the better face' (5.2.387–8). Berowne reacts both physically and emotionally, the first demonstrated by Rosaline's lines, '[h]elp! Hold his brows! He'll swoon. Why look you so pale?'[19] (5.2.392), the second by Berowne's reply to the situation

> Can any face of brass hold longer out?
> ...
> Nor never come in visor to my friend,
> ...
> By this white glove—how white the hand, God knows!—
> Henceforth my wooing mind shall be expressed
> In russet yeas and honest kersey noes.
> And, to begin: wench, so God help me, law!
> My love to thee is sound, *sans* crack or flaw.
>
> (5.2.395; 404; 411–5)

Although the colour of Berowne's face is visible to all as 'pale', the emotional state that he is suffering is not so clear: Rosaline is confused and has to ask him. It is left to the audience to divine the reason for his paleness, according to received ideas: fear on being discovered, a symptom of the love, or an indication of shame, occasioned by discovery of the duplicity of the men in trying to fool the ladies. For whatever reason, Berowne abandons here the Petrarchan language that has been a source of tension in the play. In a related move, he acknowledges the appropriateness of the conceit that the ladies have enjoyed at the men's expense:

> The ladies did change favours and then we,
> Following the signs, wooed but the sign of she.
>
> (5.2.468–9)

The men marked the ladies only by their superficial appearance and by conventional expectations of what they would be wearing according to their station and habit. Following 'fixed signs' they did not take into account more complex and variable manifestations of form, disguise, and attitude. These signs that the men miss are underlined and reiterated to the audience repeatedly, serving to heighten the failure in judgement.

The entrance of Mercadé interrupts the merriment. The scene darkens and clouds as an air of grief overtakes the previous scene of wooing. The Princess notes that '[a] heavy heart bears not a nimble tongue' (5.2.731). The Princess and her ladies must now opt out of the jovial play-making as the reality of the world is painfully pressed upon them. The King, in desperation, demands the love suit to continue as before: 'since love's argument was first on foot, / Let not the cloud of sorrow jostle it / From what it purposed' (5.2.741–3). Ever more perspicacious, Berowne explains to the ladies why the lords have acted as they did

> Your beauty, ladies,
> Hath much deformed us, fashioning our humours
> Even to the opposed end of our intents;
> And what in us hath seemed ridiculous –
> As love is full of unbefitting strains,
> All wanton as a child, skipping and vain,
> Formed by the eye and therefore, like the eye,
> Full of strange shapes, of habits and of forms,
> Varying in subjects as the eye doth roll
> To every varied object in his glance
>
> (5.2.750–9)

The men have allowed their humours and emotions to be moved by the outward beauty of the ladies. They have also allowed their vision to reign above their reason, which made them appear ridiculous to onlookers. The Princess does not agree to a hasty union and the expected structural end to the play does not occur. Instead, the men are expected to spend a penitential year improving their characters while, as Maria says, the women will be wearing black gowns of mourning. The men have to improve their emotional habits while the women contend with emotional perturbations brought on by grief.

Conclusion

The play ends with a song sung by Spring and Winter, Ver and Hiems, possibly played by Holofernes and Nathaniel. Ver mentions 'cuckoo-buds of yellow hue' (5.2.884), which is perhaps a reference to cuckoldry and jealousy (see Chapter 4). His two stanzas end with an unsettling reference to adulterous possibilities in marriage. Hiems includes references to foulness, previously associated with shame and self-loathing. 'Greasy Joan' and 'Marian's nose look[ing] red and raw' (5.2.908; 912;917), subtly point to low-born women of loose morals, perhaps even with connotations of venereal disease through mention of the afflicted nose. Such an ending to the play is difficult to reconcile, but it is, perhaps, a song designed to reinforce the raw domestic nature of emotional interactions which represent reality. Such emotionality contrasts with, and even ridicules, the lofty and ultimately unsuccessful emotional posturing of the men.

In this play, male anxieties about identity and mutability become focused on the female ability to effect external change which can mask internal states of feeling. Concerns around facial staining were focused on the female form but are enacted in this play mainly through the visible signs of emotional conflict in the men's pale and stained faces. *Love's Labour's Lost* questions the conventional wisdom that primarily associates changes of complexion with women. That reversal is reinforced in another problematic probing of the orthodoxy when the men appear disguised as foreigners, becoming the 'other' in the play's masked scene. Beyond that, the conventional red and white marking of the female face is disrupted in this play, by a sustained discourse on blackness, the theme of face-painting and, of course, by the wearing of masks. The idea of self-fashioning mentioned in the previous chapter and associated with a renewed interest in rhetoric, also allows for the possibility that the 'colours' can influence the process (Baumbach 2015, 15). *Love's Labour's Lost,* as a vehicle for considering facial expression of feeling through colour, wonderfully comments on, condones, and undermines accepted orthodoxies and social scripts. It points to emerging faults in accepted gendering on the subject. It is a play which subverts the expected reified emotional connotations by complicating colour expectations of the face. Yet, it is also a play that comments on language and its artificial embellishment, 'painted rhetoric', using cosmetics as a metaphor for obfuscation of meaning through the overuse of rhetorical elaborations.

Notes

1 Fleck (2006) discusses the slippery nature of 'blushing' and the circumstance whereby blushing can signify either innocence or shame or even both simultaneously.
2 See Derek Dunne (2016) for a discussion on the implications of blushing in the early modern period particularly in the forensic setting.
3 Writing possibly a year earlier in *The Rape of Lucrece*, Shakespeare mentions the 'art / of physiognomy' in relation to uncovering the inner character of the individual (672, 1394–5). Sibylle Baumbach notes, '[f]aces are also used to communicate emotional reactions instantly and incessantly' (2015, 17).
4 Eisaman Maus (1995) suggests that comments about interiority in the early modern period were common but the nature of interiority later came under scrutiny when the period suffered political and religious unease.
5 'to give a woman a green gown' represents depriving a woman of her virginity (OED Online, 'green gown').
6 'Maculate' meaning a blemish or an imperfection (OED Online, 'maculate').
7 One needs to consider that the verb 'made' may also refer to the 'maid' in question.
8 'Ailgna' is an anagram of 'Anglia'.
9 Farah Karim-Cooper (2006) discusses the fundamental objections to the use of cosmetics particularly in Chapter 2: *Cosmetics in Shakespeare and Renaissance Drama*.
10 Jan Ziolkowski notes that in the medieval period the 'canon fixed criteria for determining what was beautiful. It required that the damsel in question have long blonde hair; a smooth, white, moderate-sized forehead; delicate eyebrows, not joined above the nose; sparkling grey-blue eyes; a rosy or lily-white complexion; a well-formed, straight nose; a small mouth with full

red lips and white, well-spaced teeth' (1984, 1). This is the canon that was inherited by early modern writers and that was often reversed in an attempt to disrupt the orthodoxy.
11 The blazon, I am describing here, combines both the blazon, n., which is a description or representation according to the rules of Heraldry; and blazon, v., which means to inscribe (anything) *with* arms, paintings, names of distinction, set forth in colours, or in some ornamental way; to adorn as with blazonry (OED Online, 'blazon').
12 Tanya Pollard also makes a similar argument in *Drugs and Theater in Early Modern England* (2005, 93).
13 For further discussion on physiognomy in general across the corpus of Shakespearean works see Baumbach (2008).
14 Dawson (2008) notes that in the early modern period love was an infectious malady that was caught through the eyes and resulted in a physical reaction manifested by distracted spirits, liver malfunction, and general deterioration of the body.
15 Biewer (2007) also makes the point that in relation to the liver, Shakespeare uses it to describe the act of falling in love.
16 Patricia Akhimie (2021) discusses casual racism in more detail in her chapter, "Racist Humor and Shakespearean Comedy" in *The Cambridge Companion to Shakespeare and Race*.
17 For a detailed discussion on beauty in the platonic tradition, see John Vyvyan (2013).
18 Phlebotomy was specifically considered a remedy for lovesickness (Dawson 2008, 164*ff*).
19 Male swooning has a precedent in the Middle English Breton lai *Sir Orfeo*.

References

Akhimie, Patricia. 2021. "Racist Humor and Shakespearean Comedy." In *The Cambridge Companion to Shakespeare and Race*, edited by Ayanna Thompson, 47–61. Cambridge: Cambridge University Press.
Bartholomaeus Anglicus. (1582) 1976. *Batman Uppon Bartholome: His Booke De Proprietatibus Rerum*. Translated by Stephen Batman. Hildesheim; New York: Georg Olms Verlag.
Baumbach, Sibylle. 2008. *Shakespeare and the Art of Physiognomy*. Leicester: Troubador Publishing.
Baumbach, Sibylle. 2010. "Physiognomy." In *A New Companion to English Renaissance Literature and Culture*, edited by Michael Hattaway, 582–97. Chichester, West Sussex: Wiley-Blackwell.
Baumbach, Sibylle. 2015. "'Thy Face Is Mine': Faces and Fascination in Shakespeare's Plays." In *Shakespeare and the Power of the Face*, edited by James A. Knapp, 15–28. Farnham, Surrey: Ashgate Publishing Ltd.
Biewer, Carolin. 2007. "The Semantics of Passion in Shakespeare's Comedies: An Interdisciplinary Study." *English Studies* 88, no. 5: 506–21.
Calderwood, James L. 1965. "*Love's Labour's Lost*: A Wantoning with Words." *Studies in English Literature, 1500–1900* 5, no. 2: 317–32.
Caries, Walter. 1583. *A Briefe Treatise, Called Caries Farewell to Physicke*. London: Henrie Denham.
Chaucer, Geoffrey. (c1372) 2008. "The Romaunt of the Rose." In *The Riverside Chaucer*, edited by Larry D. Benson, 685–767. Oxford: Oxford University Press.

Chedgzoy, Kate. 1998. "Blackness Yields to Beauty: Desirability and Difference in Early Modern Culture." In *Renaissance Configurations: Voices/Bodies/Spaces, 1580–1690*, edited by Gordon McMullan, 108–28. Basingstoke: Macmillan Press Ltd.

Coeffeteau, Nicolas. 1621. *A Table of Humane Passions: With Their Causes and Effects*. Translated by Edw Grimeston. London: Nicholas Oakes.

Dawson, Lesel. 2008. *Lovesickness and Gender in Early Modern English Literature*. Oxford: Oxford University Press.

Dawson, Lesel. 2020. "Shame: A Lover's Complaint, Coriolanus, The Rape of Lucrece." In *Shakespeare and Emotion*, edited by Katharine A. Craik, 238–52. Cambridge: Cambridge University Press.

Dolan, Frances E. 1993. "Taking the Pencil Out of God's Hand: Art, Nature, and the Face-Painting Debate in Early Modern England." *PMLA* 108, no. 2: 224–39.

Drew-Bear, Annette. 1994. *Painted Faces on the Renaissance Stage: The Moral Significance of Face-Painting Conventions*. Lewisburg: Bucknell University Press.

Dunne, Derek. 2016. "Blushing on Cue: The Forensics of the Blush in Early Modern Drama." *Shakespeare Bulletin* 34, no. 2: 233–52.

Eisaman Maus, Katharine. 1995. *Inwardness and Theater in the English Renaissance*. Chicago, IL; London: The University of Chicago Press.

Fleck, Andrew. 2006. "The Ambivalent Blush: Figural and Structural Metonymy, Modesty, and Much Ado About Nothing." *ANQ* 19, no. 1: 16–23.

Fleissner, Robert F. 1961. "Falstaff's Green Sickness unto Death." *Shakespeare Quarterly* 12, no. 1: 47–55.

Garner, Shirley Nelson. 1989. "'Let Her Paint an Inch Thick': Painted Ladies in Renaissance Drama and Society." *Renaissance Drama* 20: 123–39.

Goldstein, Neal L. 1974. "Love's Labour's Lost and the Renaissance Vision of Love." *Shakespeare Quarterly* 25, no. 3: 335–50.

Gosson, Stephen. 1595. *A Glasse, to View the Pride of Vainglorious Women*. London: Richard Ihones.

Haydocke, Richard, trans. 1598. *A Tracte Containing the Artes of Curious Paintinge, Caruinge & Buildinge*. By Io. Paul Lomatius. Oxford: Joseph Barnes.

Iyengar, Sujata. 2005. *Shades of Difference: Mythologies of Skin Color in Early Modern England*. Philadelphia: University of Pennsylvania Press.

Karim-Cooper, Farah. 2006. *Cosmetics in Shakespeare and Renaissance Drama*. Edinburgh: Edinburgh University Press.

Karim-Cooper, Farah. 2007. "'This Alters Not Thy Beauty': Face-Paint, Gender and Race in Richard Brome's *The English Moor*." *Early Theatre* 10, no. 2: 140–9.

Karim-Cooper, Farah. 2014. "To Glisten in a Playhouse: Cosmetic Beauty Indoors." In *Moving Shakespeare Indoors: Performance and Repertoire in the Jacobean Playhouse*, edited by Andrew Gurr and Farah Karim-Cooper, 184–200. Cambridge: Cambridge University Press.

King, Helen. 2004. *The Disease of Virgins: Green Sickness, Chlorosis and the Problems of Puberty*. London: Routledge.

Knapp, James A. 2015. "Introduction: Shakespeare and the Power of the Face." In *Shakespeare and the Power of the Face*, edited by James A. Knapp, 15–27. Farnham, Surrey: Ashgate Publishing Ltd.

Lemnius, Levinus. 1581. *The Touchstone of Complexions* Translated by Thomas Newton. London: Thomas Marsh.
Loomba, Ania. 2002. *Shakespeare, Race, and Colonialism*. Oxford: Oxford University Press.
Lublin, Robert I. 2011. *Costuming the Shakespearean Stage: Visual Codes of Representation in Early Modern Theatre and Culture*. Farnham, Surrey: Ashgate Publishing Ltd.
Oxford University Press. n.d. "Oxford English Dictionary Online." Accessed August, 2021. https://www.oed.com/
Paster, Gail Kern. 1993. *The Body Embarrassed: Drama and the Disciplines of Shame in Early Modern England*. Ithaca, NY: Cornell University Press.
Phillippy, Patricia. 2006. *Painting Women: Cosmetics, Canvases, and Early Modern Culture*. Baltimore, MD: The John Hopkins University Press.
Poitevin, Kimberly. 2011. "Inventing Whiteness: Cosmetics, Race, and Women in Early Modern England." *Journal for Early Modern Cultural Studies* 11, no. 1: 59–89.
Pollard, Tanya. 2005. *Drugs and Theater in Early Modern England*. Oxford: Oxford University Press.
Potter, Ursula, Roger Bartrop and Stephen Touyz. 2009. "Pubertal Process and Green-Sickness in Renaissance Drama: A Form Furste of Anorexia Nervosa?" *Australasian Psychiatry* 17, no. 5: 380–4.
Quintilian. (95CE) 2006. *Institutes of Oratory*. Translated by Reverend John Selby Watson. Edited by Lee Honeycutt. http://rhetoric.eserver.org/quintilian/.
Sandys, George. 1632. *Ouid's Metamorphosis Englished, Mythologiz'd, and Represented in Figures. An Essay to the Translation of Virgil's Aeneis*. Oxford; London: Iohn Lichfield and William Stansby.
Schleiner, Winfried. 2009. "Early Modern Sickness and Pre-Freudian Hysteria." *Early Science and Medicine* 14, no. 5: 661–76.
Shakespeare, William. (1593) 2008. 'Venus and Adonis'. In *The Norton Shakespeare: Based on the Oxford Edition*, edited by Stephen Greenblatt et al., 601–34. New York; London: W W Norton & Company.
Shakespeare, William. (1594) 2008. 'The Rape of Lucrece'. In *The Norton Shakespeare: Based on the Oxford Edition*, edited by Stephen Greenblatt et al., 663–710. New York; London: W W Norton & Company.
Shakespeare, William. (1597) 2012. *Romeo and Juliet*. Edited by René Weis. London: Bloomsbury Arden Shakespeare.
Shakespeare, William. (1598) 2001. *Love's Labour's Lost*. Edited by H. R. Woudhuysen. London: The Arden Shakespeare.
Shakespeare, William. (1600) 2007. *Much Ado about Nothing*. Edited by Claire McEachern. London: Bloomsbury Arden Shakespeare.
Shakespeare, William. (1609) 2015. *Shakespeare's Sonnets*. Edited by Katherine Duncan-Jones. London: Bloomsbury Arden Shakespeare.
Starobinski, Jean. 1981. "Chlorosis–The 'Green Sickness'." *Psychological Medicine* II: 459–68.
Stubbes, Phillip. 1583. *The Anatomie of Abuses*. London: Richard Jones.
Trigg, Stephanie. 2007. "'Shamed Be...': Historicizing Shame in Medieval and Early Modern Courtly Ritual." *Exemplaria: A Journal of Theory in Medieval and Renaissance Studies* 19, no. 1: 67–89.

Twycross, Meg and Sarah Carpenter. 2002. *Masks and Masking in Medieval and Early Tudor England.* Aldershot, Hampshire: Ashgate Publishing Ltd.

Vyvyan, John. 2013. *Shakespeare and Platonic Beauty.* London: Shepherd-Walwyn (Publishers) Ltd.

Wright, Thomas. (1624) 1986. *The Passions of the Mind in General.* Edited by William Webster Newbold. New York: Garland.

Ziolkowski, Jan. 1984. "Avatars of Ugliness in Medieval Literature." *The Modern Language Review* 79, no. 1: 1–18.

3 'There's something in his soul / O'er which his melancholy sits on brood'

Senses, science, and the imagination

Hamlet opens in darkness as the night watch scene unfolds. Francisco says that he is 'sick at heart' (1.1.7) while Barnardo exclaims '[h]ow now, Horatio, you tremble and look pale' (1.1.52). It is easy to surmise that Horatio may be pale from fear as the circumstances of the ghost's apparition unfold. Moving from the passions Horatio relies on the veracity of his vision to provide a sensible meaning to the ghost they had witnessed

> Before my God, I might not this believe
> Without the sensible and true avouch
> Of mine own eyes.
>
> (1.1.55–7)

Horatio is depending on the truth of vision and convinces those around him of the same. However, the early modern audience is familiar with the unreasonable and untruthfulness of the images witnessed by the eyes. Indeed, previously Marcellus stated that Horatio had said it was

> but our fantasy
> And will not let belief take hold of him
> Touching this dreaded sight twice seen of us.
> Therefore I have entreated him along
> With us to watch the minutes of this night
> That, if again this apparition come,
> He may approve our eyes and speak to it.
>
> (1.1.22–8)

Horatio has acknowledged the inadequacies of the sense of sight but he also creates a contradiction by claiming his own sight cannot be at fault. This opening paradox foregrounds multiple contradictions and paradoxes that are not only confined to sight but spread across all the major concerns of the play. These concerns are complicated by classical notions of vision and colour, compounded by a reliance on humoral theory, and sit prominently in a discussion of emotional transactions and their chromatic signifiers.

DOI: 10.4324/9781003198246-4

Scientific theories

Rudimentary scientific observations may have influenced some theories surrounding the origins and composition of colour. Dryness and moisture were thought to contribute to the formation of colours since heat was seen to create clearness and brightness, the basis for the colour white. If cold and dry conditions prevail then black is created. But the colour black is also created when the heat that burns has moisture because the moisture turns to black smoke and the matter becomes earthy and thick. Moist things are the cause of black colour and this explains why black is seen by the eye (Bartholomaeus [1582] 1976). There are contradictory notions at play but for the most part two qualities predominated in each humour. In this paradigm, blood was similar to air because it had the qualities of heat and moisture; phlegm displayed coldness and moisture like water; yellow bile was similar to fire having qualities of heat and dryness; while the melancholic humour had qualities of cold and dryness (Hoeniger 1992, 102). Crooke identifies a similar process but insists that colours arise only from the perspicuity and the opacity of the elements proportioned together and not 'from heat, cold, humidity and siccity as some thought' (1615, 687). When Bartholomaeus applies his colour theory to facial colouring, the physicality of colour becomes even more conflated with humoral and elemental theory. He describes skin colouring as arising in either of two ways: 'sometimes of humours inward, and sometimes of passions of the soule' ([1582] 1976, cap. 10). The humoral colours are evidenced, for example, when hot humours become cool and then the red colour changes to white or pale. And passions of the soul are evident by the colour they produce: for example, anguish or dread cause the heart to close and draw the heat inwards leaving the outer parts pale.

The use of colour transcended the metaphorical by signifying a representation of actual physical and psychophysical states. Humoral states involved an understanding of nature and how one's body fitted into the natural world. When various colours flagged humoral concepts and situations, the colours become a shorthand that represented the humoral state. Humours were thought of as bodily substances physically present within the body and as affective temperaments or mutable passions.[1] Writing in 1586, Timothy Bright noted '[t]he perturbations are taken commonlie to rise of melancholy, choler, bloud, or fleume; so that men of hastie disposition we call cholericke: of sad, melancholicke: of heauie and dull flegmaticke: of merie and chearfull, sanguine' ([1586] 1969, 80). The humours themselves were conceived of as specifically coloured fluids which existed in different quantities depending upon the state of balance. Each coloured humour related to a temperament and explicitly to the emotional characteristics of that temperament. It was understood that the elemental and humoral features had a direct influence on the passions and bearing of the individual. *Hamlet* and its melancholic eponymous protagonist rely heavily on a colour scheme privileging black, dark, and night.[2] This accords with Bright's view that 'the qualities of melancholie bodies [are] altered by this grosse, earthie and darke humour' (129). Patricia Parker notes

> [m]ultiple forms of blackness might be expected in these early texts not just because of their preoccupation with sullying, soiling, or fouling but because of the explicit identification of melancholy, mourning, tragedy, and death with racialized figures of blackness in the period. Melancholy – identified with the 'black' humor of *atra bilis* or 'black bile' – was aligned with 'waste' and 'Moors'.
> (2003, 137)

Humoral theory was still accepted and circulated as physiological and psychological doctrine in the early modern period and the teachings of Galen were mediated through various treatises and compendia.[3]

In the main, Shakespeare adheres to Galenic theory and does not appear to subscribe to newer influences and ideas. His work reflects Galen with an ease that assumes audience familiarity with the concepts (Hoeniger 1992, 71). In keeping to the traditional Galenic theory underpinning understandings of vision, Shakespeare tapped into widely-held views which made it possible for him to transmit emotional ideas through the metaphor of colour, since he was playing to an audience who were familiar with the codes to which he appealed. Through the broad popularity of Galenic notions, the majority of the audience could understand the relation of colour to emotion in similar ways. Noga Arikha notes 'the humoural tradition did not only underpin the medical arts: it was a form of self-understanding in a broader sense. Poetry and black bile were compatible, without being reducible to each other' (2007, 121). When a character was described as either sanguine, phlegmatic, choleric, or melancholic the audience would have an expectation of their temperament and appearance. Indeed, Prince Harry describes Falstaff as 'This sanguine coward, this bed-presser, this horse-back-breaker, this huge hill of flesh' in *King Henry IV, Part 1* (2.5.223–5). Such a description echoes the words of Harington who describes the sanguine character as '[g]ame-some Lou[ing] Wine, and Women, and all recreation … Inclining to be fat, and prone to laughter, Loues mirth and Musick, cares not what come after' (1624, stanza 54). There is, however, a tension between the unpredictability of the human body and mind and the well-documented static theories that described the science behind the behaviour. In a world that favoured the use of binaries in intellectual thought – good versus evil, God versus the Devil, black versus white – the body and the mind shared a nexus in humoral theory that often confounded a simple binary reading. Indeed Parker suggests that the 'early texts of *Hamlet* repeatedly construct such oppositions – of white and black, heaven and hell, angel and devil – and simultaneously undo these polarities' (2003, 149).

Thomas Newton translated Levinus Lemnius' work, *The Touchstone of Complexions*, into English in 1581. Lemnius writes with certainty about the relationship between complexion, temperament, and humoral qualities. The title of his book suggests that health and well-being rely on outer bodily health and also inward health of the mind. He maintains that men in whom the humours of blood and choler dominate have a hot nature coupled with reddish skin, dark hair, and a tendency to be warlike. These men are proud, rash, and lecherous. Men in whom phlegm and melancholy dominate have a cold and unhealthy disposition with cold skin and flabby white flesh. These men are stupid and cowardly. Men dominated by both yellow and black bile have a dry temperament, also deemed to be unhealthy, resulting in a yellowish skin, and they sleep badly and have bad memories. Those with a moist temperament are healthier and these men are cheerful with pale hair but are not very brave and are also prone to lechery (Lemnius 1581, 108). In all of his descriptions, there is a heavy reliance on the physical colouring of the individual, since colour has a central role in recognition of the humoral traits. In *Hamlet*, this coding of humoral emotional states is also chromatically linked. Hamlet, when told by Horatio, Marcellus, and Barnardo about the ghostly appearances of the old King Hamlet, focuses on the emotional expression of the ghost and its attendant colours. He is concerned with the traces of colour which might explain the passions of his father's ghost.

> HAMLET: What looked he – frowningly?
> HORATIO: A countenance more in sorrow than in anger.
> HAMLET: Pale, or red?
> HORATIO: Nay, very pale.
>
> (1.2.229–32)

Hamlet and Horatio use humoral knowledge along with the 'countenance' of the face to try and establish the feelings of the ghost King. Here, the pale face is associated with grief, not with fear or envy, but its paleness may also refer to the ghost's existence as a soul undergoing purgation as a dead 'shade'. The complexion's colouring raises possibilities of emotional understanding and affect but it does not offer definitive answers because of the multiple contexts of interpretation and experience that are available.

Such preoccupation with humours is repeated throughout the play, for example, when Polonius takes the opportunity to question Ophelia about the nature of her relationship with Hamlet. Ophelia admits Hamlet has made advances saying, '[h]e hath, my lord, of late made many tenders / Of his affection to me' (1.3.98–9). Polonius is horrified and replies, '[a]ffection? Pooh, you speak like a green girl / Unsifted in such perilous circumstance' (1.3.100–1). Polonius is suggesting that Ophelia is immature and inexperienced in emotional matters particularly those relating to men and love. Pale watery green hints also at a phlegmatic character, moist and dull of sense, and green-sickness in young women. Claudius also uses 'green' when referencing the memory of his late brother, old King Hamlet. The grief and mourning of that reference are linked to the 'green girl' Ophelia who will suffer grief and mourning. She will also cause it through her emotional involvement in a destructive political and familial scenario. Polonius warns

> I do know
> When the blood burns how prodigal the soul
> Lends the tongue vows. These blazes, daughter,
> Giving more light than heat, extinct in both
> Even in their promise as it is a-making,
> You must not take for fire.
>
> (1.3.116–9)

Polonius may be highlighting the sanguine character of the lover given the references to red in the form of blood and fire, but he and the wider audience know that Hamlet is initially afflicted by the darker, blacker shades of melancholy, to which Ophelia also will succumb.

Later, Hamlet displays an 'antic disposition' with the royal audience at the beginning of 'The Mousetrap' to demonstrate his emotional state. Creating a paradox, he purports to eschew melancholy while continuing to wear the mourning clothes which he has called the 'trappings' of grief and melancholy.[4] Claudius, close to being exposed as a murderer, retires in some distress during play. Guildenstern conveys to Hamlet that '[the King] – is in his retirement marvellous distempered' (3.2.294). When asked whether distemper was the cause, he replies, 'No, my lord, with choler' (3.2.296). The choleric disposition is posited as that which is most lacking in reason and control. In this instance, Gail Kern Paster notes 'Guildenstern might easily have used *anger* to describe Claudius's passion in the first place... But 'choler' – body fluid and raging motion, yellow bile and anger – keeps Claudius's emotions strongly within the flesh' (2004, 51). It is the humours that are disturbed causing the perturbations suffered by Claudius through the words and actions of the players. The control that a reasoning man should apply is not apparent in Claudius; his balance has been upset to reflect a preponderance of yellow bile. At this point, Hamlet attempts to change his own humoral balance in preparation for taking his revenge on Claudius, having been unable to do so thus far despite the urging of the ghost. He says, '[n]ow I could drink hot blood / And do such business as the day / Would quake to look on' (3.2.380–2). According to Thomas Wright ([1601] 1986), seeing the red blood would affect a susceptible individual to heat and rages. Hamlet's imagination tends towards the even more horrible thought of drinking hot blood, which seems in terms of humoral tendency quite at odds with the excess of melancholy he was suffering from previously, but could possibly be understood as a drastic cure for it, or a sudden reaction. Emily Anglin suggests that such flashes of choleric violence marry the character of Hamlet with the thematic structure of the play

> *Hamlet*, then, is a melancholic play not just in terms of its famous representation of a melancholic character, but also because in its dramatic structure and plot it displays the same seemingly contradictory qualities as its Saturnine hero – intellectual paralysis undergirded by a potential for rash violence.
>
> (2014, 1)

After Hamlet stabs Polonius, references to red blood continue. Gertrude says, 'O, what a rash and bloody deed is this!' (3.4.25) while Hamlet replies '[a] bloody deed – almost as bad, good mother, / As kill a king and marry with his brother' (3.4.26–7). At this point within the play, the colour red has overtaken references to black.

While praying, Claudius struggles with the guilt that he endures over his brother's murder. He cries

> What if this cursed hand
> Were thicker then itself with brother's blood?
> Is there not rain enough in the sweet heavens
> To wash it white as snow?
>
> (3.3.43–6)

Claudius is talking figuratively about the consequences on his soul and also his conscience. He is using a refinement of the proverb suggesting that it is impossible to wash the Ethiope white. However, there is also the colour referencing of blood-red to consider; as Harington suggests, the complexion of the choleric person is red. The choleric temperament is violent, ambitious, malicious, and also prone to lying (Harington 1624, stanza 58). Since the temperament is ingrained bodily and mentally, it follows that Claudius would be unable to wash himself, and in particular his hand, the instrument of the murder, clean. When Claudius continues, saying 'O wretched state, O bosom black as death' (3.3.67), it is conceivable that emotionally he is referencing the evil that has made him sinfully black through his choleric actions. This idea is supported when Hamlet says

> Then trip him that his heels may kick at heaven
> And that his soul may be as damned and black
> As hell whereto it goes.
>
> (3.3.93–5)

Hamlet, knowing of the murder, does not want to give Claudius a chance to unblacken his soul, nor does he want to take revenge on a man who has made his peace with God. Instead, Hamlet will wait until Claudius is in a sinful state, unable to repent, and kill him, thereby condemning Claudius to hell. Ultimately, however, Claudius chooses to reject his conscience and Hamlet unwisely does not move at this point to take his revenge before it is too late.[5]

Passions and vision

In 1601, the first edition of Thomas Wright's *The Passions of the Mind* appeared (followed by editions in 1604, 1620–21, and 1630).[6] Wright declares

> Without any great difficulty may be declared how Passions seduce the Will; because the wit being the guide, the eye the stirrer, and director of the Will, which, of itself being blind and without knowledge, foloweth that the wit representeth, propoundeth, and approveth as good; and as the sensitive appetite foloweth that the direction of the imagination, so the Will affecteth for the most part that the understanding persuadeth to be best.
>
> (2.2.3–11)

Wright explains how the eye and everything it sees have such an impact on the will through the movement of the passions. The eye as the stirrer takes hold through seeing, reading, and memory of objects. The eye stirs the passions through its ability to influence the imagination and through this avenue, the will. The will is convinced by the wit that what it is being shown is both good and true. The Ghost of old King Hamlet echoes this sentiment saying, '[c]onceit in weakest bodies strongest works' (3.4.110). The will can be persuaded to believe all that the eye presents to it as true, so it behooves men to use reason to regulate what the eye sees. It was also accepted that it was important to self-regulate humoral effects where possible (Rogers 1576; Mornay 1602). The danger for the unwitting is the entry of evil into one's body. Such an early modern viewpoint was supported by the word of God transmitted via the Bible. The eyes had the capacity to allow evil to enter one's heart and it was necessary to guard against this (Cranmer 1541; Luke 11: 33–6). Wright is concerned about the sense of sight because the Holy Ghost was aware of the far-reaching capacity of the sense of vision. The visual sense above all creates an imprint on the imagination and is most likely to move the passions.

Shakespeare plays on this idea in *King Lear* when Gloucester says, '[w]oes by wrong imaginations lose / The knowledge of themselves' (4.6.281–2). Indeed in *Hamlet*, Claudius says '[Hamlet's] loved of the distracted multitude, / Who like not in their judgement but their eyes' (4.3.4–5). With the power vision possesses it is well positioned to move people to goodness but also, in the unwary, to evil. Wright's advice is not to gaze on such things as may offend God, or at the very least to pass over them quickly ([1601] 1986, 5.1.49–69). Crucially, a visually emotional moment can also move the passions. When Jacob saw Joseph's cloak sprinkled with blood, Jacob was moved to sorrow. Wright surmises that in this case it was a personal sorrow about Joseph's fate that moved Jacob, but that an audience may be moved to an abstract state of grief by such a colour given their knowledge of the story (5.1.91–9). Wright also makes it clear that every passion is potentiated by emotions already present within the person. So, when we love we are pleased by the sight of everything fortunate which befalls our loved ones and when we hate we cannot abide anything fortunate to befall the person of our hatred. One can conclude that colour cues can affect the passions, since Wright emphasises the ease with which material signs revive and stir up former passions (5.1.191–203).

Wright privileges the senses in providing the external impetus to movement of the soul, which results in what he calls 'Passions, and Affections, or perturbations, of the mind' ([1601] 1986, 1.2.14-1). Crucially this happens because when the affections or passions are 'stirring in our minds they alter the humours of our bodies, causing some alteration in them' (1.2.28–31). The sense of sight together with all the other senses allow actions to occur within a man's soul, and this is crucial to my argument suggesting that colours affect the passions and cause a change in emotions. Wright continues by stating that perturbations are those which trouble the soul, corrupting the judgment and seducing the will; those which affect the soul to the good are called affections. Passions operate within the sphere of both reason and the senses but he maintains that there is more affinity between passions and the senses. The explanation is that since childhood the senses and passions have been intertwined but reason was only added later.[7] For Helkiah Crooke, vision and colour are inextricably linked

> [T]he Eye is not affected by the species,[8] but by the colour, according as it is more or less splendent or enlightened, for all enlightened things do dissipate, by reason that our ayry and splendent spirits do vanish into that light which is like unto them: So white things, because they haue much light doe dissipate the spirits, but blacke doe gather them because they are contrary to the spirits.
>
> (1615, 669)

It is clear that the spirits that can be seen peeping out through the eyes are influenced by the shades of colour presented to them. Crooke gives a much abridged version of the colour and vision theory previously expounded by Grosseteste, through Bartholomaeus, saying '[s]ight doth perceive nothing but white and blacke; for Red, Yellow, skycoloured, and other such like, are not contrary but intermediate colours, and so of the rest' (1615, 669). Crooke also ponders the paradoxical situation that while some conditions such as jaundice cause the vision to become yellowed, and a blow to the eye resulting in a blood collection causes the vision to be reddened, colours of the individual eye (green, blue, or black) do not cause vision to be skewed in this way. He reconciles this anomaly by explaining that in the first example the whole eye becomes coloured, while in the eye colour that we are born with this colour is a vestigial reminder of the spirits that were dissipated or dispersed in the body.[9]

Reason, control, and the power of the mind

Because reason can be applied to passions, it becomes important to know oneself and how one's reason can be controlled. During the early modern period awareness of oneself became an important phenomenon, with the adage '*nosce teipsum*' (know thyself) gaining popularity.[10] Dealing with this topic, Anthony Munday translated a French treatise in 1602 called, *The true knowledge of a mans owne selfe* (de Mornay 1602). Crooke also mentions the importance of every man knowing himself in his preface to book eight. Crucially for Crooke it is through self-understanding that the faculty of sensation is understood, as it is dispersed throughout the whole system and frame of the body. In Crooke's view we must be able to understand the senses in order to use our minds and have engagement with discourse (1615, 647). Our first introduction to the idea of control and emotional response in the play, comes when Claudius enters to a fanfare which proclaims him as the King of Denmark. Claudius advocates a measured approach to grief at the passing of the Hamlet, the old King, his brother

> Though yet of Hamlet our dear brother's death
> The memory be green, and that it us befitted
> To bear our hearts in grief, and our whole kingdom
> To be contracted in one brow of woe,
> Yet so far hath discretion fought with nature
> That we with wisest sorrow think on him
> Together with remembrance of ourselves.
>
> (1.2.1–7)

Within his opening lines, there is a determined lack of references to the black heaviness of grief while the mention of green strikes a discordant note. Green, while signifying the newness of old Hamlet's death, also hints at Claudius' irresponsibility and latent sexual immaturity. Claudius also suggests a public pattern of behaviour which befits a grieving nation, yet since the pattern is reduced to something to be replicated in 'one brow of woe' it becomes a staged emotion without a truthful base negating the possibility of an individual response.

Wright urges that 'the humours *be kept* in a due proportion' ([1601] 1986, 1.4.61–2 101), suggesting a certain amount of individual and/or external agency can be pressed into service to carry out that moderation. Later in the play, when the players are directed by Hamlet on how to perform in front of the King and Queen, Hamlet insists that 'in the very torrent, tempest and as I may say the whirlwind of your passion, you must acquire and beget a temperance that may give it smoothness' (3.2.5–7). It is understood that the players can perform passions to excess; to provide a smoother, more coherent performance their passions can and should be kept in check. While Hamlet is cognizant of the individual's ability to control passions, he is accused by Claudius of being unable to do so himself

> But to persever,
> In obstinate condolement is a course
> Of impious stubbornness, 'tis unmanly grief,
> It shows a will most incorrect to heaven,
> A heart unfortified, a mind impatient,
> An understanding simple and unschooled
>
> (1.2.92–7)

The accusation does not, of course, take into account exactly what a reasonable grieving period should be. Claudius insists that Hamlet is choosing to behave in this manner through obstinacy, a potentially offensive slur. He suggests that Hamlet's mind is simple and childlike, echoing the commonplace that reason comes after childhood. To be considered mature in this paradigm, Hamlet needs to control his passions. In Claudius' opinion, Hamlet should be keeping those passions under control by exerting his will and intelligence. There is a suggestion that such excessive grief has a feminising effect. David Houston Wood says '[t]he cool propensities of the black bile of melancholy within the humoral theory ... were understood to cause in the male a movement away from the heat associated with masculinity and toward the chilled temperature associated with the feminine' (2009, 85) another slur on Hamlet's character.

Wright's exhortation accords with early modern notions of self-awareness since fluctuations in an individual's emotional behaviour and well-being could also cause fluctuations in the societal body. Individuals, especially those expected to lead the state, were particularly required to control the greater excesses of passion for the public good. To this end, Gertrude urges, '[g]ood Hamlet, cast thy nighted colour off, / And let thine eye look like a friend on Denmark' (1.2.68–9). The idea of the individual does not override other constraints in early modern society – such as social position, gender, and other cultural limitations – which also shaped the emotional actions and reactions of the person. Laertes later references such ideas of public duty in his conversation with Ophelia, warning her to guard herself against Hamlet's advances

> but you must fear,
> His greatness weighed, his will is not his own.
> He may not, as unvalued persons do,
> Carve for himself, for on his choice depends
> The safety and health of this whole state,
> And therefore must his choice be circumscribed
> Unto the voice and yielding of that body
> Whereof he is the head.
>
> (1.3.16–23)

Laertes's awareness of the constraints that surround the emotional choices open to a prince indicates another reason why Hamlet's expression of emotions may be no sure guide to his future actions.

Polonius, too, has pricked the conscience of Claudius. Unwittingly, he has carried out Hamlet's intentions, as Claudius' aside shows

> How smart a lash that speech doth give my conscience!
> The harlot's cheek beautied with plastering art
> Is not more ugly to the thing that helps it
> Than is my deed to my most painted word.
>
> (3.1.49–52)

In this first admission of guilt, Claudius uses the trope of painted colours and the anti-cosmetic didactic common in the early modern period to confess his culpability (see Chapter 2). Farah Karim-Cooper notes 'Claudius not only acknowledges his duplicitousness through cosmetic imagery, but more significantly, he sees his actions as an 'art', and the 'word', the unit of communication and ideological signification, as something that is easily painted' (2006, 186). Claudius relies on the trope of colour as a rhetorical embellishment which can be used for both proper and improper advantage, and combines it with the groundswell of opinion which railed against the duplicity of women who create false countenances with artificial means.

The ideas that Claudius grapples with are re-articulated almost immediately by Hamlet when he enters and delivers his soliloquy on vacillating between action and inaction, the meaning of life and the meaning of death. Hamlet ponders what is at the root of indecision saying

> Thus conscience does make cowards –
> And thus the native hue of resolution

> Is sicklied o'er with the pale cast of thought,
> And enterprises of great pitch and moment
> With this regard their currents turn awry
> And lose the name of action.
>
> (3.1.82–7)

In Hamlet's consideration of conscience, we are again returned to images of bodily ill-health and its related colours. The effects of a disturbed or guilty conscience cause facial pallor by disturbing the humoral balance. The outwardly discernible facial paleness indicates the involvement of emotions in the health of the whole body.

In this paradigm, those male courtiers that seek to observe, manipulate, and control the passions of those around them, are themselves emotionally out of control. The expectation of control in a performance of emotions is underscored by Hamlet's view on the reality of emotional control. When talking to Horatio he extolls the virtues of control whilst simultaneously acknowledging the difficulties of maintaining such control

> And blest are those
> Whose blood and judgement are so well co-meddled
> That they are not a pipe for Fortune's finger
> To sound what stop she please. Give me that man
> That is not passion's slave and I will wear him
> In my heart's core – ay, in my heart of heart –
> As I do thee.
>
> (3.2.64–70)

Horatio figures as the steadfast character who exemplifies reason and control.

Controlling emotions with reason was complicated by the effects of the imagination, the imagination being strongly linked to passions (Burton 1896, 1.2.3.1–2). According to Wright, the imagination and consequently the passions are moved in three ways: 'by humours arising in our bodies, by external senses and secret passage of sensual objects, by the descent or commandment of reason' ([1601] 1986, 5.1.8–15). Michel de Montaigne was also interested in the power of the imagination, quoting a medieval philosophical axiom, '*Fortis imaginatio generat casum*,' or 'a powerful imagination generates the event' (1991, 109). He says that if he witnesses someone who is suffering, the same suffering is produced in him. He asserts that 'when imaginary thoughts trouble us we break into sweats, start trembling, grow pale or flush crimson; we lie supine on our featherbeds and feel our bodies agitated by such emotions; some even die from them' (110). The power of the imagination could exert a body to a physical and chromatic reaction when the mind is open to such events. All these tracts lead to the conclusion that the early modern eye is not only a moral sign but also an active moral agent. The early modern imagination is a pliable and highly responsive organ. Imagination and reason both intrigued and concerned people because of the undue influence that could be exerted on the will. Synthesising colour in the mind involved, on occasion, relating colour to humoral and elemental involvement whilst understanding its influence on the imagination.

If the imagination can cause movement, then it becomes a facility that requires careful monitoring and balance. This is a dynamic, fluid relationship that works on balances and imbalances to produce effects. Hamlet echoes this sense of balance when describing an 'o'ergrowth of some complexion' which causes the break-down of 'the pales and forts of reason' (1.4.27–8). In the scientific treatises, and echoed in Hamlet's words, there is a cognitive effect that figures in the transaction. The catalyst for the dynamism of the relationship appears to be either a sense or memory of an object

> First, then, to our imagination cometh by sense or memory some object to be known, convenient or disconvenient to Nature; the which being known ... in the imagination, which resideth in the former part of the brain (as we prove when we imagine anything) ... where they pitch at the door, signifying what an object was presented, convenient or disconvenient for it. The heart immediately bendeth either to prosecute it or to eschew it, and the better to effect that affection draweth other humours to help him; and so in pleasure concur great store of pure spirits; in pain and sadness, much melancholy blood; in ire, blood and choler; and not only, as I said the heart draweth, but also the same should that informeth the heart, residing in other parts, sendeth the humours unto the heart to perform their service in such a worthy place.
>
> (Wright [1601] 1986, 1.11.9–26)

Horatio views the ghostly vision as a portent of disaster but in his description he draws on the machinations of the imagination described above, saying '[a] mote it is to trouble the mind's eye' (1.1.111). The spectre of the old King is an irritation to the mind's eye (the imagination) which again casts doubt on its truth, given the unstable and unreliable nature of the imagination itself. Despite that, Horatio is convinced it is an omen of disaster, like the murder of Julius Caesar whose end was foretold in bloody astrological events (1.1.112–6).

Performance of emotions

When the players arrive, Hamlet calls for 'a passionate speech' (2.2.369–70). He has a particular speech in mind which tells of the death of Priam. In order to remind the players, he recites his version of the speech, which is particularly passionate and, crucially, laden with humoral colour references

> The rugged Pyrrhus, he whose sable arms,
> Black as his purpose, did the night resemble
> When he lay couched in th'ominous horse,
> Hath now this dread and black complexion smeared
> With heraldry more dismal, head to foot,
> Now is he total gules, horridly tricked
> With blood of fathers, mothers, daughters, sons,
> Baked and impasted with the parching streets
> That lend a tyrannous and a damned light
> To their lord's murder; roasted in wrath and fire,
> And thus o'ersized with coagulate gore,
> With eyes like carbuncles, the hellish Pyrrhus
> Old grandsire Priam seeks.
> (2.2.390–402)

Hamlet aims to motivate the players he is addressing to provide their audience with an affective re-enactment of the play. The blackness of melancholy and dread in this passage is quickly superseded by the red blood and gory gules of murder and death. Fiery red is used to emphasise the underlying depth of wrath and anger. Hamlet's version of the story to the players is remarkably more colourful and colour-marked than the speech that the player then delivers. Hamlet's version flags humoral states and acts to provide an emotive impetus for the player to create an equally emotional rendition, albeit with less emphasis on colour. In Hamlet's retelling, the humoral colours of red and black ebb and flow to create wide fluctuations in balance. Paster notes that the name 'Pyrrhus' comes from Greek and means flame-coloured or yellowish-red, reflecting the contemporary colours of the choleric individual (2004, 35). Paster also suggests 'that Shakespeare's version of the fall of Troy … comes in the key colors and thermal markers of early modern humoralism, as the black complexioned Pyrrhus, his armor coated with the drying blood of his victims, raises his sword over Priam's milky head' (35). Of course, this also relates to the colourful world of heraldry. Keir Elam notes 'the heraldic colour code provides Hamlet, among others (as well as Shakespeare himself) with one of his many sources of lexical abundance, a rich storehouse of synonyms – "sable" for black, "gules" for blood red, "azure" for light blue – and they literally colour his discourse' (2017, 44). This allows the audience, within the confines of the emotional community formed by the play, to understand and perhaps be affected by the emotives used by Hamlet. Hamlet is setting up the imagination of the audience, through his colour-filled performance, to be receptive to the upcoming emotional message of The Mousetrap.

Richard Meek notes

> Hamlet, who first appeared to us in black, must – like Pyrrhus – end up covered in blood in order to become an 'authentic' revenger. It is worth emphasizing, then, that this is not simply an extraneous or ornamental digression, given this identification between Pyrrhus and Hamlet. Pyrrhus is, like Hamlet, a son in search of revenge.
>
> (2009, 100)

Meek also points out that Pyrrhus pauses before killing King Priam. Even Pyrrhus, like 'a painted tyrant' (2.2.418), with a suggestion of emotional stasis or even of insincerity, is momentarily unable to act, 'and like a neutral to his will and matter, / Did nothing' (2.2.419–20). Possibly associating the story of Hecuba, who laments a husband killed by a 'malicious Pyrrhus', with Hamlet's already emotional state, Polonius is moved to say, 'Look where he has not turned his colour and has tears in's eyes' (2.2.457–8). Polonius could be referring to the player's tears, as Hamlet later does, but alternatively he may be directing others to notice the changing colour of Hamlet's complexion before he urges the player to stop. He does not indicate which colour it has changed to, but he does intimate that the change is due to a heightened emotional state. The scene suggests why Hamlet struggles to find the rage necessary for revenge: he is gripped by melancholy. As Kristine Steenbergh writes, '[i]t is characteristic of the prince's humoral economy that he is more receptive to Hecuba's grief then to Pyrrhus' choler' (2011, 107). In terms of relationality of emotion to action, there is a clear change in the emotional register of the humours from Hamlet's speech to the player's lines on Hecuba (2.2.443–55). While Hamlet's speech indicates a black melancholy overcome by a blood-red choleric state, the player's Hecuba displays an active grief consumed by tears and noise. She runs 'barefoot up and down, threatening the flames / With bisson rheum' (2.2.443–4). Tanya Pollard notes that the performance of female grief offers a distinctively different model from male grief, suggesting that 'while the ghost warns his tragedy will freeze and stiffen its audiences, Hecuba's tragedy promises the opposite effect: it will melt, liquefy, even douse the flames' (2012, 1062).

The player concludes by saying,

> The instant burst of clamour that she made
> (Unless things mortal move them not at all)
> Would have made milch the burning eyes of heaven
> And passion in the gods.
>
> (2.2.453–6)

The player has used the rhetorical idea of actively portraying an emotion in order to evoke an emotional response in the audience. Hamlet notes the skill of the player, but he relates the player's performance to his own perceived lack

> Is it not monstrous that this player here,
> But in a fiction, in a dream of passion,
> Could force his soul so to his own conceit
> That from her working all the visage wanned,[11]
> – Tears in his eyes, distraction in his aspect,
> A broken voice, and his whole function suiting
> With forms to his conceit – and all for nothing –
> For Hecuba?
> What's Hecuba to him, or he to her,
> That he should weep for her? What would he do
> Had he the motive and that for passion
> That I have? He would drown the stage with tears
> And cleave the general ear with horrid speech
>
> (2.2.486–98)

Evidently, the player has the ability to change his complexion to one of pallor and wring tears from his eyes. However, Hamlet, instead of having the necessary ability to perform and communicate the depth of his emotions which far eclipses that of the player, counts himself as 'pigeon-livered' and lacking in gall to confront Claudius. Hamlet believes his thoughts should be more passionate and inclined to action. Steven Mullaney notes 'Pyrrhus's choler is not, after all, the focus of Hamlet's attention; it is not what he is disturbed by. He reacts entirely to the *player's* theatrical tears, which are 'real' despite the fact that they are feigned' (2015, 60). Hamlet is preoccupied by the player who can control his own emotions and effect an emotional change in others. This preoccupation can be explained because the play, which focuses on family interactions and loyalties, privileges the performance of emotions above so-called genuine emotions which can never be verified.

Hamlet uses the notion of the passionate orator moving his audience when constructing the 'play within a play' trap for Claudius. Hamlet shares his plan saying

> Hum, I have heard
> That guilty creatures sitting at a play
> Have by the very cunning of the scene
> Been struck so to the soul that presently
> They have proclaimed their malefactions.
>
> (2.2.523–7)

The story of Ibycus and his murderers had set a literary precedent for this kind of entrapment. Ibycus was an ancient Greek lyric poet whose murderers were caught because of their guilty and fearful reactions while sitting in the theatre.[12] While Hamlet uses the same idea, in the context of early modern fascination with passions and self-knowledge it becomes a direct comment on self-control and the regulation of emotions. Claudius lacked self-control when he murdered the old King Hamlet and again when confronted by the players' performance. Within this play there is a consideration of the performance of emotions and how that performance can mobilise passions.

Hamlet, contradictions, and confounding science

The paradox of personal and public grief unfolds after Claudius addresses Hamlet '[h]ow is it that the clouds still hang on you?' (1.2.66). Claudius' concern is that Hamlet is not following the emotional regime or scripts prescribed by the court.[13] Hamlet's emotions are portrayed through a mourning palette of dark and grey, not the show of emotion demanded by either Claudius or Gertrude. Gertrude urges

> Good Hamlet, cast thy nighted colour off
> And let thine eye look like a friend on Denmark.
> Do not for ever with thy vailed lids
> Seek for thy noble father in the dust.
> Thou knowest 'tis common all that lives must die,
> Passing through nature to eternity.
>
> (1.2.67–73)

The spirits emanating from Hamlet's eye should deliver an air of political stability. Instead, blackness envelops Hamlet; the 'clouds' and 'nighted colour', and the 'inky cloak' which surrounds him, foreground the melancholy that consumes him. Gertrude does not acknowledge the possibility that there is an involuntary component to his grief. She questions why grief, common to all, seems to take such a particularly outward expression in Hamlet. Hamlet notes the contradiction

> 'Seems', madam – nay it is, I know not 'seems'.
> 'Tis not alone my inky cloak, cold mother,
> Nor customary suits of solemn black,
> Nor windy suspiration of forced breath,
> No, nor the fruitful river in the eye,
> Nor the dejected haviour of the visage,
> Together with all forms, moods, shapes of grief,
> That can denote me truly. These indeed 'seem',
> For they are actions that a man might play,
> But I have that within which passes show,
> These but the trappings and the suits of woe.
>
> (1.2.76–86)

Hamlet indicates the black colour of the clothes he is wearing, possibly in defiance of a ruling by Claudius. But he tries to make it clear that the black represents the melancholy and grief experienced by a bereaved son. With Hamlet's speech, we are told that black is the colour which best represents his grief and we are warned about the incongruity between actually experiencing melancholy and a false state which can dissemble melancholy if one understands the signifiers. Passion becomes more suspect of counterfeit when one is aware of the trappings, ornaments, and embellishments needed to create it. What is interesting here is that Hamlet points to all the signifiers of grief – black funerary clothes, weeping and a dejected appearance – as mere show and ornaments of grief, but he maintains that his grief will continue even if he dispensed with them. By making this point, Hamlet emphasises the difference between a real internal passion and an outward sign. A spectator might even consider that if the vision of outward signs is potentially such an unreliable guide to true inner feelings, then Hamlet's own claims to authentic emotions are impossible to judge.[14] Underlying the presence of the passions is the suspicion that his performance may indeed be just that, a performance of the melancholic being. As Ross Knecht suggests, the real action here may be the outward show, while Hamlet's interior passions remain unnamable passions (2015, 47).

Hamlet indicates to his mother that these shows of grief, the colour black being an example, may not always indicate the truth of a person's feeling. The conclusion is that the outward appearances are so powerful that they not only make a reality in themselves but can also point to a false reality. The emotional power of colour symbolism thus becomes a force to be feared as much as it is trusted. Colour can lead to false conclusions and must be viewed with respect and intelligence. Anglin notes

> early modern melancholy (along with other humours) was both embedded deeply within early modern structures of thought, but could also – because of this rich network of intimate familiarity with humoral meaning – be worn on a person's surface as well as borne deep within the soul, and it was donned like an inky cloak for social purposes ranging from the sartorial to the political.
>
> (2014, 3)

Hamlet's awareness of the embeddedness of these structures allows him to create a rapport with the audience. He uses public signifiers to confound the characters around him while creating an ultimately more truthful relationship through his soliloquies. Anglin continues saying 'Hamlet's controlled, metatheatrical use of these stage conventions aids in a performance of melancholy which allows him to instead establish private communication between himself and the audience, leaving in the dark those characters who like to reduce his condition to simple, manageable terms for interpretative purposes' (2014, 2).

Hamlet assured those around him that although his outward façade used the common tropes of grieving, he suffered deep inward grief; yet after hearing about the murder of his father from the ghost, Hamlet decides to use those very tropes to create a situation where he can entrap the guilty. He says, '[a]s I shall perchance hereafter shall think meet / To put an antic disposition on' (1.5.169–70). His 'antic disposition' highlights the unknowable veracity or duplicity of expressions of humoral passions. Passions can be learned and after the learning process they can be externalised without the internal mirrored emotion being present, but the choice to make such a display may in itself be read as a true sign of what it purports to 'put on'.

The antic disposition that Hamlet assumes is described in detail by Ophelia, who is distressed and convinced by Hamlet's behaviour

> Lord Hamlet, with his doublet all unbraced,
> No hat upon his head, his stockings fouled,
> Ungartered and down-gyved to his ankle,
> Pale as his shirt, his knees knocking each other,
> And with a look so piteous in purport
> As if he had been loosed out of hell
> To speak of horrors, he comes before me.
>
> (2.1.75–81)

In this passage, there is the commonplace description of the lover's version of melancholy. The disheveled appearance includes 'fouled' stockings, and in this reference, there is a hint of black bile, since both dirt and gross humours can be indicated by this word (OED, 'foul'). While his paleness, however achieved, is assumed to reflect the accepted countenance of the lover,[15] an audience may also remember the pale ghost reflecting grief and death. Hamlet has convincingly played the part and both Ophelia and Polonius are certain of what ails Hamlet. Polonius observes

> This is the very ecstasy of love,
> Whose violent property fordoes itself
> And leads the will to desperate undertakings
> As oft as any passions under heaven
> That does afflict our natures.
>
> (2.1.99–103)

Polonius is certain that the violence of Hamlet's passions can be explained under this rubric. His conviction is unshakeable and he holds it until his death at the hands of Hamlet. Polonius recounts the stages of Hamlet's love sickness to the King and Queen as fact

> And he, repelled, a short tale to make,
> Fell into a sadness, then into a fast,
> Thence to a watch, thence into a weakness,
> Thence to a lightness, and by this declension
> Into the madness wherein now he raves,
> And all we mourn.
>
> (2.2.143–8)

Knecht suggests that the melancholy expressed by Hamlet follows a pattern that can be understood in terms of patterns of grammar that were understood by all who were conversant with the Grammar School system (2015, 41). Such a pattern is clearly elaborated by Polonius as the set piece for love sickness. Yet Hamlet, understanding the expected progression of his behaviour, declares to Rosencrantz and Guildenstern that he is 'but mad north-north-west. / When the wind is southerly I know a hawk from a handsaw' (2.2.315–6). He teasingly admits to an assumed madness, but in terms that might either seem to confirm its reality or to be part of a further 'show'. Again a conflict between seeming and being arises, casting doubt on the truth of Hamlet's emotional appearance, but simultaneously affirming the truth of Ophelia's. Carol Thomas Neely suggests

> [t]he stylistic distinction between Hamlet's feigned madness and Ophelia's actual madness is emphasized by other distinctions. When he is not feigning and especially in his soliloquies, Hamlet is presented as fashionably introspective and melancholy whereas Ophelia, distract, acts out the madness he only plays with.
>
> (2004, 54)

Before Hamlet can enact his plan to ensnare Claudius with The Mousetrap, he himself is the subject of entrapment at the hands of Polonius and Claudius, with Ophelia featuring as a knowing pawn. Polonius urges Ophelia to

> Read on this book
> That show of such an exercise may colour
> Your loneliness. We are oft to blame in this –
> 'Tis too much proved that with devotion's visage
> And pious action we do sugar o'er
> The devil himself.
>
> (3.1.43–8)

Polonius alludes to the performative nature of Ophelia's trap while suggesting that such actions are not uncommon. The verb 'to colour' is used as a means of explaining Ophelia's reading alone while walking in the lobby. Colour here, while it may mean 'to express' or 'to explain' equally suggests 'to portray in a false light' or 'to disguise', draws attention tangentially to the usefulness of colour in general to create meaning (OED Online, 'colour'), and in this case meaning that is false to the point of sinfulness.

Paleness continues to figure when Hamlet is exhorting Ophelia not to marry. If she does, he says, 'be thou as chaste as ice, as pure as snow, / thou shalt not escape calumny' (3.1.135–6). Ophelia is associated with pale whiteness both through her chastity and innocence but also humorally through her femininity, which is traditionally cast as a pale and moist disposition, and principally because she is kept continually in a state of fear and apprehension. In Hamlet's counsel to her, he suggests that emotionally she is a victim of her own circumstances, and that only by being aware and guarded to the point of withdrawal will she be safe. Then having made the point that she is at risk, Hamlet proceeds to carry out the very attack that he warns her against. He begins by referring to the commonplaces of the anti-cosmetic movement: 'I have heard of your paintings well enough. God hath given you one face and you make yourselves another' (3.1.141–2). In these words, Hamlet is suggesting that paleness that heralds a woman's (and therefore Ophelia's) innocent disposition, is merely painted on, a counterfeit. The pretence of purity denoted by a pale made-up face belies the wanton woman beneath. In this scene it is difficult to discern the emotions of Hamlet under the 'antic disposition' he is assuming. Ophelia is convinced that Hamlet intends no personal malice but is instead overcome by the madness of melancholy. She laments

> O, what a noble mind is here o'erthrown!
> The courtier's, soldier's, scholar's eye, tongue, sword,
> Th'expectation and rose of the fair state,
> The glass of fashion and the mould of form,
> Th'observed of all observers, quite, quite down.
>
> (3.1.149–53)

Ophelia gives a thoughtful construction of a Prince in describing how far Hamlet has strayed from this ideal. Indeed her speech suggests that Hamlet was the embodiment of this ideal and possibly a happier temperament before the present upheavals.[16] Claudius, alone, however, is unconvinced that Hamlet's performance relates to love sickness saying, '[l]ove! His affections do not that way tend' (3.1.161). He does concede that it is some form of melancholy, but the subject of that melancholy has yet to be revealed. However, Polonius remains convinced that Hamlet's grief has 'sprung from neglected love' (3.1.177).

Hamlet then moves to accuse his mother of betraying his father by prostituting herself in an act of incest with her brother-in-law. Despising what he sees as feigned innocence, he says

> Such an act
> That blurs the grace and blush of modesty,
> Calls virtue hypocrite, takes off the rose
> From the fair forehead of an innocent love
> And sets a blister there
>
> (3.4.38–42)

The obvious gloss for these words is that Gertrude's act of marrying Claudius removes her chaste virtue and brands her as a diseased prostitute. Her maidenly blushes can be considered hypocritical as her love is not an innocent love. In a contemporary humoral framework, the rose and white colour suggests the sanguine nature, whose complexion Harington describes as 'Roses ioyn'd to Lillies bright' (1624, stanza 58). A rosy sanguine temperament is also inclined to have an appetite for wine and sex. It may be suggested that in Gertrude the sanguine humour abounds too much, explaining her behaviour as one who has gone too far and should be publicly shamed for her actions.

Hamlet continues to berate his mother drawing again on scientific frameworks. He cries

> And batten on this moor? Ha, have you eyes?
> You cannot call it love, for at your age
> The heyday in the blood is tame, it's humble
> And waits upon judgement, and what judgement
> Would step from this to this?
>
> (3.4.65–9)

He points to the humours which are affected by age and contain less blood and fire. Her declining age should mean a less sanguine temperament. Both humours and vision should be tempered by reason, but Hamlet accuses Gertrude of lacking it. He contrasts the goodness of his father's fair face with the black Moorish representation of his uncle. Parker notes that the comparison is the 'point of departure for his mother's decline'; she has moved from her relationship with unsullied Old King Hamlet to blackened Claudius (2003, 129). Blackness signifies a moral stain but also the effect of the feminised humour of melancholy, a product both of her grief and of her incontinent female ways. Hamlet is attempting to 'purify' the maculate or spotted Queen (Parker 2003, 130). He demands that she feels the disgrace she has brought on herself, asking 'O shame, where is thy blush?' (3.4.79).

The Queen responds by accepting his accusations

> O Hamlet, speak no more.
> Thou turn'st my very eyes into my soul
> And there I see such black and grieved spots
> As will leave there their tinct.
>
> (3.4.86–9)

Gertrude is forced towards introspection by Hamlet to examine those passions which she had sought to conceal from the state, her son, and ultimately herself. Her inward glance reveals a discolouration, a physical expression of her guilt and grief that causes her discomfort and concern. Hamlet's talk of his stained mother recalls his own position as a melancholic, since Timothy Bright describes melancholics, '[o]f colour they be black, according to the humour whereof they are nourished, and the skinne always receaueing the blacke vapors, which insensibly do passe from the inward parts, from the inward parts, taketh die and staine therof' ([1586] 1969, 128). Since a person's 'spirit' was thought to have an active role in obtaining visual images, the 'spirit' was liable to blame when those images proved to be false. When Gertrude tells Hamlet that, '[f]orth at your eyes your spirits wildly peep' (3.4.110), she feels she can see Hamlet's inner spirit overflowing from his eyes. The spirit or air was the pneuma which circulated within the body with the humours. It was also vital to life (Arikha 2007, 183). Gertrude has noticed the change in Hamlet's humoral temperament at this point and says 'O gentle son, / Upon the heat and flame of thy distemper / Sprinkle cool patience' (3.4.118–20). She is suggesting that his humours are too dry and hot and need to cool down; and by 'sprinkle', she suggests that he needs more moisture. Hamlet is distracted by the Ghost and acutely aware that he has not carried out the Ghost's wishes. He is afraid that he will lose his resolve if the Ghost looks upon him. If this happens Hamlet says, 'what I have to do / Will want true colour, tears perchance for blood' (3.4.121–6). Here, 'colour' may mean character or justification but the literal meaning might be closer to humoral discourse, as Hamlet needs the colour of blood to fire him up rather than the watery paleness of the phlegmatic constitution.

While Hamlet was focused on his inner self to this point, he now becomes more focussed on a plan of action and, in doing so, becomes a dangerous opponent for Claudius. The danger is apparent to Claudius who again has a bodily reaction with a blood-red focus. Claudius wants Hamlet to be killed on arrival to England, saying

> Do it, England!
> For like the hectic in my blood he rages
> And thou must cure me.
>
> (4.3.63–5)

Only action will cure Claudius of his raging choler which was muted in the prayer scene but reignited after the killing of Polonius. In contrast, Hamlet is still unsure about how to proceed, saying

> How stand I then
> That have a father killed, a mother stained,
> Excitements of my reason and my blood,
> And let all sleep
>
> (4.4.55–61)

This speaks to the paradoxes that permeate the play, and Hamlet, yet again, is soon resolved to overcome his indecisiveness, telling himself that 'from this time forth / My thoughts be bloody or be nothing worth' (4.4.64–5), his chromatic references throwing off the melancholic black in favour of blood-red.

Before Hamlet can act, Ophelia falls prey to a madness which, like Hamlet's, is difficult to ascribe to a single cause, considering how she has been treated by Hamlet, Polonius, and Claudius. The King is convinced it is occasioned by the death of her father, perhaps compounded by the sudden nature of his burial which the King observes was done 'but greenly' (4.5.83). Laertes later refers to Polonius' 'obscure funeral' which did not include the proper rites (4.5.205–7). Polonius was disposed of just as summarily after death as he was in dying. Ophelia describes his shroud in pure white terms, struggling to reconcile her view of him as a loving father and the way in which he was disposed. These considerations, according to Claudius, 'divided [Ophelia] from herself and her fair judgement' (4.5.86). Laertes, on hearing the news, picks up the theme of conscience and sin, professing 'vows to the blackest devil, / Conscience and grace to the profoundest pit' (4.5.130–1). Conscience being the axis on which the action has turned in the play, Laertes understands that revengeful rage and a lust to kill are against good conscience. However, Claudius is able to manipulate Laertes' conscience, suggesting that Laertes must hesitate and hear exactly towards whom his rage needs to be directed. Laertes' choleric temperament abounds in images of blood-red. He is willing to feed his friends on his own blood. This aligns him with Hamlet who earlier claimed to be ready to drink 'hot blood'. Both young men are manipulated or exploited by Claudius, although neither of them know it at this point. Laertes describes his rage in corporeal humoral terms, asking for heat to dry up his brain and the salt from his tears to burn out the sense and virtue of his eye. In this moment he asks to have a hot choleric rage, and for his sight to be unmediated by his intellect. He does not want to be controlled by his reason.

Claudius continues to manipulate Laertes suggesting that Hamlet is jealous of Laertes' sword skills. Claudius uses the metaphor of sables and weeds to represent the *gravitas* of settled age. Here, we are reminded of the suit of sables Hamlet wished to wear to express his continuing grief and melancholy, and also his graveness beside the carousing Claudius. Claudius continues to prick at Laertes saying

> Laertes, was your father dear to you?
> Or are you like the painting of a sorrow,
> A face without a heart?
>
> (4.7.105–7)

Claudius implies that Laertes' sorrow might not be real and that he is using the performance of sorrow of which Hamlet was previously accused. We are reminded of the player who played 'painted Pyrrhus' and was able to perform counterfeit emotions. By suggesting to Laertes that he is all show, Claudius stirs Laertes' passions. Laertes is convinced '[t]o cut his [Hamlet's] throat i'th'church' (4.7.124) in order to prove his love for his slain father. He then becomes a pawn in the complex and vengeful plan constructed by Claudius, but before their diabolical plan can be enacted there comes the tragic news of Ophelia's death.

Ophelia, in her dying, encapsulates the phlegmatic female, cold and moist. Gertrude in her description of the river bank where the drowning took place talks of 'our cold maids' (4.7.169) and of Ophelia falling 'in the weeping brook' (4.7.173). The lyrical description of Ophelia slipping from a floating wretch to a drowning soul recalls Harington's description of the phlegmatic '[i]n sleepe, of Seas and riuers dreaming oft' (1624, stanza 61). Laertes and Gertrude echo each other's utterances of the word 'drowned' until Laertes makes his pronouncement

> Too much of water hast thou, poor Ophelia,
> And therefore I forbid my tears. But yet
> It is our trick – nature her custom holds
> Let shame say what it will. [Weeps] When these are gone
> The woman will be out.
>
> (4.7.183–6)

Laertes notes the feminine association with water and implicitly with whiteness: it was held that '[t]he watrie Flegmatique are faire and white' (Harington 1624, stanza 58). Out of consideration for the overabundance of moisture that has led to this moment, Laertes wishes to stifle his tears. However, in an involuntary outpouring of grief, Laertes weeps. He acknowledges that there is some shame in the feminised act of weeping but also that by doing so he will be purged of the weak woman within. Momentarily his fiery red rage is drowned.

After the brief funeral rites, Laertes, distressed that his sister cannot be granted the full ceremonies as a suicide, says 'lay her I'th'earth, / And from her fair and unpolluted flesh / May violets spring' (5.1.227–9).

The idea of purple violets conjures up youthful love, grief, death, and royalty. However, her fair flesh will soon be rotted, and possibly too quickly, due to the superfluity of water. She was fair and phlegmatic, and 'water is a sore decayer of your whoreson dead body' (5.1.162). Hamlet, becoming cognizant of the unfolding scene, interjects 'What is he whose grief / Bears such an emphasis ... This is I, / Hamlet the Dane' (5.1.243–4; 246–7). Laertes, blaming Hamlet for the occasion of Ophelia's death, attacks Hamlet. Perhaps grasping the machinations of another in the moment, Hamlet calmly replies

> I prithee take thy fingers from my throat,
> For, though I am not splenative rash,
> Yet have I in me something dangerous
> Which let thy wisdom fear, Hold off thy hand.
>
> (5.1.249–52)

The 'something dangerous' in him is causing a humoral imbalance and he urges Laertes to let reason control his anger since Hamlet is ready to fight over the question of who loved Ophelia more. The Queen does not believe Hamlet's emotional outpourings, calling them 'mere madness' (5.1.273). The audience, privy to Hamlet's soliloquies, can sense the contradiction and tension here. His performance of madness was accepted by those around him but his frenetic grief on the death of Ophelia is questioned.

In conversation with the courtier, Osric, Hamlet contrives to contradict him in an echo of the 'cloud' conversation with Polonius (2.2.169*ff*). The significance of the discussion is what it reveals about Hamlet's self-assessment of his constitution and also the disclosure of Claudius' plan. After trying to persuade Osric that the weather is cold, although from the discussion it appears to be a hot day, Hamlet conflates the weather with his present temperament. Hamlet says, '[b]ut yet methinks it is very sultry and hot, or my complexion' (5.2.84–5). Hamlet's teasing of Osric reminds us that he is tending towards hot choler and away from the cold melancholy. In reply to the invitation to duel, Hamlet replies, 'I will win for him if I can; if not, I will gain nothing but my shame and the odd hits' (5.2.157–8). Hamlet is aware that the encounter will be a passionate one but the extent of those passions is as yet unknown. The idea that a loss would result only in personal shame and minor scrapes is not borne out by the subsequent dialogue between Horatio and Hamlet. While shame is seen as a prerequisite for female modesty, in early modern terms, men were warned against revealing an outward sense of shame (Filipczak 2004, 79). Horatio urges Hamlet to follow his reason saying, '[i]f your mind dislike anything, obey it' (5.1.195) but Hamlet is keen to follow the determinist pathway and let the events unfold.

During the duel, '[t]hey bleed on both sides' (5.2.289), and the King declares that the Queen 'swoons to see them bleed' (5.2.293). The frantic duelling is augmented with the mentions of bloody red until the realisation dawns that poison has been used. Once this happens, the emotional red colour scheme is muted momentarily while Laertes and Hamlet exchange forgiveness. In this moment, Hamlet notes that it is the onlookers who look pale '[y]ou that look pale and tremble at this chance, / That are but mutes or audience to this act' (5.2.318–9).

The paleness supports the calm with which Hamlet approaches his death in the midst of the violent carnage. With the arrival of Fortinbras the blood-red register reappears as he surveys the havoc saying

> O proud Death,
> What feast is toward in thine eternal cell
> That thou so many princes at a shot
> So bloodily hast struck?
>
> (5.2.348–51)

Horatio echoes the reference referring to Fortinbras' 'bloody question' (5.2.359) and the 'carnal, bloody, unnatural acts' (5.2.365). The play which began in a black melancholy ends with the red blood choler and its effects.

Conclusion

There are approximately 50 black or dark references in *Hamlet* compared, for example, with approximately 14 in *Coriolanus*. There is, however, much less mention in *Hamlet* of blood or the colour red, which can be related specifically to the sanguine character, as well as intense passion, blood ties, and loyalty. In *Macbeth*, by contrast, where ideas of loyalty, blood ties, and excessive passions abound, there are approximately twice as many references to blood. The discourse of blood in *Hamlet* is muted and framed by absence rather than its presence. Hamlet focuses instead on his lack of gall and fire (in itself a choleric element but often signified by burning red) which defines his indecision and inactivity. Within the framework of scientific theories, *Hamlet* works both in tandem with and in opposition to these theories to heighten emotional registers affecting dramatic tension. *Hamlet*, as a canonical text for illustrating humoral affect and expressions of self and inwardness, provides many opportunities to see how colour registers are used within an early modern English concept of emotions. Many of *Hamlet*'s characters express strong personal emotions and reflect upon the consequences that these emotions have upon them. There is a particular self-awareness required for this to be possible. Combined with ideology surrounding reason and will, the performance of emotions became a much-examined

106 Senses, science, and the imagination

phenomenon. Colour, the humoral body, vision, and imagination were inextricably entwined in the early modern period producing an emotional register that was paradoxically coherent and contradictory.

Notes

1. In this work *On the Natural Faculties*, Galen describes at length the physical role of humours in relation to the body, including a detailed description of the synergy with the digestive system. He also describes the impact of warmth, cold, moistness, and dryness (1952).
2. For an overview on modern philosophy in relation to Hamlet's melancholy see Andrew Cutrofello (2014).
3. See Wright ([1601] 1986); Harington (1624), Bartholomaeus ([1582] 1976); Taavitsainen (2011). Noga Arikha notes that in '1521, there appeared for the first time a Latin translation of the short book by Galen that focused on the determination of temperaments by the four elements, *De temperamentis et de inaequali in temperie*. The translator, Thomas Linacre, was a famous English physician who had studied medicine at Padua and had been instrumental in founding the London College of Physicians a few years earlier, in 1518' (2007, 140).
4. The Oxford English Dictionary Online states that trappings refers to a cloth or covering spread over the harness or saddle of a horse or other beast of burden, often gaily ornamented; or ornaments; dress; embellishments; external, superficial, and trifling decoration. It also has the meaning of the action of being trapped. (OED Online, 'trapping').
5. Alexander Dunlop (2020) considers Claudius' conscience in further detail in his article "Fooles of Nature: The Epistemology of *Hamlet*".
6. Interestingly this heralds a coincidental connection with Shakespeare as Valentine Sims was Thomas Wright's printer and he also printed five Shakespeare quartos, including the 1603 bad quarto of *Hamlet*. The second edition of *The Passions of the Mind* is dedicated to Henry Wriothesley, third Earl of Southampton, the dedicatee of *Venus and Adonis* (1593) and *The Rape of Lucrece* (1594).
7. 'Three sorts of actions proceed from men's souls: some are internal and immaterial, as the acts of our wits and wills; others be mere external and material, as the acts of our senses (seeing, hearing, moving, etc.); others stand betwixt these two extremes and border upon them both; the which we may best discover in children, because they lack the use of reason and guided by an internal imagination, following nothing else but that pleaseth their senses'. (Wright, [1601] 1986, 1.2.1–10).
8. 'The outward appearance or aspect, the visible form or image, *of* something, as constituting the immediate object of vision'. (OED Online, 'species').
9. Crooke also comments that vision and colour are particularly fascinating to men as man is the only creature that has diverse eye colour whereas other creatures eyes are all alike depending on their kind – the oxen have black eyes and the sheep have watery eyes (1615, 673).
10. Alison Thorne declares that it 'is generally accepted that the end of the sixteenth century was a crucial moment in the formation of the individual self, a moment when the subject acquired a sharper sense of its particularity and its power to shape or "fashion" its own identity' (2000, 104).
11. The meaning of 'wan' is discussed in Chapter 2.
12. The cranes in Plutarch's '*Plutarch's Morals: Ethical Essays*' cried 'Behold the avengers' as they flew overhead and the murderers were unable to hold their

tongues and admitted to the murder (1896). There are copies of the work in Latin and in English published in sixteenth- and seventeenth-century London.
13 Erin Sullivan (2020) discusses the implications of Hamlet's departure from the expected emotional customs in her chapter 'Grief' in *Shakespeare and Emotion*.
14 For further discussion on inwardness see Katharine Eisaman Maus (1995). Maus examines theories of inwardness in her book beginning with reference to Hamlet's speech about the trappings of grief.
15 See Chapter 2 for a description of paleness by Bartholomaeus.
16 For further discussion of a happier Hamlet, see Richard Strier (2021).

References

Anglin, Emily. 2014. "'Something in Me Dangerous': *Hamlet*, Melancholy, and the Early Modern Scholar." *Shakespeare* 13, no 1: 1–15.
Arikha, Noga. 2007. *Passions and Tempers: A History of the Humours*. New York: Ecco: Harper Collins.
Bartholomaeus Anglicus. (1582) 1976. *Batman Uppon Bartholome: His Booke De Proprietatibus Rerum*. Translated by Stephen Batman. Hildesheim; New York: Georg Olms Verlag.
Bright, Timothy. (1586) 1969. *A Treatise of Melancholie*. Amsterdam; New York: Da Capo Press, Theatrum Orbis Terrarum Ltd.
Burton, Robert. 1896. *The Anatomy of Melancholy*. Edited by Arthur Richard Shiletto. London: G. Bell.
Cranmer, Thomas. 1541. *The Byble in English*. London: Edwarde Whitchurch.
Crooke, Helkiah. 1615. *Mikrokosmographia: A Description of the Body of Man*. London: William Iaggard.
Cutrofello, Andrew. 2014. *All for Nothing: Hamlet's Negativity*. Cambridge, MA: The M. I. T. Press.
de Montaigne, Michel. 1991. *The Complete Essays of Michel De Montaigne*. Edited and translated by M. A. Screech. London: Allen Lane.
de Mornay, Philippe. 1602. *The True Knowledge of a Mans Owne Selfe*. Translated by A. M. London: William Leake.
Dunlop, Alexander. 2020. "Fooles of Nature: The Epistemology of *Hamlet*." *English Literary Renaissance* 50, no. 2: 204–31.
Elam, Keir. 2017. *Shakespeare's Pictures: Visual Objects in the Drama*. London: Bloomsbury Arden Shakespeare.
Filipczak, Zirka Z. 2004. "Poses and Passions: Mona Lisa's 'Closely folded' Hands." In *Reading the Early Modern Passions: Essays in the Cultural History of Emotions*, edited by Gail Kern Paster, Katherine Rowe, and Mary Floyd-Wilson, 68–88. Philadelphia: University of Pennsylvania Press.
Galen. 1952. *On the Natural Faculties*. Translated by Arthur John Brock. Cambridge, MA: William Heinemann Ltd.
Harington, Sir John, trans. 1624. *The English Mans Doctor*. By Henricus Ronsouius. London: Thomas Dewe.
Hoeniger, F. David. 1992. *Medicine and Shakespeare in the English Renaissance*. Newark: University of Delaware Press.
Karim-Cooper, Farah. 2006. *Cosmetics in Shakespeare and Renaissance Drama*. Edinburgh: Edinburgh University Press.

Knecht, Ross. 2015. "'Shapes of Grief': Hamlet's Grammar School Passions." *ELH* 82, no. 1: 35–58.
Lemnius, Levinus. 1581. *The Touchstone of Complexions*. Translated by Thomas Newton. London: Thomas Marsh.
Maus, Katharine Eisaman. 1995. *Inwardness and Theater in the English Renaissance*. Chicago and London: The University of Chicago Press.
Meek, Richard. 2009. *Narrating the Visual in Shakespeare*. Farnham, Surrey: Ashgate Publishing Ltd.
Mullaney, Steven. 2015. *The Reformation of Emotions in the Age of Shakespeare*. Chicago, IL: University of Chicago Press.
Neely, Carol Thomas. 2004. *Distracted Subjects: Madness and Gender in Shakespeare and Early Modern Culture*. Ithaca, NY: Cornell University Press.
Oxford University Press. n.d. "Oxford English Dictionary Online." Accessed August, 2021. https://www.oed.com/
Parker, Patricia. 2003. "Black Hamlet: Battening on the Moor." *Shakespeare Studies* 31: 127–64.
Paster, Gail Kern. 2004. *Humoring the Body: Emotions and the Shakespearean Stage*. Chicago, IL: University of Chicago Press.
Plutarch. 1898. *Plutarch's Morals: Ethical Essays*. Translated by Arthur Richard Shilleto. London: George Bell and Sons.
Pollard, Tanya. 2012. "'What's Hecuba to Shakespeare?'" *Renaissance Quarterly* 65, no. 4: 1060–93.
Rogers, Thomas. 1576. *A Philosophicall Discourse, Entituled, The Anatomie of the Minde. Nevvlie Made and Set Forth by T.R.* London: Andrew Maunsell.
Shakespeare, William. (1598) 2009. *King Henry IV, Part 1*. Edited by David Scott Kastan. London: Bloomsbury Arden Shakespeare.
Shakespeare, William. (1611) 2006. *Hamlet*. Edited by Ann Thompson and Neil Taylor. London; New York: Bloomsbury Arden Shakespeare.
Steenbergh, Kristine. 2011. "Emotion, Performance and Gender in Shakespeare's *Hamlet*." In *Sexed Sentiments: Interdisciplinary Perspectives on Gender and Emotion*, edited by Willemijn Ruberg and Kristine Steenbergh, 93–116. Amsterdam; New York: Rodopi.
Strier, Richard. 2021. "Happy Hamlet." In *Positive Emotions in Early Modern Literature and Culture*, edited by Cora Fox, Bradley J. Irish and Cassie M. Miura, 21–43. England: Manchester University Press.
Sullivan, Erin. 2020. "Grief." In *Shakespeare and Emotion*, edited by Katharine A. Craik, 211–23. Cambridge: Cambridge University Press.
Taavitsainen, Irma. 2011. "Dissemination and Appropriation of Medical Knowledge: Humoral Theory in Early Modern English Medical Writing." In *Medical Writing in Early Modern English*, edited by Irma Taavitsainen and Paivi Pahta, 94–114. Cambridge: Cambridge University Press.
Thorne, Alison. 2000. *Vision and Rhetoric in Shakespeare: Looking through Language*. Basingstoke: Macmillan Press Ltd.
Wood, David Houston. 2009. *Time, Narrative, and Emotion in Early Modern England*. Farnham, Surrey: Ashgate Publishing Ltd.
Wright, Thomas. (1601) 1986. *The Passions of the Mind in General*. Edited by William Webster Newbold. New York: Garland.

4 'Not black in my mind, though yellow in my legs'

Bodies, clothes, colour, and passions in *Twelfth Night*

While Orsino is indulging in his unrequited love for Olivia, he frames his conversation around flowers and songs to mark his affection. But as Orsino's outlook changes, his language, and colour-coding become more muted and sombre and inclined towards melancholy and deathly gloom. Since it was an early modern commonplace that music had an impact on mood and temperament (Ficino [1489] 1989),[1] Orsino requests a gloomy song hoping it would relieve his passion more than light airs. The song that Feste sings to Orsino uses imagery and, more significantly, an item of clothing that associates white and black with death, grief, and sadness:

> My shroud of white, stuck all with yew,
> ...
> Not a flower, not a flower sweet
> On my black coffin let there be strewn.
>
> (2.4.55; 59–60)

An article of clothing, the shroud marks the emotional mood. As a voluminous androgynous covering, it indicates both purity, and, in its physicality, anonymity – in death identity is lost. The mood that has been created by the change in song tempo and lyrics is continued by Viola/Cesario who cryptically describes to Orsino her hidden love for him

> She never told her love.
> But let concealment like a worm i'th'bud
> Feed on her damask cheek.[2] She pined in thought,
> And with a green and yellow melancholy
> She sat like Patience on a monument,
> Smiling at grief.
>
> (2.4.109–14)

Viola laments her own unrequited love through references laced with colour and cloth. Her unrequited love takes the form of 'patient female suffering' alluding to the well-known figure, 'patient Griselda' (Jardine 1983, 182).

DOI: 10.4324/9781003198246-5

110 Bodies, clothes, colour, and passions

This suffering takes the form of 'resignation and waiting' (184). By mentioning the damask textile, Viola denotes a pink or light red damask rose cheek colour which was consumed and destroyed by the withering worm of concealment (OED Online, 'damask'). Because damask was a rich fabric mainly composed of silk, Viola suggests that her status is higher than the role she currently occupies. Often, through sumptuary laws, damask lay in the realm of titled ladies. With an elevated status, the role of a courtly lover fits her standing. Viola colours her melancholy in green and yellow – an interesting choice combining the green sickness of the forlorn virgin and the bitterness of yellow gall, creating a melancholic figure eaten away by grief, losing the first bloom of her beauty. Concealment, and in Viola's case disguise, has destroyed her soft rosy cheek. The colour choice allows a more complex blending of states indicating a sensitive emotional register.

Shakespeare presents a complex relationship between characters, their bodies, and their clothing; one that offers a subversive response to the common idea, expressed by Polonius in *Hamlet*, that 'the apparel oft proclaims the man' (1.3.73). In this chapter, I discuss culturally received ideas surrounding the body and its coverings in the early modern period. I examine how Shakespearean characters both respond to colour in costuming and exploit expected responses to it in ways that highlight the complications and emotional potential within the early modern body/clothes relationship. I also look at tensions that arise when the body and its clothing are read as signifiers and how cultural assumptions around clothing, and in particular coloured clothing, augment emotional transactions that take place. The emotional register potentiated and represented by clothing and the body can be uncovered by exploring the relationship between clothing and bodily references, colours, and the emotions displayed around both. References to clothes and the body in *Twelfth Night* were used specifically both to demonstrate and affect this relationship. For Jones and Stallybrass, *Twelfth Night* suggests a radical vision of how clothes are central to self-fashioning, particularly when Viola remembers and 'resurrects' her brother by wearing his 'fashion, colour, [and] ornament' (2000, 198). Clothes represent the material and also the transferability of the material, in this case from brother to sister. This also means that while the emotion can be represented by an item of clothing, it can also be put on and taken off at will when a character wants to exhibit a real or even false emotion. To some extent, the rapidly changing costumes of the play mirror the rapidly changing fashions of the early modern period, which have in some ways 'obscured the sense in which clothes were seen as printing, charactering, haunting' (Jones and Stallybrass 2000, 4).

The dangers of frivolity were linked particularly to clothing and fashion by Elizabeth I in a 1574 proclamation

> The exceffe of apparel, and the fuperfluitie of uneceffary foreyne wares therto belongyng, nowe of late yeeres is growen by fufferance

to fuche an extremitie, that the manifeſt decay, not onely of a great part of the wealth of the whole Realme generally is like to folow [...] but alſo particularly the wafting and undoyng of a great number of young Gentlemen otherwiſe feruiſable, and other feekyng by ſhewe of apparel to be eſteemed as Gentlemen.

Elizabeth I marks concerns that young gentlemen were living above their means swayed by the allure of fine clothing, which was liable to lead them down a frivolous path to generational financial ruin. This will then have an impact on the realm itself. These concerns were linked to practices on the stage in a variety of pamphlets. For example, when Rainolds writes on the subject of cross-dressing he aligns it with a comment against dressing above one's station in life

Likewise in apparell, that which cometh vpon the backe, dishonesteth not the man; yet, if men wear costilier garmentes then they ought, they are dishonested by their riotous and vnmodest behaviour. And so, if anie man doe put on Womans raiment, hee is dishonested and defiled, because he transgresseth the boundes of modestie and comelinesse, and weareth that which Gods law forbiddeth him to weare.

([1599] 1972, 16)

Behaviour, activities, and language marked social position and approval but social position was also dependent on wearing appropriate clothing (Everett 1995, 200; Escolme 2012, 139). By putting on inappropriate clothing, a man's very person is defiled. Macbeth, when he is made Thane of Cawdor, asks '[w]hy do you dress me in borrowed robes?' (1.3.116). He considered it inappropriate as he thought the present Thane was still *in situ*. Banquo explains that Macbeth is not yet comfortable in his elevated social position and '[n]ew honours come upon him, Like our strange garments, cleave not to their mould, But with the aid of use' (1.3.147–9).

By the middle of the sixteenth century, sumptuary laws included regulation of clothing, indicating how influential clothing, as a signifier, was perceived. Stage costuming used codes embedded in the sumptuary laws to indicate the social order and moral codes that were being transgressed (Lublin 2011, 5). Alan Hunt notes 'clothing exhibits a capacity to communicate about such matters as age, social status, gender and national identity, but may also operate within an emotive register being capable of representing mood, playfulness, eroticism, nationalism and a range of sentiments' (1996, 59). While codes were clearly defined in the statutes, it was not uncommon for these codes to be contravened when communicating a social or emotional message. On the Shakespearean stage, costumes constructed the wearers according to conventions of rank, gender, and occupation. However, as in society, while the dress code existed it was constantly violated (MacIntyre 1992, 41). The shape and materials of clothing, including the colours and the fabrics used in them, were normative signifiers for a person's social status, and as such, they were regulated by the state for the societal good. These regulations offered a means to signify social position on the stage, which then could be manipulated creating dramatic tension. The meaning of clothing could also be read according to other normative codes that indicated moral qualities or emotional well-being (Ashelford 1988, 7; Hunt 1996, 59) Antitheatricalists grappled with the power that fashion had adding it to their argument against play-going. Anthony Munday, in his diatribe against plays and the theatre, *A Second and Third Blast of Retrait from Plaies and Theaters*, warns that '[a]l vncleanes is fhowed at plaieng; al luxurioufnes at wreftling; at tumbling al vnfhamefaftnes; al madnes in caues' ([1586] 1973, 34). The uncleanliness, vanity, and shamelessness promoted through such recreational activities needed to be rooted out for the greater good. Focusing specifically on vanities encouraged by theatre going, William Prynne (1633) notes the detrimental effects on the vulnerable youth whose minds are corrupted by exposure to the vices of the playhouse. Continued engagement in this activity will change the behaviours and morals of those who persist in attending.

In *Twelfth Night*, there is a fascination with not only clothing but also the materials from which they were fashioned and the way in which they could be deployed to support emotional registers. For example, Feste uses the metaphor of diverse-coloured taffeta to underline Orsino's inconstancy. The mention of this particular material also indicates in part the Duke's social standing and identity, according to sumptuary laws of the time

> Now the melancholy god protect thee, and the
> tailor make thy doublet of changeable taffeta, for thy
> mind is a very opal. I would have men of such constancy
> put to sea.
>
> (2.4.73–6)

Feste's use of coloured referencing to express intellectual ideas beyond simple inconstancy, indicates a familiarity with the various meanings of 'changeable taffeta'. The connotations of 'taffeta' include 'florid', 'bombastic', and 'overdressed', as well as the material quality of the fabric, which changes colour depending on the light and the angle of the viewer (OED Online, 'taffeta'). All of these meanings add depth to his description of Orsino while staying close to the play's material preoccupation with clothes and their physical aspect. Feste, by using the precious opal and the valuable cloth suggests a reverence for Orsino whilst ironically indicating Orsino's inconstancy. Indeed, the opal was used figuratively to express variety and change (OED Online, 'opal').

Olivia, when she is about to receive Viola/Cesario, demands her veil to cover her face (1.5.160). She wishes to announce her state of grieving by covering the most expressive part of her body, her face, from view. Although it is not stated, it is likely that she is attired in black clothing to further accentuate her state of mourning. Viola/Cesario, however, wise to the fact that clothes can conceal defects and deficits, wishes to gaze upon Olivia's face during the transaction: 'let me see your face' (1.5.223). Olivia agrees, saying 'we will draw the curtain and show you the picture' (1.5.226). Olivia compares her unveiling to taking the dust covers off to reveal the painting beneath.[3] As she is in mourning for her brother, she is guilty of unveiling herself; by exposing her face, her desire for Viola/Cesario leaves her open to public exposure and, therefore, shame. The metaphor becomes less flattering when we recall Sir Toby addressing Sir Andrew similarly, saying '[w]herefore have these gifts a curtain before 'em? Are they like to take dust…?' (1.3.120–2). In Sir Toby/Sir Andrew exchange, we are invited to laugh at Sir Andrew as his hidden talents border on the ridiculous. There is also a mutable level of surface reality exposed in Olivia's face since in a painting colour can be applied at will, and the outward countenance can be painted according to the owner's desires. The colours used can denote various emotional states such as embarrassment, guilt, and love. Olivia and Viola/Cesario discuss the nature of Olivia's face

> VIOLA: Excellently done, if God did it all.
> OLIVIA: 'Tis in grain, sir, 'twill endure wind and weather.
> VIOLA: 'Tis beauty truly blent, whose red and white
> Nature's own sweet and cunning hand laid on.
>
> (1.5.229–32)

Viola/Cesario says that Olivia's looks are pleasing if they are natural and fashioned by God. There is a hint that she suspects the counterfeiting actions of cosmetics before Olivia affirms that is from nature. This view is ironic since they have had a conversation that plays on learning lines and being an actor, and in reality, Olivia is a boy actor who would be wearing quite significant makeup, while Viola/Cesario is a boy actor playing a girl playing a boy. The reference to fabric dyeing methods ('in grain') accords with the play's focus on costume and clothing. 'In grain' signifies a process that produces a dyed material of some permanence while 'blent' refers to blended or mixed paints. Olivia echoes the sentiments of Berowne, discussed in Chapter 2, who notes that his love alone will not be worried about the ravages of the weather on the colouring of her face. The conversation is multi-levelled, tracing the line between real and counterfeit facial appearance, and implicitly questioning the link between emotional expression and discernable facial colouring. In this exchange, both Olivia and Viola/Cesario use clothes to conceal physical and emotional conditions.

Clothing and the body beneath

In the medieval period, there were concerns related to clothes and the body. The sin of pride could be located in the clothing which adorned the body. Geoffrey Chaucer describes this sin at length in *The Parson's Tale*

> Now been ther two maneres of Pride: that
> oon of hem is withinne the herte of man, and
> that oother is withoute.
> ...
> For certes, if ther ne hadde be no synne
> in clothyng, Crist wolde nat so soone have
> noted and spoken of the clothyng of thilke
> riche man in the gospel.
>
> ([c1396] 2008, X. (I).408–13)

Chaucer continues to numerate in detail the sins and evil that such pride in clothing brings, including the expense, the vanity it instils, and the inappropriate design of the clothing for purpose. Such a diatribe against ostentatious clothing is possible in an atmosphere where a discourse on proper clothes-wearing was commonplace. Later in 1586, Munday claimed that

> [s]inne hath always a faire cloake to cover his filthie bodie. And therefore he is to be turned out of his case into his naked skin, that his nastie filthie body, and stinking corruption being perceaued, he might come into the hatred and horror of men.
>
> ([1586] 1973, 44)

Although Munday is talking about the devil, the devil he speaks of is connected with the theatre, and moreover, is intimately connected with the body and clothing which can deceive. Munday was, himself, both an actor and a playwright, but when sponsored by the city to attack the stage he did not hesitate to do so in his work. He insisted that his contempt for the stage stemmed from his intimate knowledge of its arts and therefore, the sins inherent in the activity (Hill 2004, 46).

The puritanical campaign to stamp out the theatre in early modern England gained further currency from erudite men such as John Rainolds writing persuasive tracts which had, at their root, the 'deep-seated conviction of man's natural inclination towards evil and the belief that the visual and auditory attractions to the stage appeal directly to his depraved nature' (White 1988, 48). Rainolds, whose letters on the subject were published in 1599, was concerned about the effect playing a particular role a number of times might have on the actors themselves

> The care of making a shew to doe such feates, and to doe them as lively as the beasts them selues in whom the vices raigne, worketh in

the actors a maruellous impression of being like the persons whose qualities they express and imitate: chiefly when earnest and much meditation of sundry dayes and weekes, by often repetition and representation of the partes, shall as it were engraue the things in their minde with a penne of iron, or with the point of a diamond.

([1599] 1972, 19)

The argument goes beyond the idea that the passions are moved in the theatre during a single performance. Instead, it maintains that there is the danger that the actor's character can be permanently altered by continuous exposure to the roles acted out on the stage. The acting, which includes the wearing of clothes suited to the role, moulds the mind, body, and character of the actor.

The other concern regarding clothing arises when there is cross-gendered costuming. Philip Stubbes, a puritan pamphleteer, writes in *The Anatomie of Abuses*

Our apparel was given to us as a signe distinctive to discerne betwixt sexe and sexe; and therefore, one to weare the apparell of another sexe, is to participate with the same, and to adulterate the veritie of his owne kinde. Wherefore, these women may not improperly bee called *hermaphroditi*, that is Monsters of both Kindes, halfe women, halfe men.

(1583, sect. 'A curse for Apparell')

Stubbes describes women who indulge in cross-dressing, but there is an implicit reference to both sexes. Either gender can blur its approved lines, while creating a false aspect which cannot be trusted. Jones and Stallybrass note

Stubbes wants clothes to place subjects recognizably, to materialize identities for the onlooker and wearer alike. But he is forced to recognize what he deplores: that clothes are detachable, that they can move from body to body. That is precisely their danger and their value.

(2000, 5)

Shakespeare exploits this value in comedic moments that a blurred gender line can bring. For example, Orsino, not realising that his new attendant is, in fact, Viola, a girl, says

Dear lad, believe it
For they shall yet belie thy happy years
That say thou art a man. Diana's lip
Is not more smooth and rubious. Thy small pipe

Is as the maiden's organ, shrill and sound,
And all is semblative a woman's part.

(1.4.29–34)

The fact that Orsino is noting so-called female features in the boy actor playing Viola/Cesario speaks to the moment of comedy but also the dangers noted by the pamphleteers who are convinced that this mutability of form laid down permanent changes. Gender identities would have been harder to define as it was thought that the physical boundaries themselves were mutable and subject to the influence of the fabric they are clothed in. Will Fisher suggests that 'clothing materialized gender along with other, more corporeal, features, and both were essential' (2010, 13). The fact that gender differences were not fixed created a tension exploited by early modern dramatists.

Clothing on stage could disrupt gender leading to off-stage cross-dressing practices that render bodies inscrutable. In the *Merchant of Venice*, Jessica alludes to these concerns when she is eloping with Lorenzo

I am glad 'tis night you do not look on me,
For I am much ashamed of my exchange.
But love is blind, and lovers cannot see
The pretty follies that they themselves commit,
For, if they could, Cupid himself would blush
To see me thus transformed to a boy.

(2.6.35–40)

As with Viola, Jessica is a boy playing a woman who is, in turn, playing a boy. Her transformation, as she calls it, would be a risk since it may well change her relationship with Lorenzo due to the transgression of gender boundaries. Tracey Sedinger notes, 'erotic difference (sexuality) is not reducible to sexual difference (gender): crossdressing mobilizes a libidinal investment in the play (erotic difference) not reducible to the real sex of the boy-actor' (1997, 66). In itself, the doubling of cross-dressing would have been a comic moment with an underlying significance about contemporary issues of the body, not necessarily confined to gender concerns. Jessica's speech points to Ovid's warning about darkness hiding the true nature of the body – in this case, its gender, confused by the boy-actor – and also to erotic love untempered by reason.[4] Jessica's assertion indicates that a physical transformation has been made to the body's plasticity underneath its outer coverings. Lisa Jardine maintains that 'the double entendres of these speeches [Jessica's and other similar speeches] by blushing heroines (played by boys) as they adopt male dress to follow their male lovers are both compatible with the heterosexual plot, and evocative of the bisexual image of the "wanton female boy"' (1991, 63). Because of the complex malleability of the body, Rainolds warns against the 'unclean affections' that cross-dressing can provoke. He says, 'that the putting of Womens attire on men, may kindle sparkes of lust in vncleane affections: I saide not, in all mens affections, but in some; not in sanctified, but in vncleane' ([1599] 1972, 34). Although there was an acceptance of the boy-actors to a certain extent, the practice did not come without concerns.

Keir Elam maintains that, for an intensive reading of the body, the only framework available was Galen's theory of the humours (2008, 52). I propose that equally significant is the concept of the mutability and porosity of the body's surface. In the early modern period, the surface of the body was perceived as a liminal physical and figurative space that hid, displayed, and enacted emotions. The physicality of the body relied heavily on clothing, and the *Twelfth Night* leans into this space. Throughout the play, colours can be observed to enable and augment the emotional register of the physical and figurative space that is the body.

Desire, pride, and chromatic metaphors

Orsino relies quite heavily on metaphors steeped in chromatic significance to describe his love plight. He introduces the trope of the love hunt and the myth of Actaeon[5] before lamenting the lack of returned affections from Olivia, 'How will she love when the rich golden shaft / Hath killed the flock of all affections else / That live in her' (1.1.34–6). The golden colour represents the gold-tipped arrow of Cupid which can wound, causing love to flourish. Appositely here, Cupid's arrow has killed off all hope of love; all other emotions have been stifled in the wake of the death of Olivia's brother. Olivia has vowed to grieve for seven years for her brother, allowing no one to 'behold her face at ample view, / But like a cloistress she will veiled walk (1.1.26–7).[6] In scene two, Viola enters and coincidentally uses the word 'gold', as she wishes to reward the ship's captain, who suggests that there is a good chance that her brother Sebastian may have survived the shipwreck (1.2.16). Viola repeats the name 'Orsino' after the captain mentions him, linking the eventual lovers by both their names and their references to 'gold' and 'golden', a colour associated with value and beauty.[7] In the play, gold becomes associated with the precious and often elusive emotion of love. After her verbal reference to gold, Viola physically produces gold and gives it to the captain on stage. Viola is using the currency to pay for an emotional transaction: the hope that her brother, whom she loves dearly, is alive. Only 22 lines earlier in Orsino's lament, gold is mentioned in association with the production and paradoxically the absence of love. A close connection is forged between gold and the emotion of love and loyalty in the context of the characters and physical presence of Orsino and Viola. Viola now vows to become a servant to Olivia, in the guise of a woman. She asks that the captain, '[c]onceal me what I am, and be my aid / For such disguise as haply shall become / The form of my intent' (1.2.50–2). The male clothes will conceal her female form and also her intentions while she is disguised as a servant. As in classical literature, and medieval and early modern romances, her disguise will keep her safe until her circumstances improve. Later, Sebastian uses an implicit reference to gold to denote emotions of love and loyalty when referring to his relationship with Olivia, '[t]his is the air, that is the glorious sun./ This pearl she gave to me' (4.3.1–2), and then Antonio, '[h]is counsel now might do me some golden service' (4.3.8). The various fluid bodies on stage are linked through connected colours and emotions.

An emotional response to Olivia is activated in Malvolio through the gulling orchestrated by Maria. The relationship, in Malvolio's understanding, begins with his receipt of a forged letter, ostensibly from Olivia but actually penned by Maria. When he thinks he is alone, he reveals his inner desire for Olivia, and simultaneously a humoral imbalance and lack of restraint, which ultimately exposes him to shame. He says, 'Maria once told me she [Olivia] did affect me, and I have heard herself come thus near, that should she fancy it should be one of my complexion' (2.5.21–4). Maria has prepared a trap which relies, in part, on Malvolio having a complexion (colour, humoral state, and emotional character) which he believes would be attractive to Olivia. Imagining his marriage to Olivia has taken place, he considers how this will change his status, and envisages himself in an elevated state marked in part by his sumptuous garments. He pictures himself '[c]alling my officers about me in my branched / velvet gown, having come from a day-bed where I have / left Olivia sleeping' (2.5.44–6). Feelings of pride and vainglory motivate him to consider the 'branched velvet gown' which, according to the sumptuary laws, only barons' sons and knights were allowed to wear.[8] Branched velvet, material that is patterned with branches or flowered foliage, suggests an image of vernal green opulence.[9] Green evokes youth and hopefulness but also is associated with love, joy, and the greensickness of young maidens. All of these passions may be implicated in the gown which Malvolio imagines covering his body, hiding his true social position. Dympna Callaghan notes that in 'the Renaissance the mimicking of social superiors by wearing their clothes was as much a violation of natural order as the assumption of a sexual identity other than that dictated by one's anatomical destiny' (2000, 32). Malvolio's wish for sumptuous clothing is as much a transgression as the deception wrought by Viola. He swells with the proud vision of a youthful self – successful in securing Olivia. Malvolio's bombastic pride and hubris incite both anger and amusement in his eavesdroppers, indicating the unpredictability of emotional response as the trick is, in fact, proceeding as well as Maria hoped for. Malvolio's audience could not have expected a better response.

Malvolio, after his wooing attempt, is incarcerated in a dark chamber and tormented by his malefactors who conspire to convince him that he is, indeed, suffering from madness. At this moment, not only is Malvolio hidden from view but so also is his body and the transgressing yellow stockings. His outward show of desire is nullified by visual absence. To bait Malvolio, Maria brings a curate's costume onstage consisting of a gown and a false beard, which Feste dons to become the embodiment of 'Sir Topas' thus focusing the audience's attention on the costume and the body. Elam notes in the 'List of Roles', that the name among several connotations may refer to the madness relieving qualities of the topaz stone or it may reflect the motley colours of Feste in his fool's garments, as the gemstone was changeable in colour, ranging from yellow, green, and white (2008, 159). Feste, himself, notes the failings of his bodily appearance for the role

> I am not tall enough to become the function
> well, nor lean enough to be thought a good student, but
> to be said an honest man and a good housekeeper goes
> as fairly as to say a careful man and a great scholar.
>
> (4.2.6–9)

However, Maria remarks that Feste might have fulfilled his role without the disguise since Malvolio could not see him (4.2.63–4). This leads one to conclude that the donning of the costume was mainly important for Feste, to help him to embody the role of the curate. The clothes helped to fashion the assumed character beneath. The psychological assault upon Malvolio is marked by numerous references to black and darkness. Malvolio states '[t]hey have laid me here in hideous darkness' (4.2.29–30), to which Feste replies, '[s]ayst thou that house is dark?' (4.2.33–4). Feste describes the windows as 'lustrous as ebony' (4.2.39). The conversation continues with the word dark/darkness mentioned a total of eight times. I suggest that the continued use of the dark/black colour impresses upon the audience the madness and the melancholic state that the malefactors are trying to induce in Malvolio. It also suggests the idea that the blackness is hiding Malvolio's body and therefore some of the shame that he had experienced earlier. Indeed this body has been, as Patricia Akhimie describes, 'imagined as the appropriate locus for expressions of fear, anger, jealousy, and anxiety' (2018, 30), and hiding corporeal expression of emotions can also disguise the motivations of his tormenters. As Malvolio comes to terms with the situation and the place of blackness, the colouring of the passage also changes. At this point, it is evident that Malvolio will not be swayed into a melancholic state of madness, as he asks for both ink and paper and, crucially, light. The 'light' references seem to brighten the sombre predicament that Malvolio finds himself in, and allow him to maintain a grip on his own sense of right and sanity.

Malvolio uses his colour referencing to counteract the blackness highlighted previously in the conversation.

Viola and imprinting the body

The opening scene of *Twelfth Night* features Orsino describing the lovesickness he is suffering because of his unrequited love for Olivia. His description mentions the violet as a metaphor for the food of love; 'O, it came o'er my ear like the sweet south / That breathes upon a bank of violets, / Stealing and giving odour' (1.1.5–7). The fleeting smell of the violet is identifiable not only with his love for Olivia but also because Viola as violet is interchangeable with 'viola' as the name for the flower (OED Online, 'viola'). Viola will enter his life with the same stealth and will remain elusive until the play climaxes. The colour purple is suggested through the violet hue of the blossom itself. The regal purple of her namesake hints that Viola's social standing is more elevated than the page costume which she assumes for a large portion of the play. 'Viola' and 'Olivia' are also interchangeable as the two names are almost anagrams of each other, and this interchangeability foreshadows how later Orsino's love for Olivia will be swapped by his love for Viola. Viola or the violet is also an epithet for the Virgin Mary, aligning Viola with thoughts of chastity and pure love (University of Michigan n.d., 'viola'). The chastity is of an enforced nature, as Viola comes to Orsino in the guise of a male imprinted onto the female body.

Viola as Cesario, is marked as male by her clothing making her form interchangeable with that of her twin, Sebastian. Antonio, the seacaptain who befriends Sebastian, articulates the often ephemeral nature of shame and betrayal after he mistakes Viola for Sebastian. Feeling that he has been abandoned by Sebastian he says

> Thou hast, Sebastian, done good feature shame.
> In nature there's no blemish but the mind:
> None can be called deformed but the unkind.
> Virtue is beauty, but the beauteous evil
> Are empty trunks o'erflourished by the devil.
>
> (3.4.363–7)

In this assertion, the shame of evil-doing is irreconcilable with a beautiful body. The outward form of the body should reflect an inner virtue. Coupled with this sentiment Antonio notes the part that the mind plays in the outward expression of the body; thinking evil makes it so, and should, in his view, be as discernible as the black devil which causes the inner evil to spill over into that aspect of the body visible to the public. Antonio's outburst leads Viola to understand that the incident has arisen because her brother lives. She notes

> He named Sebastian. I my brother know
> Yet living in my glass. Even such and so
> In favour was my brother, and he went
> Still in this fashion, colour, ornament,
> For him I imitate.
>
> (3.4.376–80)

Viola notes that their bodies were so alike that his form appears to her every time she looks in a mirror. She has strengthened the resemblance by imitating his clothes, including their colour and ornamentation, to keep his memory alive. In this case, then, clothes – their colour and style – serve not only to disguise Viola's vulnerable female state, but act as a physical representation of an emotional bond, and a means of preserving her brother.

Meanwhile, around the time Olivia marries Sebastian, mistaking him for Cesario, there arises confusion amongst many characters regarding the person who they think is either Cesario or Sebastian. The misunderstanding continues until both characters appear on stage together. Orsino's reaction is '[o]ne face, one voice, one habit and two persons: A natural perspective that is and is not' (5.1.212–3). Evidently Viola's disguise, both in terms of gender and clothing, perfectly matches that of her brother – echoing Viola's earlier statement that Sebastian is 'living in my glass' (3.4.377). In this case, the clothes, not the mind and the form, make the man, both in terms of gender and identity. No one questions Viola's performance as a man; even Antonio cannot tell the two apart, '[h]ave you made a division of yourself? / An apple cleft in two is not more twin / Than these two creatures. Which is Sebastian?' (5.1.218–20). The conversation reveals Viola's identity and gender. However, she wants to delay the reunion proper while she is clad in male attire. Her body and her psychological being are influenced by her outerwear

> If nothing lets to make us happy both
> But this my masculine usurped attire,
> Do not embrace me till each circumstance
> Of place, time, fortune, do cohere and jump
> That I am Viola – which to confirm,
> I'll bring you to a captain in this town,
> Where lie my maiden weeds
>
> (5.1.245–51)

The notion that the clothes are exerting a significant pressure on her being is established by the fact that she will be confirmed as Viola only when attired in her feminine wear. Callaghan states, '[t]o divest oneself of the appropriate signifiers is to alter one's essence, to adulterate God-given nature. From this point of view, the soul resides in the clothes ... for all humanity' (2000, 33).

Viola resolves her male/female position by the end of the play when she finds Sebastian. What is startling is the fact that Viola has to offer Sebastian proof about her identity before he will acknowledge her as his lost sister. As Mary Thomas Crane notes, 'meaning in *Twelfth Night*, like desire, is neither a rigidly confining system nor a slippery field of play; both meaning and desire offer both possibilities, a field of choice anchored by the plenitude of conceptualization itself' (2001, 115). It is the slipperiness of Cesario's gender, under male outer clothing, which proves male to Olivia and female to Orsino that appropriately channels Orsino and Olivia's passions. They both mature and learn to desire a partner who will temper their excesses. Orsino, upon realising Viola/Cesario's gender, admits he has feelings for her/him. However, Orsino wishes to see Viola in her 'woman's weeds' (5.1.269). Orsino is colluding with Viola in the fallacy that becoming a woman again relies on the outer coverings of the body. He will make a union with Viola when Malvolio releases the captain who has possession of Viola's clothes. Ownership of the clothes appears to be an important part of the transaction as the moment of transformation cannot be made by way of random feminine clothing. Jones and Stallybrass note that the play is inherently dependent upon Malvolio's releasing the Captain so that the latter can provide Viola's clothes, which are necessary to transform her from Cesario back into a woman (2000, 199). They note '[t]he failure to persuade Malvolio to release the Captain from prison leads to the failure to translate Cesario back into Viola. Viola remains Cesario because her clothes inscribe her as "a man"' (200).

Orsino states 'golden time convents, / A solemn combination shall be made / of our dear souls' (5.1.375–7), At this moment, Orsino, with his reference to gold previously representing love, may mean that his love is in every way reliant on Viola's transformation. It is a valiant effort for determination but his construction appears to suggest a conditional situation without any certainty. The hesitancy may also be a product of Viola's reluctance to embrace female subservience and a bewildered Orsino's inability to enforce his will. In this construction, the clothes become a significant part of the transaction. Most early modern women relied on clothing from fathers, husbands or those in a position of power. As Cristine M. Varholy notes when women 'used clothing to alter their identities through costume or disguise unbeknownst to their sexual partners, their behavior was perceived as threatening and was denounced, in part, because it disrupted clothing's perceived ability to signify a stable relationship, much as violations of the sumptuary laws disrupted clothing's perceived ability to signify a stable class identity' (2008, 7).

The vulnerable body

Each of the characters in *Twelfth Night* contributes to the discussion of the vulnerable body and its relationship to colour. When Feste enters colours are immediately foregrounded. Maria chides him for being absent from the household. Feste demonstrates his penchant for colour/clothing referencing when he reacts to Maria's chiding, saying '[l]et her hang me. He that is well hanged in this world needs to fear no colours' (1.5.4–5). Feste manages to incorporate feelings of fear, loyalty, and swaggering bravado within his colour reference. He may be alluding to worldly deceptions and/or the hangman's noose, but also to the colours which represented either the livery of a particular household or flags of factions at war. There is also a hidden allusion here to the deceptive qualities of colours that do not reveal the wearer's true emotional state, such as mourning weeds which indicate sorrow but could be used to promote such a façade to the world. Maria points out that the saying 'I fear no colours' originated in a military context and Feste is either demeaning the saying or alternatively he is in a significant amount of trouble on account of his truancy. Feste later proclaims, *'cucullus non facit monachum*[10]*–* that's as much to say as I wear not motley in my brain' (1.5.51–3). Such a notion is demonstrable in opposition to ideas posed by Thomas Wright on the subject

> Extraordinary apparel of the body declareth well the apparel of the mind; for some you have so inconstant in their attire that the variety of their garments pregnantly proveth the fickleness of their heads; for they are not much unlike to Stage-players, who adorn themselves gloriously like Gentlemen, then like clowns, after as women, then like fools, because the fashion of their garments maketh them resemble these persons.
>
> ([1601] 1986, 4.2.6.376–81)

Wright suggests that fickleness in fashion choices reflects the fickle state of one's mind. In his assessment of the situation, Wright condemns both the stage player and the individual who mimics him. Feste, however, is expressing, through received wisdoms, that his demeanour is not a reflection of the motley colours of his outer garments. This is despite both the accepted porosity of the mind to the material influences on the body, such as clothing, and also to the fact that some chose their outer garments in order to reflect an inner reality. With his words, Feste is highlighting these tensions to the audience.

On the subject of love, Orsino declares he is the embodiment of the stock lover:

> For such as I am all true lovers are,
> Unstaid and skittish in all motions else
> Save in the constant image of the creature
> That is beloved.
>
> (2.4.17–20)

He does not suggest anything particular about his own love for Olivia but instead is insistent that the tropes are present; his emotional disarray, his need for melancholic love music, and his proposed withdrawal from company to 'sweet beds of flowers' (1.1.39). He also advises Viola/Cesario on the subject of taking a lover

> Then let thy love be younger than thyself,
> Or thy affection cannot hold the bent;
> For women are as roses, whose fair flower
> Being once displayed doth fall that very hour.
>
> (2.4.36–9)

There are hints of the inconstancy and superficiality in Orsino's passions since he views love as being possible only in the presence of a young, physically perfect woman. Once the woman's beauty begins to diminish passions also dwindle. The women are compared to roses, drawing together metaphorically the Petrarchan perfection of white and red blooming in the cheek, the fleeting nature of the body's perfection and of love itself, and the idea of a plucked or deflowered bloom. Further underlying the theme of a misalignment between a bodily surface and an emotional interior, Olivia falls in love with Viola as Cesario. Viola is aghast: '[f]ortune forbid my outside has not charmed her' (2.2.18). She acknowledges that being disguised is a wickedness that creates desperate problems for those involved. Although Viola admits that Olivia is physically beautiful, she posits Olivia is guilty of pride.

Sir Andrew Aguecheek, presented as a stock character, the fool, discusses his dancing ability when he appears onstage. The first part of his name, which plays upon the early modern term for fever, suggests a somewhat pale and sickly complexion (OED Online, 'ague'). His self-portrait reveals an inconstant character who 'delight[s] in masques and revels sometimes altogether' (1.3.109–10). Sir Toby describes Sir Andrew as having a leg excellent for the galliard, a galliard being 'a quick and lively dance in triple time'. However, the word could mean 'valiant, hardy; 'stout', sturdy; lively, brisk, gay, full of high spirits; having a gay appearance, spruce; a man of courage and spirit; a gay fellow, and a man of fashion' (OED Online, 'galliard'). Sir Toby applies the term to Sir Andrew jokingly, as the latter is, of course, none of these things, indicating the vulnerable body on show. Sir Andrew replies regarding his leg saying that '[a]y, 'tis strong, and it does indifferent well in a flame-coloured stock' (1.3.129–30). In this case, the clothing also serves to draw attention to the body while allowing emotional and character conclusions to be made. Elam's textual note here suggests that in this instance 'flame' refers to a colour, and while it is unclear the exact colour being mooted it does anticipate the yellow stockings which will be worn by Malvolio

(2008, 180). Materially stockings point to a new direction in legwear prominent in the late Elizabethan era.[11] Jane Schneider notes

> [w]orsted wool lay behind the most important fashion innovation of the Elizabethan era – knitted stockings – which, by 1600, were displacing imported silk and woolen hose. Manufactured in several of England's wool-producing districts, they dared to come in multiple colors, some even 'striped with a fiery red.' Phillip Stubbes... railed that even children 'are not ashamed to weare hose of ... greene, red, white, russet, tawny and els what, whiche wanton light colors, any sober chaste Christian ... can hardly without any suspicion of lightnesse at any time weare.'
>
> (2000, 119)

The mention of 'flame' (even if 'flame' means diverse colours as emended in the Oxford edition) in this context may indicate Sir Andrew's changeability and also his disarrayed mind, as diverse colours were often associated with motley, being a fool, and inconstancy. In a play that is very conscious of social standing and the role of clothes, this exchange mentioning diverse-coloured stockings in conjunction with his interest in the superficial pursuits of dancing and masques, marks Sir Andrew as a fickle and inconstant character. Sir Andrew's psychological and emotional characterisation has been directly related to his body and the coverings he chooses to wear. Demonstrating his characteristics, Sir Andrew states he will allow himself a month to woo Olivia, indicating his willingness to reassign his affections after a short period.

In the early modern period, excessive ornamentation in the form of clothing was thought to lead to the sin of pride. Stubbes writes that pride

> is tripartite, namely [...] pryde of the hart, the pride of the mouth, & the pryde of apparel, which ... offendeth God more than the other two. For as pride of the heart & mouth is not opposite to the eye, nor visible to the sight, and therefor intice not others to vanitie & sin ... so the pride of apparel, remaining in sight, as an exemplary of evil, induceth the whole man to wickednes and sinne.
>
> (1583, sect. 'Three sorts of pride')

He regards vanity with respect to one's clothing as a particularly wicked sin of pride because its manifestation entices others to sin similarly. It is the public display that can cause the most offence as it affects the wearer and, crucially, the onlooker. The sin of apparel is closely linked to that unstable sense, vision. Another contemporary, Munday, notes '[t]here cometh much euil in at the eares, but more at the eies, by these two open windows death breaketh into the soule' ([1586] 1973, 96). The eye takes visual information to the imagination and to the mind where reason processes it. Of course that reason can be swayed by the affections. Stubbes reports that the sin of pride in one's apparel is committed

> [b]y wearyng of Apparell more gorgeous, sumptuous & precious than our state, calling or condition of lyfe requireth, whereby, we are puffed up into Pride, and inforced to thinke of our Selues, more than we ought, being but uile earth and miserable sinners. And this sinne of Apparell (as I haue sayde before) hurteth more then the other two: For the sinne of the heart, hurteth none, but the Author, in whom it breedeth, so long as it bursteth not forth into exterior action.
>
> (1583, sect. 'Pride, vainglorious')

The sin of pride works its evil particularly in Malvolio through his public display of strange apparel. Indeed, in Malvolio's first appearance, the seeds of his sin are sown as Olivia says to him, 'you are sick of self-love, Malvolio, and taste with a distempered appetite' (1.5.86–7).

Malvolio demonstrates the most complex relationship with the body and its clothing, usually referenced in relation to his emotional connection with Olivia and his own feelings around that transaction. The gulling which he undergoes is directly related by Maria to Malvolio's perception of himself, his body, and a love relationship with Olivia

> I will drop in his way some obscure epistles of
> love, wherein by the colour of his beard, the shape of
> his leg, the manner of his gait, the expressure of his
> eye, forehead and complexion he shall find himself
> most feelingly personated.
>
> (2.3.150–4)

Maria points also to the importance of colour in this relationship, which she expands upon when the trick takes form. Emphasising Malvolio's corporeality is central to the trick: 'rationality and the body are disassembled at the same time' (Salkeld 1993, 75). The embodiment and expression of emotions require Malvolio to engage completely, both physically and psychologically.

Reading aloud from the letter, which proves to be his downfall; Malvolio quotes 'She thus advises thee that sighs for / thee. Remember who commended thy yellow stockings and / wished to see thee ever cross-gartered' (2.5.148–50). Since Olivia appears to abhor the colour 'yellow', it is difficult to reconcile the reference to a previous recommendation of the yellow stockings. Perhaps in happier times, Olivia admired an ensemble worn by Malvolio which included the yellow stockings without giving it much thought or, as with Maria telling Malvolio that Olivia felt love for him, she may also have told him an untruth about the colour which Malvolio is now happy to misremember. Notwithstanding, it is clear that emotional circumstances have a bearing on a person's response and Malvolio's belief in the untruth was fuelled by his personal desires. Aristotle framed this circumstance by saying, 'when people are feeling friendly and placable, they think one sort of thing; when they are feeling angry or hostile, they think either something totally different or the same thing with a different intensity' ([c350BCE] 1984, 1377^{b}32–1378^{a}1, 2194). Despite the joke being wholly Maria's, any earlier praise from Olivia to Malvolio suggests that Malvolio was previously trying to impress Olivia with his dress and lends weight to his gullibility around the forged letter. His outlook was coloured by germinal feelings of love and attraction to Olivia.

Given his simmering emotions, Malvolio embraces the false letter

> I do not now fool
> myself, to let imagination jade me; for every reason
> excites to this, that my lady loves me. She did commend
> my yellow stockings of late, she did praise my leg
> being cross-gartered, and in this she manifests herself
> to my love, and with a kind of injunction drives me
> to these habits of her liking. I thank my stars, I am
> happy. I will be strange, stout, in yellow stockings, and
> cross-gartered, even with the swiftness of putting on.
>
> (2.5.159–67)

With alacrity, Malvolio switches from a hint of green in his branched velvet gown (discussed earlier) to yellow self-referential colour-coding. The yellow stockings are important to Malvolio; for him they are an effective signifier of emotional expression. He is unaware that, in this, he is being manipulated and, in fact, they will not convey the meaning he expects. To begin understanding the meaning of the stockings, it is necessary to consider the commonplace cultural associations of the colour yellow. Richard Haydocke, in 1598, makes a pre-Christian link between yellow with the sun, and, therefore, with warmth and fruitfulness

> Yeallowe, insomuch as it noteth a kinde of hope and reioicing, hath giuen occasion to some, to apply the signification of desire and ioy thereunto. ... By occasion of this colour, the *Athenians* called the morning hope. For the daily renewing of *Charon* (though he were very olde) they assigned him yeallow sailes, and of the colour golde, as *Homer* writeth. The new married wiues of the *Romanes* ...used to adorne their heads with a vaile of this colour called Flamen, to shew that they hoped to beare children.
>
> (3.16, 120)

In this account by Haydocke, we also get an understanding of the close relationship between yellow and gold and why it is possible to conflate the two in meaning and description. There is also a link to joy and desire which suits Malvolio in his current frame of mind and his hopes for a fertile union. M. Channing Linthicum notes that '[y]ellow in hose or footwear had three meanings in drama: love, marriage, and jealousy after marriage. Its connection with love probably grew out of its association with Hymen' (1963, 10.1). One classical writer who associates Hymen, god of marriage, with saffron yellow is Ovid. In *The Metamorphoses*, Ovid writes, '[t]hence through the boundless air Hymen, clad in a saffron mantle, departed and took his way to the country of the Ciconians, and was summoned by the voice of Orpheus, though all in vain' ([8CE] 2005, 10.1–4). Through such references, it's easy to see how yellow, closely related to saffron, became associated first with the god of marriage and therefore with love. Ben Jonson (1596–1637) represents rustics in yellow stockings on their wedding day, possibly indicative of hope of marriage, which correlates with the ancient English custom that an elder, unmarried sister of a bride must dance in yellow stockings at her sister's wedding to avert ill-luck and get a husband. After marriage, yellow hose signified jealousy because of unfaithfulness (Tilley 1950, 63; Linthicum 1963, 48).

Christian clergy, who saw yellow as impure, sought to attach negative connotations to the colour by aligning it with clay, from which the body was made and therefore, with earthly passions (Linthicum 1963, 15).[12] Bartholomaeus also has very particular views on various colours exhibited in the body. He notes that saffron colour in the body had some potent physical effects arising from disturbed humours

> Saffron colour dieth and coloureth humours and licours more than citrine, and betokeneth passing heate and distemperaunce of bloud in the licour by medling of cholera, as it fareth in them that have the Jaunders, their urine hath yeolowe spume, & they have yeolow eyen, & their skinne is foule and citrine.
>
> ([1582] 1976, cap.16)

Indeed, this accords with the later opinion expressed generally in the play that Malvolio was afflicted by a disturbance to his humours, a case of the yellow outerwear affecting the inner passions.

Shakespeare uses yellow in diverse ways across his works. In *Love's Labour's Lost*, yellow points to both spring and the mocked figure of the cuckold:

> And cuckoo-buds of yellow hue
> Do paint the meadows with delight,
> The cuckoo then, on every tree,
> Mocks married men
>
> (5.2.884–7)

He also uses it variously in his work to represent autumn and ageing[13]; yellow bile and a choleric temperament; and also the radiance of gold. In a popular ballad from 1586, the husband of a suspicious woman wants to go back to his carefree bachelor days, a desire which is signalled by his yearning for yellow hose. Towards the end of the ballad, it is the jealous wife who is cast as wearing the yellow stockings (Giese 2006, 237). Yellow stockings were also worn by wives who wished to expose their wandering husbands to public censorship, as described in a popular lyric, indicating that the practice was well known in popular culture (237). Yellow hose, then, could be worn to empower a husband who wished to have a carefree single life, or a wife who hoped to expose a partner's infidelity. In *Twelfth Night*, however, Maria gains power in the emotional transaction through her superior psychological strength in persuading Malvolio to don the yellow stockings and in so doing emasculate himself.

Malvolio is willing to cast himself actively in the role of a lover and adopt the colours preferred by his love object, a fashion in Elizabethan times. Sir Philip Sidney in *Astrophel and Stella* complains about this practice, lamenting the superficiality of the court ladies who believe it necessary for their men to demonstrate their love for them by wearing their colours (Sidney [1591] 1947, 193; Ashelford 1988, 102). By falling for the trick, Malvolio is demonstrating the Elizabethan ideal of love and the pitfalls that arise when that love is not available in all three forms: the senses, the imagination, and the intellect. However, of all the characters in *Twelfth Night*, Malvolio is the most constant in love despite its misdirection. Here again his donning of the yellow stockings signifies this trait since heraldry used yellow to indicate faith and constancy (Ferne 1586, 169; Linthicum 1963, 47). However, as R. S. White points out, it is not only Malvolio who is misdirected in his love, as both Orsino and Aguecheek share an unrequited love for Olivia; Olivia desires a transgendered Cesario; and, until her true sex is revealed, Viola has an impossible love for Orsino (2016, 144).

The engineers of the trick are wholly satisfied that it has been successful in bringing out into the open Malvolio's desire for Olivia, and they express immediate joy and elation at Malvolio's gullibility. In addition to wearing the yellow stockings cross-gartered, a style and colour which offends Olivia's eye, they have also instructed Malvolio to smile upon Olivia's face, despite the melancholy which she is suffering upon her brother's death. Malvolio clearly wishes to be, and also, be seen, as a lover, unlike Feste, who tells us that the machinations of his mind are *not* to be divined through his appearance. Feste's intentions are inscrutable, while the sober steward is easily swayed by the vacillations of his emotions, and is motivated by both pride and possibly love to then experience shame and humiliation. An early modern audience, with a cultural understanding of the significance of the yellow stockings, would have appreciated the way the conspirators' plan satirises and subverts

Malvolio's desire for sexual domination. Malvolio's yellow stockings may come to suggest subservience, embarrassment, and perhaps even the yellowing colours of ageing (Giese 2006, 241). The clothing mediates between the body and the external, and as a cultural reference is a key means of deepening the audience's understanding in this instance.

The encounter between Olivia and Malvolio is prefaced by Olivia's request that her sober and respectful servant be sent for, as Malvolio's temperament is one which suits her melancholic disposition. Malvolio enters, smiling and duly cross-gartered in yellow stockings, as prescribed in the stage directions.[14] Olivia, shocked and concerned says, '[w]hat is the matter with thee?' To which Malvolio replies, '[n]ot black in my mind, though yellow in my legs' (3.4.23–6). Malvolio is categorically stating that he is not affected by madness (yellow choleric and black melancholic bile) but instead, by drawing attention to his stockings, he is inviting us to categorise his demeanour with reference to the cultural associations of the yellow stockings. By mentioning that the stockings are causing some obstruction in the blood, Malvolio is indicating that his flesh and blood is resisting the form of clothing that he wishes to be seen wearing for Olivia's love approval.[15] For Malvolio, they have become an emblem of the love he feels for Olivia and also of the covert love he thinks she has for him. The clothes also help to construct the madness from which he is believed to be suffering. His shame will not develop until he becomes aware of the disconnect between his feelings and the reality of the situation, since 'a sense of shame is knowledge of what is shame-producing; it operates as a form of restraint and forbearance' (Fernie 2002, 9). In fact, Olivia feels moved to pity and perhaps exasperation, rather than love, tempered by a sense of loyalty. She says, '[l]et some of my people have a special care of him; I would not have him miscarry for the half of my dowry' (3.4.59–61). However, her concern, perhaps restrained by her social position or her own emotional distraction, is short lived. Later it appears she has not tried to rehabilitate the situation that Malvolio found himself in, for she exclaims

> fetch Malvolio hither.
> And yet, alas, now I remember me,
> They say, poor gentleman, he's much distract.
> A most extracting frenzy of mine own
> From my remembrance clearly banished his.
> How does he, sirrah?
>
> (5.1.274–9)

Olivia is initially shocked, perhaps, by Malvolio's behaviour. His behaviour is also indicative of the shame that can be experienced once one allows excessive passions to take hold. This is a powerful reminder to Olivia that she needs to hide her own desires and imbalances from public scrutiny. When Olivia later dismisses her loyal servant to his fate, it may be to avoid her own shame. Malvolio's public engagement with his emotions allows her shame to go unnoticed. In public, she can avoid being 'shamed'. Malvolio, as her steward, is best placed to observe her compromised behaviour with Viola/Cesario. Her shame is found at the nexus between her private and her public appearance and demeanour, and in this regard she has shown herself to be very similar to Malvolio, a connection from which she would like to distance herself from.

Malvolio is tricked into appearing cross-gartered in yellow stockings like a lover to signify his new role, contrasting with the customary black of his steward's office (Gurr 2009, 241).[16] This colour combination, black and yellow, used by Malvolio to signify his love, is even more inappropriate because it was often associated with mourning, and may, therefore, have been read by Olivia as an insult to the memory of her brother.[17] The Malvolio subplot is a colourful addition to the play. Certainly, John Manningham noted in his diary, after seeing a performance of *Twelfth Night* in 1602, that the play revolved around a scheme to gull the steward into believing that his mistress was in love with him (rather than around the love triangle between Orsino, Olivia, and Viola) ([1602] 1978, 48). To Manningham, Malvolio's wearing the yellow stockings as a symbol of being shamed is more important than the intrinsic emotions of the other more prominent characters. Shame, more than other emotions, relies on a performative aspect and a transaction between the sufferer and an audience (Hobgood 2014, 134). Without the complicit attention of other characters and also the audience, Malvolio's public display would not have resonance. The onstage exposure of his carnal excesses has left him open to shame (Coeffeteau 1621, 493). For Malvolio, the yellow stockings are not only a sign of his love for Olivia but also a catalyst for emotions of love, excitement, and happiness within Malvolio himself. Ultimately they signify shame as they visually draw attention to his emotional position through the overt display of colour-coding.[18] Wearing the yellow stockings encourages Malvolio to feel these emotions internally and act them out emotions externally, in accordance with Jean MacIntyre's opinion that 'within a role, costume change almost always reflects an inward change' (1992, 13).[19]

Shame continues as an omnipresent emotion in the play even towards its close. Amongst several references to shame in the play, the most poignant is Malvolio's letter to Olivia from his incarcerated position, in which he says, 'I have your own letter that induced me to the semblance I put on, with the which I doubt not to do myself much right or you much shame' (5.1.300–3). It is interesting to note the terminology he uses to describe his emotional outpourings which accompanied the physical wearing of the yellow stockings. He includes both actions with the phrase 'the semblance I put on', an action that is intrinsically associated with dressing and counterfeiting. By allowing himself to be persuaded into the scheme and to conduct himself accordingly, he has been shamed, humiliated, and emasculated as he tried to promote the imagined relationship he had with Olivia. 'In other words', as Allison P. Hobgood argues, 'Malvolio's shame, for one, is driven not entirely by his own baseness but by the weakness, fear, and shame of other characters in the drama' (2014, 147). His position is exacerbated by his sanity and self-awareness of the situation he has found himself in. Finally, when the truth of the jape is revealed, Malvolio's frustration is moved to become a vengeful emotion not targeted particularly at his tormentors but more generally upon the establishment, which cannot support his aspirations. He says before exiting, 'I'll be revenged on the whole pack of you' (5.1.371). His anger is fuelled by the reluctance of his audience to absolve him of his public shame, which he has tried to ameliorate by pointing out that he was manipulated into extremes of desire and public display by others. He tried to displace his internal feelings of shame with a burning fury. But unfortunately, his behaviour cannot be undone and his reputation cannot be restored. This realisation lends weight to the frustrations he feels. Ewan Fernie suggests that

> [i]t is precisely because shame is so private, so intimate a sensation, because the shamed self is *literally not fit to be seen*, that it recoils from exposure. As has been said, the crucial thing about shame is that for whatever public or private reason the subject's relation with itself has broken down. The cruelty of shaming is that it can interfere with the subject's sense of self; if it does not, one is able to brazen it out. This is a subsidiary form of shame where one is shamed in the eyes of others but not in one's own eyes, shamed but not ashamed.
> (2002, 16)

Malvolio, in light of Fernie's statement, has to exit because he cannot bear the exposure of his shame, and his self has been disrupted from a superior position within the household to that of a ridiculed figure. He had aligned himself with his social superiors, Sir Toby and Sir Andrew, a position-dependent solely on his office in Olivia's household. Malvolio's shame is 'in fact highly contingent upon an audiences' emotional collaboration' (Hobgood 2014, 129). Acknowledgement of his untenable position creates intense feelings of frustration that incapacitated his ability to interact any further on the stage.

Conclusion

The yellow stockings, mentioned nine times in total, become indicative of the effects of the emotions they are flagging and therefore a social comment on the vagaries of inappropriate love, affection, and pride. They are also emblematic of the shameful incontinence of bodily emotions.

Embedded within the emblem is a comment on the dangers of indiscriminate movement between social classes compounded by the fickle nature of fashion at court and the flagrant disregard for the sumptuary laws. (The play illustrates many moments of social status and climbing – Maria succeeds in marrying above her station, Malvolio does not.) The relationship between clothes and colours articulates emotional transactions within the play and provides both a textual and a visual means of expression, heightening the awareness of other characters to their own failings. This in turn stops them from allowing Malvolio to be redeemed from his shame in the final scene. Fernie suggests that considering

> Shakespeare's interest in shame as a psychological, an ethical and a ritual experience, a transforming moment extraordinary to behold on stage, which may motivate or complete a dramatic action, sending ripples of more or less vicarious shame through the theatre and thereby perhaps having a more positive ethical and political effect outside it.
>
> (2002, 86)

In this view, to redeem Malvolio would involve acknowledging both the onlookers' own part in his shame and also the shameful incontinence of their own personal emotions.

An examination of the emotions within *Twelfth Night* through the lens of the body, clothing, and colour references illustrates the intricate balance and complexity of feelings that can be uncovered. G. K. Hunter states

> The formality of clothing and the precision of the social meanings they can bear allow the dramatists to arrange the visual diagrams on the stage not only in clear demonstration of a closed social situation but also with indications of the instabilities that threaten that order, suggesting also perhaps something of the transformations that may be necessary before the inner pattern of desires and the outer pattern of formal relationships can be brought into a stable alignment.
>
> (1980, 33)

Examining the colour-coding that accompanies the body and its clothing in early modern drama means that further analysis is brought to bear on the emotional relationships, mentioned by Hunter. Within the emotional paradigm of the body and its coverings, colour can offer a subversive response that is not always immediately apparent. Colour can also augment the emotional transaction that is driven by the malleable relationship of the body and the environment. Clothing forms part of that environment in a unique way because of its close proximity to the body, the mind, and by association to the emotions of a person.

Notes

1. See S. Knuuttila (2004) for classical and medieval references to music.
2. The damask rose also features in Chapter 2 where it alludes to the ladies' complexions and their masking and unmasking of themselves.
3. Patricia Simons (2013) discusses the practice of veiling special pictures to show them to a chosen few, in "The Visual Dynamics of (Un)veiling in Early Modern Culture".
4. Myrrha is attracted to her father and becomes consumed with guilt, shame, and desire. Her nurse stops her from hanging herself and instead conspires to deliver Myrrha to her father's bed under cover of darkness. The darkness hides both her body and her true identity. The truth is discovered when her father, wishing to recognize his new mistress, brings in a light, exposing the sins of both (Ovid [8CE] 2005, X.298-502).
5. See Ovid, *Metamorphoses: Books I-VII*, ([8CE] 2004) for the full story of Actaeon.
6. Crane (2001, 103) suggests that Olivia is hidden, veiled by her house itself using it as a form of concealment.
7. The golden age was a time in history when everyone behaved correctly and punishments did not exist. There were no wars, food from the earth was plentiful, and spring was everlasting. (Ovid [8CE] 2004, 1.89*ff*).
8. Hunt provides a breakdown of the sumptuary law issued in 1559 (1996, 119). Elizabeth I made 19 proclamations dealing with excess of apparel between 1559 and 1597. Lublin provides a table summarizing Queen Elizabeth's 1597 Sumptuary Proclamation, in *Costuming the Shakespearean Stage* (2011, 46).
9. The Musée des Arts Décoratifs, Paris, holds an early sixteenth-century Florentine green velvet material fragment showing a pattern of interlaced chestnut branches on ivory silk ground enriched with silver thread.
10. The cowl does not make the monk.
11. Roze Hentschell (2008) examines the English cloth industry particularly from as an industry of immense cultural significance, contributing to an emerging national identity.
12. Jones and Stallybrass note that '[y]ellow, in fact, had long been associated not only with satanic flames but also with the clothes that Judas wore. In Giotto's *Betrayal of Christ*, for instance, Judas embraces Christ, he covers him in his yellow robes' (2000, 66).
13. Shakespeare uses yellow in sonnets 17, 73, and 104 when describing autumn or approaching death.
14. Duncan Salkeld notes that Malvolio 'cuts a notably similar figure to Hamlet, who enters Ophelia's chamber, unbraced, fouled, downgyved, knock-kneed, stares, shakes her hand, sighs and nods, and then leaves. Both characters, not surprisingly, are declared mad' (1993, 7).
15. Paster discusses the obstruction in terms of the humoral manipulation; see *The Body Embarrassed* (1993, 216).
16. Rodney Stenning Edgecombe suggests that Malvolio is supposed to be depicted as a wasp and therefore a sexual aggressive annoyance to Olivia; see "Shakespeare's *Twelfth Night*" (1997, 200–2).
17. 'The colours of the doublet, yellow and black, are significant as they symbolize sadness at the departure of a loved one. Ann Clifford recorded in her diary that she wore a black nightgown and yellow waistcoat when her husband went away' (Ashelford 1988, 103).
18. John Gouws concludes that the combination of a reference to puritan cross garters and yellow youthful lovers is designed on any level to render Malvolio

a source of ridicule in "Dressing Malvolio for the Part" (1991). G. P. Jones suggests that there is puritan lampooning at play because of the cross gartered look, see "Malvolio Flouted and Abused" (2004).
19 On humility and clothing, Stubbes wrote '[t]han seeing that our apparel was giuen us of god to cover our shame, to keep our bodies from cold, and to bee as pricks in our eies, to put us in mind of our frailites, imperfections and sin, of our backsliding from the commaundements of god and obedience of the highest, and to excite us the rather to contrition, and compunction of the spirit, to bewayle our misery, & to craue mersy at the mercifull hands of God' (1583, chap. 'The fall of Adam,' sect. 'Wherfor our apparell was geuen us').

References

Akhimie, Patricia. 2018. *Shakespeare and the Cultivation of Difference: Race and Conduct in the Early Modern World*. New York: Routledge.

Aristotle. (c350BCE) 1984. "Rhetoric." In *The Complete Works of Aristotle the Revised Oxford Translation*, edited by Jonathan Barnes, translated by W. Rhys Roberts. Princeton, NJ: Princeton University Press.

Ashelford, Jane. 1988. *Dress in the Age of Elizabeth I*. London: B. T. Batsford Ltd.

Bartholomaeus Anglicus. (1582) 1976. *Batman Uppon Bartholome: His Booke De Proprietatibus Rerum*. Translated by Stephen Batman. Hildesheim; New York: Georg Olms Verlag.

Callaghan, Dympna. 2000. *Shakespeare without Women: Representing Gender and Race on the Renaissance Stage*. London: Routledge.

Chaucer, Geoffrey. (c1396) 2008. "The Parson's Tale." In *The Riverside Chaucer*, edited by Larry D. Benson, 287–328. Oxford: Oxford University Press.

Coeffeteau, Nicolas. 1621. *A Table of Humane Passions: With Their Causes and Effects*. Translated by Edw Grimeston. London: Nicholas Oakes.

Crane, Mary Thomas. 2001. *Shakespeare's Brain: Reading with Cognitive Theory*. Princeton and Oxford: Princeton University Press.

Edgecombe, Rodney Stenning. 1997. "Shakespeare's *Twelfth Night*." *Explicator* 55: 200–2.

Elam, Keir. 2008. "Introduction." In *Twelfth Night*, by William Shakespeare, edited by Keir Elam, 1–153. London: Bloomsbury Arden Shakespeare.

Elizabeth I. 1574. *By the Queene*. London: By Newgate Market, next vnto Christes Churche, by Richard Iugge.

Escolme, Bridget. 2012. "Costume." In *Shakespeare & The Making of Theatre*, edited Stuart Hampton-Reeves and Bridget Escolme, 128–45. Basingstoke: Palgrave Macmillan.

Everett, Clare. 1995. "Venus in Drag: Female Transvestism and the Construction of Sex Difference in Renaissance England." In *Venus and Mars: Engendering Love and War in Medieval and Early Modern Europe*, edited by Andrew Lynch and Philippa Maddern, 191–212. Nedlands, Western Australia: University of Western Australia Press.

Ferne, John. 1586. *The Blazon of Gentrie*. London: Printed by John Windet, for Toby Cooke.

Fernie, Ewan. 2002. *Shame in Shakespeare*. London; New York: Routledge.

Ficino, Marsilio. (1489) 1989. *Three Books on Life*. Translated by Carol V. Kaske. Binghamton, NY: Medieval & Renaissance Texts & Studies.

Fisher, Will. 2010. *Materializing Gender in Early Modern English Literature and Culture*. Cambridge: Cambridge University Press.

Giese, Loreen L. 2006. "Malvolio's Yellow Stockings: Coding Illicit Sexuality in Early Modern London." *Medieval & Renaissance Drama in England* 19: 235–46.

Gouws, John. 1991. "Dressing Malvolio for the Part." *Notes and Queries* 38, no. 4: 478–9.

Gurr, Andrew. 2009. *The Shakespearean Stage 1574–1642*. Cambridge: Cambridge University Press.

Haydocke, Richard, trans. 1598. *A Tracte Containing the Artes of Curious Paintinge, Caruinge & Buildinge*. By Io. Paul Lomatius. Oxford: Joseph Barnes.

Hentschell, Roze. 2008. *The Culture of Cloth in Early Modern England: Textual Constructions of a National Identity*. Aldershot, Hampshire: Routledge.

Hill, Tracey. 2004. *Anthony Munday and Civic Culture: Theatre, History, and Power in Early Modern London: 1580–1633*. Manchester: Manchester University Press.

Hobgood, Allison P. 2014. *Passionate Playgoing in Early Modern England*. New York: Cambridge University Press.

Hunt, Alan. 1996. *Governance of the Consuming Passions*. Basingstoke: Macmillan Press Ltd.

Hunter, G. K. 1980. "Flatcaps and Bluecoats: Visual Signals on the Elizabethan Stage." *Essays and Studies* 33: 16–47.

Jardine, Lisa. 1983. *Still Harping on Daughters: Women and Drama in the Age of Shakespeare*. Sussex; New Jersey: The Harvester Press; Barnes & Noble Books.

Jardine, Lisa. 1991. "Boy Actors, Female Roles, and Elizabethan Eroticism." In *Staging the Renaissance: Reinterpretations of Elizabethan and Jacobean Drama*, edited by David Scott Kastan and Peter Stallybrass, 57–67. New York and London: Routledge.

Jones, G. P. 2004. "Malvolio Flouted and Abused." *English Language Notes* 42: 20–6.

Jones, Ann Rosalind and Peter Stallybrass. 2000. *Renaissance Clothing and the Materials of Memory*. Cambridge; New York: Cambridge University Press.

Jonson, Ben. 1606. *Hymenaei: Or The Solemnities of Masque*. London: Valentine Sims for Thomas Thorp.

Knuuttila, Simo. 2004. *Emotions in Ancient and Medieval Philosophy*. Oxford: Oxford University Press.

Linthicum, M. Channing. 1963. *Costume in the Drama of Shakespeare and his Contemporaries*. New York: Russell & Russell.

Lublin, Robert I. 2011. *Costuming the Shakespearean Stage: Visual Codes of Representation in Early Modern Theatre and Culture*. Farnham, Surrey: Ashgate Publishing Ltd.

MacIntyre, Jean. 1992. *Costumes and Scripts in the Elizabethan Theatres*. Edmonton: University of Alberta Press.

Manningham, John. (1602) 1976. *The Diary of John Manningham of the Middle Temple 1602–1603*. Hanover, New Hampshire: University Press of New England.

Munday, Anthony. (1586) 1973. *A Second and Third Blast of Retrait from Plaies and Theaters*. New York and London: Garland Publishing Inc.
Oxford University Press. n.d. "Oxford English Dictionary Online." Accessed August, 2021. https://www.oed.com/
Ovid. (8CE) 2004. *Metamorphoses: Books I-VII*. Translated by Frank Justus Miller. Cambridge, MA: Harvard University Press.
Ovid. (8CE) 2005. *Metamorphoses: Books IX-X*. Translated by Frank Justus Miller. Cambridge, MA: Harvard University Press.
Paster, Gail Kern. 1993. *The Body Embarrassed: Drama and the Disciplines of Shame in Early Modern England*. Ithaca, NY: Cornell University Press.
Prynne, William. 1633. *Histrio-Mastrix*. London: Edward Allde, Augustine Mattewes, Thomas Cotes and William Iones for Michael Sparke, and are to be sold at the Blue Bible, in Greene Arbour, in little Old Bayly.
Rainolds, John. (1599) 1972. *The Overthrow of Stage-Plays*. New York; London: Johnson Reprint Corporation.
Salkeld, Duncan. 1993. *Madness and Drama in the Age of Shakespeare*. Manchester: Manchester University Press.
Schneider, Jane. 2000. "Fantastical Colors in Foggy London: The New Fashion Potential of the Late Sixteenth Century." In *Material London ca.1600*, edited by Lena Cowen Orlin, 109–28. Philadelphia: University of Pennsylvania Press.
Sedinger, Tracey. 1997. "'If Sight and Sound Be True': The Epistemology of Crossdressing on the London Stage." *Shakespeare Quarterly* 48, no. 1: 63–79.
Shakespeare, William. (1598) 2001. *Love's Labour's Lost*. Edited by H. R. Woudhuysen. London: Bloomsbury Arden Shakespeare.
Shakespeare, William. (1600) 2010. *The Merchant of Venice*. Edited by John Drakakis. London: Bloomsbury Arden Shakespeare.
Shakespeare, William. (1602) 2008. *Twelfth Night*. Edited by Keir Elam. London; New York: Bloomsbury Arden Shakespeare.
Shakespeare, William. (1606) 2015. *Macbeth*. Edited by Sandra Clark and Pamela Mason. London: Bloomsbury Arden Shakespeare.
Sidney, Philip. (1591) 1947. "Astrophel and Stella LIV." In *Silver Poets of the Sixteenth Century*, edited by Gerald William Bullett, 173–225. London: Dent.
Simons, Patricia. 2013. "The Visual Dynamics of (Un)veiling in Early Modern Culture." In *Visual Cultures of Secrecy in Early Modern Europe*, edited by Timothy McCall, Sean Roberts, and Giancarlo Fiorenza, 24–53. Kirksville, Missouri: Truman State University Press.
Stubbes, Phillip. 1583. *The Anatomie of Abuses*. London: Richard Jones.
Tilley, Morris Palmer. 1950. *A Dictionary of the Proverbs in England in the Sixteenth and Seventeenth Centuries: A Collection of the Proverbs Found in English Literature and the Dictionaries of the Period*. Ann Arbor: University of Michigan Press.
University of Michigan. n.d. "The Middle English Dictionary Online." Accessed August 2021. http://quod.lib.umich.edu/cgi/m/mec/med-idx?type=id&id=MED51203
Varholy, Cristine M. 2008. "'Rich Like a Lady': Cross-Class Dressing in the Brothels and Theaters of Early Modern London." *Journal for Early Modern London* 8, no. 1: 4–34.

White, Paul. 1988. "Calvinist and Puritan Attitudes Toward the Stage in Renaissance England." *Explorations in Renaissance Culture* 14, no. 1: 41–55.

White, R. S. 2016. "Smiles That Reveal, Smiles That Conceal." *Shakespeare* 12, no. 2: 134–47.

Wright, Thomas. (1601) 1986. *The Passions of the Mind in General.* Edited by William Webster Newbold. New York: Garland.

5 'O well-painted passion'
Cultural commonplaces of colour and affective patterns in *Othello*

The central point of *Othello* hinges on both a chromatic reference and an emotional state. Iago, with rhetorical command and a reliance in part on accepted chromatic associations, has unsettled Othello and warns him

> O beware, my lord, of jealousy!
> It is the green-eyed monster, which doth mock
> The meat it feeds on.[1]
>
> (3.3.167–9)

Iago warns against what he fully expects and wishes to happen, that the colour of jealousy will take possession and influence Othello's more rational parts. In rhetorical terms, Heinrich Plett suggests that this is the moment of Iago's *propositio*, the naming of the topic, which comes when he says 'O, beware of jealousy' (2004, 462). Not only does this naming figure as a rhetorical device but it also brings attention to emotion as a form of practice (Scheer 2012, 213). Green, which has previously been associated with hope, joy, and youth, is now associated not only with jealousy but also with the visual proof of that emotional state through references to the eye and the issues associated with trusting the sense of sight (OED Online, 'green-eyed'). But to fix one meaning undermines the complexity of the relationship of green to the wave of emotions conjured up by this reference. It is pertinent to note 'desire' as one meaning coming from the Middle English word *grenen*, which means to green or grow, but also to desire or to long for something (University of Michigan n.d., 'grenen'; OED Online, 'grenen'). There is also the greenness of Othello's socialisation in Venetian society, as well as the green hope Othello wants to feel for his union with Desdemona. His eyes are clouded by the green vision of jealousy as the monster, from the Latin *monstrare* 'to show', demonstrates to him evidence that obscures reality. Jealousy is the point on which the play turns. The scene continues as an homage to jealousy, which is mentioned five more times in quick succession; Othello demands ocular proof although it is clear that his vision has become an unreliable sense.

DOI: 10.4324/9781003198246-6

Iago is now in control as Othello has been overwhelmed by misplaced jealousy. As Thomas Wright, in *The Passions of the Mind in General*, says

> the passions not vnfitly may be compared to green spectacles, which make all things resemble the colour of greene; euen so, he that loueth, hateth, or by any other passion is vehemently possessed, iudgeth all things that occur in fauour of that passion.
> ([1601] 1986, 2.1.37–9)

From now on every interaction Othello has with Desdemona will be 'coloured' by the jealousy he feels. Indeed later, perhaps in a moment of truth, Iago says to Othello 'oft my jealousy / Shapes faults that are not' (3.3.150–1), a fact he uses to his own advantage to convince Othello of Desdemona's guilt. Emilia makes this very same point regarding jealousy saying

> But jealous souls will not be answered so:
> They are not ever jealous for the cause,
> But jealous for they're jealous. It is a monster
> Begot upon itself, born on itself.
> (3.4.159–62)

Little does Emilia know that she is both echoing Iago's words, and unwittingly mentioning the presence of a monster who is, in fact, her husband whose final appearance demonstrates his evil machinations.

In *Othello* cultural associations with the colour green help construct affective patterns that an audience can be expected to interpret. In this final chapter, I examine some of the cultural commonplaces of the early modern period that provide a supportive framework for this and other patterns. Regarding visual experience as closely linked to social experience is key to my explanation of the place of colour in the affective patterns and emotional register of *Othello*. It is important to consider the social context of the technologies of colour, as they can be gleaned from contemporary commonplaces, since these technologies form some of the mechanisms employed in forming personal and cultural identities. While others negotiate the question of race in Shakespeare's plays through ideological frameworks, I will look at race through the use of chromatic references designed to elicit emotional responses.[2] These references and others work to form an undulating colour arc in the play as the use of colour works synergistically with the emotional register. I will also delve into the influence of contemporary visual culture in *Othello*, especially through reference to the material colours mentioned in emblem collections but also through some social constructions of colour prevalent in the early modern period. With these thoughts in mind, I will start by examining the social circumstances that may have shaped the meaning of 'Moor' in *Othello*, and analyse the term's emotional resonance in the context of contemporary visual culture. It is important to outline the complexity surrounding a term which is mentioned a total of 45 times in the play. Along the way I point to ways in which ideas examined in previous chapters influence the chromatic emotional arc in tandem with the cultural commonplaces.

The cultural landscape in early modern London

From medieval traditions, the early modern period inherited a complex set of cultural relationships with the colour 'black'. Many medieval church wall paintings featured devils with black-coloured skin.[3] These images were also found in illuminated manuscripts, alabaster tablets, and painted windows. More particularly, in *The Discovery of Witchcraft* Reginald Scott says 'a damned soule may and dooth take the shape of a blacke moore, or of a beast, or of a serpent, or speciallie of an heretike' (1584, Book 1, Chapter XXVIII, 26). In early Tudor England, black people physically appeared on the social landscape in minor numbers, for example, in 1501 as part of Catherine of Aragon's retinue, and as skilled labourers during the time of friendly relations between Spain and England (Habib 2008, 63). In the 1570s, according to Imtiaz Habib, Africans appeared as commodities in Elizabeth I's household, initiating the appearance of Africans in personal bondage to the Elizabethan ruling class (2008, 74). Meanwhile in 1585, *The Barbary Company* was founded to facilitate commercial ventures between England and Morocco, although the licence expired without renewal in 1597. The physical record documented in London between 1585 and 1590 from household accounts, government proclamations, legal records and parish entries, to name a few, shows the low numbers for black people at this time. The terms 'blackamoor' and 'negro' are used in these records without distinction. Sensationally in 1589, at the wedding of James VI and Anne of Denmark, a 'blackamoor' appeared in coloured dress carrying a sword while four naked 'blackamoors' danced in the snow, the four later dying of pneumonia (Habib 2008, 316). The entire record indicates their servile position, with little social engagement beyond spectacle and death. However, despite low physical numbers, Virginia Mason Vaughan notes, 'for Londoners in 1594, caught in a continuing war with Spain and facing seriously for the first time the dangers of territorial expansion, anxieties about cultural exchange were very real' (1997, 177).

The physical record of black people across London changes towards the end of the sixteenth century. Where previously the record mainly noted spectacle, deaths, and servitude, now the record mentions legal cases concerning carnal relations, marriages, and a royal proclamation deporting 'blackamoors' from England.[4] The social landscape was further complicated by the presence of an elite Moor in London. The portrait of Abd el-Quahed ben Messaoud ben Mohammed Anoun, ambassador to Elizabeth I from Muly Hamet, shows the Moroccan ambassador aged 42, and was possibly painted during the six months he spent in London during 1600/01 while negotiating an alliance against Spain. The portrait itself features a black and white colour scheme through the garments worn by the sitter and the hues used in creating the facial image. This muted colouring is not unexpected in relation to a representation of the Moor since it played into cultural ideas fomenting around race and its relationship to character. The Ambassador's presence brought the regal Moor to the attention of Londoners. Previous concerns around 'otherness' were now complicated by the realisation that the Moors were potential allies against the Spanish and could boast a nobility previously unacknowledged and unwitnessed at such close proximity (Skura 2008, 302). A cultural lineage and a religious tradition now elevated some African groups, while others were associated with a dearth of religion and culture (Loomba 2002, 81). In the wake of such contradictions, Shakespeare's *Othello* appears on the stage, perhaps even prompted by the ambassadorial visit. *Othello* was crafted in this period within the system of cognitive and motivating structures that governed the negotiation of cross-cultural exchanges, both emotionally and socially. Shakespeare also had access to other influential resources such as John Pory's 1600 translation of John Leo's *A Geographical Historie of Africa*.[5] Leo, a Moor himself brought up in Barbary, wrote about his countrymen, and his description resonates with certain aspects of Othello's character, for example, an interest in sorcery (Pory 1600, 27).

Adept at confounding the accepted polemic notions and disturbing traditional cultural mores, Shakespeare distributes the accepted traits of the dark-skinned 'other' among many of the characters in *Othello*, both black and white (Barthelemy 1994, 93), asking the audience to examine their emotional reaction to the Moor in the play (Dadabhoy 2021). Indeed, Sibylle Baumbach notes 'the art of physiognomy in this particular play is approached from very different angles whereby both its advantages and its perils come into view' (2008, 145). Iago vilifies Othello in a late Elizabethan London where Othello might not be 'the other' but part of the social fabric.[6] Iago is an incipient racist, following Ian Smith's definition which states '[r]ace presumes a cultural contestation, a struggle predicated on power, whose familiar terms are located along an axis of color' (1998, 170). By presenting Othello as part of society, audiences are further prompted to decipher the meaning of blackness in the context of both a literal colour and a figurative term for evil within a subtly changing *habitus* which is stretching its boundaries. However, the actions of Othello himself play an integral part in promulgating both the accepted discourse and an alternate, more complex discourse that questions accepted orthodoxies. Although Vaughan has stated that '[m]iscegenation ... becomes a marker for a variety of social problems, and *Titus Andronicus* established a pattern that would be repeated in English and American literature and culture for centuries' (2005, 50) I argue that subtle historical changes affected the London social field at the turn of the seventeenth century, as exemplified by the ambassador's visit and the record of Moors in servitude, getting married, and having sexual relationships, sometimes with white people. The effects of these changes can be seen in the interrogation of accepted cultural and emotional discourses in *Othello*. The Moor's blackness is both questioned and compromised within a framework of cross-cultural exchanges marked by new negotiation and organisation of colour references.

Race: colouring the Moor

It is important to note that at this point in history, the word 'Moor' had no clear racial status, and was much more a marker of the exotic than of colour (Hunter 1978, 40). Blackness, and the term blackamoor, could include all those at the periphery; a pagan 'other' in opposition to a white civilised Christian. Indeed, as far back as the Crusades, the religious 'other', the Saracen, was depicted as dirty and often black (Loomba 2002, 25).[7] The Christian tradition of black coloured skin even suggested that faith could wash away the staining caused by sin. The early church father Augustine says that 'Ethiopians... [are] black in their natural sinfulness; but they may become white in the knowledge of the Lord' (Saint Augustine in Hunter 1978, P.L. xcii, col.938). The explanation for dark pigmentation in this context is associated with the transgressions of Cham, son of Noah, who became dark skinned for his sins and inhabited the liminal edges of the earth in a position of servitude. In this paradigm, Ambereen Dadabhoy notes, '[b]lackness emerges as a visible sign in a manner that religious – Islamic – difference does not' (2014, 126). In the early modern context, Vanessa Corredera observes that

> [c]onceptions of alterity in the Renaissance do not *have* to be considered as race. But by recognizing the varied, contradictory ways people consider and conceive of race, we open up the possibility that these conceptions can be understood racially even if individual racial ideologies do not neatly align with strict definitions of the term.
> (2016b, 44)

Corredera suggests elsewhere that the signification of blackness articulates 'opposing approaches to blackness in the Renaissance. On the one hand, blackness does not have to be the defining facet of identity; on the other hand, blackness works as the principle marker of both appearance and inward nature' (2016a, 95).

The English stage became an important medium to probe the emotional reaction to encroaching 'otherness', not least through references to the blackamoor. The contradictions located within Othello's character serve to highlight the competing tensions within the broader community. The social context of colour in this fermenting period makes much of the competing ideologies of skin colour. In *Othello*, such ideologies are probed in relation to social inclusiveness and personal and public identity. By the time *Othello* was staged, audiences, like those who had enjoyed *Titus Andronicus*, were familiar with blackface devils on stage. However, unlike the characterisation of Aaron in *Titus Andronicus*, which reflects many stock characteristics, there is more complexity surrounding Othello's ethnicity, religion, and more fundamentally his character. Disturbingly, in *Othello*, it is Iago the white Venetian who embodies evil. Distinct from Aaron, who is complicit in his own construction of evil, it is Iago who painstakingly constructs an edifice of evil for and around Othello.

The term 'Moor' represents a form of blackness both visually and imaginatively. A linguistic marker, situated in both cultural and ethnic paradigms, is emphasised in the opening lines when Iago uses the descriptor 'Moor' three times without naming Othello. This sets up Othello's Moorish background as a key consideration. The term refers to many nuanced valences related to received wisdoms, all of which Iago relies upon to advance his case with Roderigo and subsequently with Brabantio. On the first occasion that Iago refers to Othello by name in public, it is notable that he says 'black Othello' (2.3.29) insisting upon the chromatic marker. Emily C. Bartels notes that '[d]espite his demonizing rhetoric, the difference to which Iago responds is political rather than racial, and the alienation his own rather than Othello's' (1990, 450). It is the promotion of Cassio or perhaps a suspected affair between Othello and Emilia which has precipitated Iago's machinations, since he feels professionally and personally marginalised. However, whatever Iago's motivations, he is socially and culturally astute and uses germinal ideas of racial otherness to advance his own schemes. Iago urges Roderigo to inflame the emotions of Desdemona's father by rousing Brabantio out of bed with poisonous and vexing tales. Iago cautions to change up the vexations lest 'it may lose some colour' (1.1.72), linking the rhetorical meaning of the term with racially based emotion in this context. Roderigo is urged to keep the scene emotionally heightened. Iago is using his own abilities of rhetorical persuasion to convince Roderigo to a course of action.[8] Conversely a loss of colour suggests that the emotional strength of the encounter will also be diminished. This concept is crucial to the movement of colour that the play employs to maintain its varying emotional tone. What follows is a fast-paced and highly charged scene which serves to distress and agitate Brabantio even before he discovers the loss of Desdemona.

Previously Roderigo has described Othello as 'the thicklips' (1.1.65), a pejorative reference to a black African, despite a certain ambiguity around the ethnic background of Othello. However, Iago brings a visual picture to Brabantio that plays on a reference both to Othello's background and the stereotypical position which he occupies in this space. Iago says '[e]ven now, now, very now, an old black ram / Is tupping your white ewe!' (1.1.87–8). Not only is the black colour emphasised but there is also an implicit reference to woolly hair, [9] and lustful lascivious behaviour in the bestial image of the ram.[10] The image contrasts the evil associations of black with the unstained virtuous white of Desdemona, implying that Othello has violated or dirtied the unsullied Desdemona. Iago reinforces the image by shouting to Brabantio, 'your daughter and the Moor are now making the beast with two backs' (1.1.114–5). Roderigo augments the image by saying 'your fair daughter' is transported '[t]o the clasps of a lascivious Moor' (1.1.120; 124).[11] Desdemona's whiteness is a source of her attraction but also a source of her undoing. The continual references to the fair whiteness of Desdemona are confounded by her sexual attraction to Othello. She is defying the Petrarchan image of the fair lady love who remains chaste and unobtainable. As Iago takes his leave of Roderigo he again refers to Othello as 'the Moor' (1.1.145). When Brabantio appears from aloft he also uses the term 'Moor', echoing the vocabulary of the previous two men, using the rhetorical tool of *imitatio* designed to persuade the listeners. Later, while waiting for Desdemona to exonerate him at the council meeting, Othello says he will 'confess the vices of my blood' (1.3.125). Othello is saying that he will tell the story of the courtship as truly as he confesses his sins before God. However, this may be understood instead that his blood and his bloodline cannot change its colour, always labelling him as 'other'. This is not the representation that Othello intended since he was describing what drew the pair together and not a singular vice. However, he cannot control those who hear his words. Desdemona, on her arrival, proves herself to be articulate and unabashed at the course of action that she has taken. She refers to Othello as 'the Moor my lord' (1.3.189), indicating the conventionally superior position in which she places Othello as husband and also the variable emotional register of the term 'Moor'. In reply, Brabantio reluctantly acquiesces and with regret hands over his claim on Desdemona to the 'Moor'.

Iago continues to urge Roderigo to follow through with their plot. Iago convinces Roderigo with words that resonate with both blood-red references and the trope of the Moor as a devil. He says

> Mark me with what violence she first loved the Moor,
> ...
> Her eye must be fed, and what delight
> shall she have to look on the devil? When the blood is

made dull with the act of sport, there should be, again
to inflame it, and to give satiety a fresh appetite, love-
liness in favour, sympathy in years, manners and
beauties, all which the Moor is defective in.

(2.1.220; 223–8)

Iago is urging an emotional response in Roderigo. He is also insisting that the emotional attachment Desdemona has to Othello is dependent on her ability to tolerate his skin colour, a situation which, according to Iago, is bound to be finite. When Iago is alone on stage he reveals his own affinity with the devil saying

Divinity of hell!
When devils will the blackest sins put on
They do suggest at first with heavenly shows
As I do now.

(2.3.345–8)

The evil aligned with the black devil is attested to here, but the sly and duplicitous nature that evil possesses is also revealed. Evil becomes a carapace that can be donned at will and hidden when the owner so desires. Iago's goal is to undermine Desdemona's goodness, 'I will turn her virtue into pitch' (2.3.355), tarring her virtue with his pervasive black nature. Such an encompassing evil will be the trap that ensnares all of the characters.

Othello, then, suffers from self-doubt which did not afflict him when considering matters of state. He is becoming more aware of the impact of his 'otherness' as his personal circumstances deteriorate

Haply for I am black
And have not those soft parts of conversation
That chamberers have, or for I am declined
Into the vale of years – yet that's not much –
She's gone, I am abused.

(3.3.267–71)

Until this moment, Othello has side-stepped the issue of his 'otherness'. Now it is no longer a neutral feature which can be ignored. It has become his weakness, disrupting his life and placing him in a liminal position at the edges of acceptable society which will judge him on both his actions and his colour. The emotional tempo of the play increases and in the company of Desdemona and Lodovico Othello calls Desdemona a '[d]evil!' (4.1.239) and strikes her. Lodovico is shocked but Othello exclaims 'O devil, devil! / If that the earth could teem with woman's tears / Each drop she falls would prove a crocodile' (4.1.243–5). Previously

Othello had called her a 'fair devil' but now he is fully convinced of her evil and transgressive nature. There is, to his mind, no goodness left in her and all of her deeds from this moment forth, including crying and pleading, are viewed negatively. Othello continues to talk matters of state to Lodovico while berating and undermining Desdemona

> And she's obedient: as you say, obedient,
> Very obedient. – Proceed you in your tears. –
> Concerning this, sir – O well-painted passion! –
> I am commanded home. – Get you away.
>
> (4.1.255–8)

By now Othello is convinced that all outward signs from Desdemona are false and her display of emotional anguish must be a deceit. Marguerite A. Tassi notes '[t]he painting trope is used to describe the exhibition of false passions... While this negative use of the trope damns painting as an artificial, deceitful practice, it manages to take an ambivalent stance towards playing' (2005, 33). Othello is also suggesting that Desdemona is ably articulating her deceit since painting and embellishment refer to rhetorical skills as well as fine art and the use of cosmetics. However, should he have been taking notice of her speeches Othello might have noticed she was not using rhetorical skills nor ornaments but merely stating unadorned truths. Lodovico cannot reconcile this presentation with his memories of Othello

> Is this the noble Moor whom our full senate
> Call all in all sufficient? This the nature
> Whom passion could not shake? whose solid virtue
> The shot of accident nor dart of chance
> Could neither graze nor pierce?
>
> (4.1.264–8)

Lodovico is clinging onto nobility as one of Othello's traits but is shocked by the emotional excesses. Mary Floyd-Wilson observes '[e]thnicity in the early modern period is defined more by emotional differences than by appearance: distinctions rest on how easily one is stirred or calmed – on one's degree of emotional vulnerability or resistance – or one's capacity to move others' (2004, 133). It is the lack of a temperate emotional valence which has shaken Lodovico's faith in Othello's character and may lead others to consider him in racially prejudiced terms. At this moment, Othello is unable to regulate his emotions and is not conforming to the emotional expectations of Venetian society (Scheer 2012, 214).

When Emilia enters, she realises that Othello has murdered Desdemona, and cries 'O, the more angel she, / And you the blacker devil!' (5.2.128–9), followed by '[t]hou dost belie her, and thou art a devil'

(5.2.131). Emilia hints that just as Othello cannot change his skin, so his black hue and accompanying black core cannot be affected by the veneer of white Venetian society. Emilia continues to associate Othello with dark, black actions and character saying, '[s]he was too fond of her most filthy bargain!' (5.2.153), and that he was as 'ignorant as dirt!' (5.2.160). The audience, as noted by Meredith Anne Skura, 'seem to have been no less sophisticated in juggling the literal and figurative meanings of the word "black," sometimes meaning (1) literally dark color, sometimes (2) figuratively dark (evil and/or foul), and sometimes both' (2008, 308). Such multilayered meanings are embedded in the emotional responses to the representation of Othello as a chromatically figured Moor.

Cultural commonplaces

As a developing area of research interest, 'visual culture' is described by Peter Erickson and Clark Hulse as emerging

> at the intersection of these two trajectories, one running from art history toward cultural and literary studies, the other running from literary and cultural studies toward the history of images ... if visual culture is the study of the social construction of visual experience, then equally it is the study of the visual construction of social experience.
>
> (2000, 1)

Visual culture is not limited to particular genres and locations and there are no boundaries to employing it in forms such as drama. Indeed, Chloe Porter (2011) has shown how Shakespeare engages with visual culture and in particular with both anti-visual discourses and the discourses surrounding the proper execution of the visual arts. While Marguerite A. Tassi states that '[n]o Elizabethan dramatist explored the complex, paradoxical nature of human responses to painted images as fully as Shakespeare did, nor did any of his contemporaries exploit painting's theatrical potential as extensively' (2005, 179). There are many studies on the representation of visual culture in Shakespeare's plays (Tassi 2005; Meek 2009; Porter 2013; Elam 2019). One reason is that the art of painting was understood to engage seeing, imagining, and feeling, a combination which is reflected in the words and visual cues provided in the theatre. For Thomas Wright

> to persuade any matter we intend, or to stir up any passion in a multitude, if we can aptly confirm our opinion or intention with any visible object no doubt but the persuasion would be more forcible, and the passion more potent.
>
> ([1601] 1986, 5.1.214–8)

There is no doubt that colours influence an audience. According to Haydocke, it behoves the craftsman to pay attention to the colours that are foregrounded to avoid unfortunate excesses of emotion in susceptible audiences. Already, through the medium of fine art, colour has an emotive imperative, as 'by the helpe of colours thus indiciouslie disposed, the eies of those mournefull countenances (mencioned in the former booke of *Motions*) vvil looke pale, of fooles vvanne and voide of all bloud, of angrie folks fieries, and of such as weepe blackish' (1598, 97). Like the visual culture of his period, Shakespeare's drama represents interior states of emotion by using visual and imaginative prompts related to colour playing into the idea that emotions are something that practically engage with the world. He employs colour associations drawn from contemporary art, and (consciously or subconsciously) familiar ideas from common life such as relying on the social bond of objects or the employment of emblematic references. In fact, he draws from the visual representations of royal portraits which figure the excessively white complexions as symbols of power, privilege and even divinity.[12]

The genre of emblems can equally be considered part of visual culture. Geoffrey Whitney was credited with bringing the interest in emblems to the fore in England. In 1586 he brought out his book, *A Choice of Emblemes and other Devises*. In effect, it was a tome designed to provide moralising and instructive advice to its readers. In this collection, there are 248 emblems, each accompanied by a woodcut with a motto in both English and Latin, and a poem in English. This was an important English vernacular publication as it produced for the first time a comprehensive collection of the emblems that were in common usage across Europe.[13] Within Whitney's collection there are a number that use colour references within the text as an aid to convey their message. They involve specific colour terms in literary representations and images that align them with particular emotions as I discussed in the introduction to this book. For example, Whitney notes the power of colour to move animals as a warning against indiscriminate use of colour, echoing the advice of Thomas Wright[14]

> The scarlet cloathe, dothe make the bull to feare,
> The culler white, the Olephant dothe shunne.
> ...
> All which doe showe, we no manne shoulde dispise,
> But thinke howe harme, the simplest maie deuise.
> (Whitney 1586, 143)

The power of colour to explain, mark, and move a person was emphasised through emblematic examples. Their messages were readily memorised and their lessons became commonplaces (Daly 1998, 41). I suggest that emblems, like colours, are alluded to in order to provoke consideration of a particular situation, whether in agreement or disagreement with the proposed paralleling emblem. With emblems, as in other examples of visual culture, the meaning of colour lies in the 'fickle' gaze of the individual observer; colours are potentially multivalent, waiting for their attachment to particular objects in times and places before they achieve meaning. Peter M. Daly reiterates that 'the word-emblem serves a conceptual function; it is primarily a vehicle of meaning, not a means of decoration' (1998, 112). These emblems reinforce the idea that *Othello* could be seen in some ways as belonging to the genre of morality plays (Thompson 2016, 7*ff*).

Material objects also feature as cultural commonplaces creating social bonds in their circulation and having the power to cause happiness or unhappiness (Ahmed 2010, 35). Sara Ahmed continues '[h]appy objects are passed around, accumulating positive affective value as social goods' (2010, 35). Conversely the same can be said of unhappy objects of which the handkerchief in *Othello* is one. In the early modern period, textiles were read as a sign of women's chastity and worth, through the virtuous activity required to produce them. However, in plays 'staged' textiles 'mark and then signify the contested female body, which can be possessed entirely by men and, thus reduced, may be disposed of violently' (Frye 2000, 221). Witness the significance of the circulating handkerchief. When onstage with Othello, Desdemona innocently drops her handkerchief. We know from later descriptions that the handkerchief is 'spotted with strawberries'.[15] After the exit of Desdemona and Othello, Iago and Emilia are onstage with the handkerchief which is mentioned three times between them and snatched from one to the other. It is a material presence acting as an emotive which literally flashes red staining in front of the audience. Visually and imaginatively there is an image of a pale handkerchief spotted with red. The image can arouse thoughts of lost virginal innocence, fear, and anxiety around the image of the female body and around the danger that is slowly becoming apparent for Desdemona.[16] Most importantly it is a handkerchief which, in Desdemona's possession, becomes metonymic of Othello's love which she has now lost. Its importance lies not only in its presence but also in its power to create emotional moments. As Andrew Sofer says, '[t]he handkerchief is not merely a sign but a performer in the play's action, and its physical movements and shifting emotional impact deserve as much attention as its symbolism' (1997, 368).

When the handkerchief comes into his possession, Iago contrives to leave it in Cassio's lodgings so that the dangerous thought with which he has pricked Othello's mind will 'with a little art upon the blood / Burn like the mines of sulphur' (3.3.331–2). Iago asks Othello '[h]ave you not sometimes seen a handkerchief / Spotted with strawberries, in your wife's hand?' (3.3.437–8). The mention of strawberries not only provides a flash of red imagery but it also conjures up ideas of virginity and purity represented by the fruit itself.[17] Desdemona, returning to the stage with Emilia, laments the loss of the handkerchief, saying

> Believe me, I had rather have lost my purse
> Full of crusadoes; and but my noble Moor
> Is true of mind, and made of no such baseness
> As jealous creatures are, it were enough
> To put him to ill thinking.
>
> (3.4.25–9)

This sentiment would have resonated with the London audience watching the play, who were invested in status-giving textiles. Paul Yachnin suggests, '[t]he play's stake in the handkerchief registers the theatre's participation in English society's fetishized trade in textiles' (1996, 202). While anxious about the loss, Desdemona is placing her trust in Othello's just and true nature. At this point, she sees the handkerchief more as an object than as an emotional touchstone for fidelity and desire. When Othello asks her for it and she does not have it about her, he tells a tale of an Egyptian charmer who gave it to his mother as an aid to subduing his father. The reverse was also true, that should his mother lose it his father would loathe her, as there was 'magic in the web of it' (3.4.71). Susan Frye notes the 'point of this tale, however, is not to charm but to situate the handkerchief in a narrative that parallels the suspicion and domestic violence through which Othello is now narrating his life' (2000, 223). At this point, '[m]agic or no, the handkerchief has become charged with dramatic value and danger' (1997, 370). Before he exits, Othello mentions the handkerchief six times in the scene, thus building up the anxiety and fear felt by Desdemona. Catherine Richardson notes that objects like the handkerchief 'insist upon material culture as an embodied form, one which connects bodies, one which speaks loudly about memory and grief as a desire for presence' (2011, 45).

Going forward, Iago, once more in conversation with Othello, uses repetition and suggestive pauses to draw attention to the handkerchief, putting into practice Aristotle's ideas on persuasion

> Persuasion is achieved by the speaker's personal character when the speech is so spoken as to make us think him credible. We believe good men more fully and more readily than others ... Secondly, persuasion may come through the hearers, when the speech stirs their emotions. Our judgements when we are pleased and friendly are not the same as when we are pained and hostile. It is towards producing these effects, as we maintain, that present-day writers on rhetoric direct the whole of their efforts ... Thirdly, persuasion is effected through the speech itself when we have proved a truth or an apparent truth by means of the persuasive arguments suitable to the case in question.
>
> ([c350BCE] 1984, 1356^{a}1–21, 2155)

In particular, Iago is using the second mode of persuasion to stir Othello's emotions. He produces a pained and hostile disposition in Othello, knowing that this will affect Othello's judgement. He is also playing on the fact that Othello views him as a good person. Stefan D. Keller also notes another tool used by Iago 'his preferred weapon is the figure paralipsis, pretending to pass over a matter in order to give it more emphasis' (2010, 403). Iago manages by subtle phrasing to suggest that the woman who gives away her handkerchief can also be accused of giving away her honour. Such deft conversational handling is contrasted with the emotional frenzy and incoherence felt by Othello who is reduced to stuttering '[h]andkerchief! confessions! handkerchief!' and '[c]onfess! handkerchief! O devil!' (4.1.37; 430). After his seizure, Othello is still gripped by emotional turmoil, while proclaiming himself to have patience. This turmoil is well illustrated by his word repetition and the use of red blood

> Dost thou hear, Iago?
> I will be found most cunning in my patience
> But – dost thou hear? – most bloody.
>
> (4.1.90–2)

He is underlining his conflicting patience and heightened passions. He then has to witness Bianca returning the handkerchief to Cassio, stirring him to say '[h]ow shall I murder him, Iago?' (4.1.167). Yet at that moment of ocular proof, when the handkerchief is again being passed red-spotted across the stage, Othello asks for that proof to be verified, '[w]as that mine?' (4.1.171). His passions are roused and he is unable to use his own senses. When confronted by the whole assembly Othello again mentions that he saw the handkerchief in Cassio's hand, 'an antique token / My father gave to my mother' (5.2.214–5). Emilia replies 'O thou dull Moor, that handkerchief thou speak'st of / I found by fortune and did give my husband' (5.2.223–4). At this point, Othello's intelligence is doubly challenged as he is given proof of both Desdemona's innocence and Iago's duplicity.

In *Othello*, 'ocular proof' extends not only to the handkerchief but also to faces which are equally open to misinterpretation. This finds its full expression in the use of the word 'visage' which can also be linked to emblematic wisdoms. Desdemona says 'I saw Othello's visage in his mind' (1.3.253). However, as Ambereen Dadabhoy notes 'there is a difference between Othello's visage as it is presented to the world and that which he constructs in his mind' (2014, 122). Desdemona's use of the term 'visage' here proves a problematic one for the sincerity both of her emotional attachment and also Othello's intentions. Desdemona will soon regret such confidence in her ability to see into his mind, and therefore his 'true' character, when Othello's mind is poisoned by the machinations of Iago. Furthermore, the audience has recently heard 'visage' used by Iago to outline his own duplicitous position. He maintains that his outer visage hides his true intentions and self-serving nature

> Others there are
> Who, trimmed in forms and visages of duty,
> Keep yet their hearts attending on themselves
> ...
> And such a one do I profess myself.
>
> (1.1.48–50; 54)

Much later, Othello brings Desdemona's visage into question when he says '[h]er name, that was as fresh / As Dian's visage, is now begrimed and black / As mine own face' (3.3.389–91). In fact, Shakespeare is asking the audience to consider how they interpret Othello's blackness in relation to the virtue both he and Desdemona had. These lines recall an emblem from Whitney on the subject of appearances. Although John Dixon Hunt (1989) notes that the theatre is more complex than the emblem, my point is that verbal and visual signs in the theatre could bring to mind known emblems that associated them with particular emotional responses, adding to the complexity of the theatrical experience. The motto accompanying the Whitney emblem states, '*Frontis nulla fides*, No faith in appearances' and indicates the difficulty in reading faces

> The lions roare: the Bores theire tuskes do whet.
> The griphins graspe theire tallantes in theire ire:
> The dogges do barke; the bulles, with hornes doe thret.
> The Serpents hisse, with eyes as redde as fire.
> But man is made of suche a seemlie shape,
> That frende, or foe, is not discern'd by face:
> Then harde it is the wickeds wile to scape,
> Since that the bad, doe maske with honest grace.
>
> (1586, 198)

There was an anxiety around reading emotions and reactions through the face which is captured in both this emblem and the lines in *Othello*.[18] Indeed, the last line points to Iago's earlier assertion regarding his 'visage of duty'.

As the play draws towards its climax, Othello and Desdemona are alone in their bedroom. Othello asks his wife, '[t]urn thy complexion there, / Patience, thou young and rose-lipped cherubin, / Ay, here look, grim as hell!' (4.2.63–5). His lines imaginatively address an allegorical figure, Patience, who is often imagined on a monument or a hill. In this iteration, the figure of Patience would lose her essential qualities when faced with Desdemona's infidelity. I would like to suggest another reading that conflates Patience and Desdemona as the listener to whom Othello addresses his words. If Desdemona could change her complexion, then this could indicate her changing passions. However, the instability of both the complexion of the face, and the internal humours, may also be indicated by these lines. The unstable conflation allows Desdemona's complexion to become a misread palette of the passions rather than the cold marble figure he would prefer. Both her facial appearance and her humoral complexion are in question since Othello's lines seem to privilege her outward appearance and her inner emotional qualities equally. She has changed, in Othello's mind, from the sincere maiden he married to an emotionally hollow strumpet. She is the 'weed' that is so 'lovely fair' that he wishes had never been born (4.2.68; 69). Such discourse recalls both physiognomic treatises and didactic tracts warning women of the dangers of using make-up to change their outward appearance (Stubbes 1583, under 'A particulare Discription of the Abuses of Womens apparell in Ailgna').

Othello continues to describe both her appearance and her character in a conflation that rests on the metaphor of the book, saying, '[w]as this fair paper, this most goodly book, / Made to write 'whore' upon?' (4.2.72–3).[19] Derek Dunne notes that the 'legibility of the face is at once obvious and inscrutable, as Othello reads his wife's features as a book on which her inchastity is writ large in invisible letters' (2016, 240). The image becomes an oscillation between white and black. The fair/white Desdemona is blackened internally and externally with the dark ink that inscribes 'whore' across her. Shortly after this exchange, Desdemona asks Emilia to '[l]ay on my bed my wedding sheets' (4.2.107). In a portentous move, those are the sheets which will become her burial shroud. Her murderous, evil (and black) death will be inscribed on that white linen.

Desdemona's repetition of the words 'green willow' brings to mind a pale languid green sickness, *morbus virgineus* ('virgin's disease'). The changing valence of green coincides with Desdemona's realisation that her fate has been set. Her virtue in the light of her reliance on the colour green reflects the emblem and motto, '*Virescit vulnere virtus*' or 'Virtue thrives from wounds'

> The dockes (thoughe trodden) growe, as it is dailie seene:
> So vertue, thoughe it longe be hid, with wounding waxeth
>   greene.
>   (Whitney 1586, 196)

Desdemona's virtue, though questioned and attacked, does not waver. She proclaims her innocence all the more as the accusations against her increase. Emilia brings back the juxtaposition of black and white when answering Desdemona's query about whether she would be unfaithful to her husband, saying that she would not be unfaithful 'by this heavenly light: / I might do't as well i'th' dark' (4.3.65–6). Here she echoes the emblem concerning thieves who act similarly

> When silent nighte, did scepter take in hande,
> And dim'de the daie, with shade of mantle blacke,
> What time the theeves, in priuie corners stande,
> And haue no dowte, to robbe for what they lacke
> (Whitney 1586, 130)

While the words of Emilia reflect the same sentiment as the emblem, which is understandable given the Elizabethan training that encouraged sententious and epigrammatic writing, what 'distinguishes Shakespeare's use of the commonplaces, however, is his adaptation of them to individuals, so that they are not so much presented as possessing universal validity as expressing a character's nature and response to circumstances' (Dundas 1983, 50).

After Desdemona's death, Othello is blackened inside and out, which recalls the motto, 'To wash an Ethiopian'

> Leave of with paine, the blackamore to skowre,
> With washinge ofte, and wiping more than due:
> For thou shalt finde, that Nature is of power,
> Doe what thou canste, to keepe his former hue:
> Thoughe with a forke, wee Nature thruste awaie,
> Shee turns againe, if wee withdrawe our hande:
> And thoughe, wee ofte to conquer her assaie,
> Yet all in vaine, shee turns if still wee stande:
> Then evermore, in what thou doest assaie,
> Let reason rule, and doe the thinge thou maie.
> (Whitney 1586, 150)

No amount of scrubbing will change the fundamental colouring of the blackamoor in the emblem suggesting Othello cannot escape his natural state of blackness and all that it represents.

The colour arc

Tracing the undulating arc of colour in the play plots the close relationship that colour and emotion have and the way their entwined register serves to move an audience. *Othello* opens at night with a scene which sees Iago reassuring Roderigo, that he, Iago, will help Roderigo to obtain access, both socially and sexually, to Desdemona. Iago's first word is embedded in colour – 'Sblood' ('God's blood') (1.1.4) – emotionally positioning an attentive audience to anticipate the tragedy that is about to unfold in front of them. The blood-red reference, through its martial significance, as described in Haydocke's art treatise, may be designed to encourage Roderigo to continue bravely following Iago's lead. The oath also points to spilling of Christ's blood. Similarly, violence in the play culminates in the murder of Desdemona and also the murders of Emilia and Roderigo who are killed through the machinations of Iago.

Quite soon, Iago, again through a chromatically-resonant observation, hints at the plot for the audience, describing Michael Cassio cryptically as a 'fellow almost damned in a fair wife' (1.1.20).[20] This introduces a white note into the chromatic arc. It could be that Cassio is 'almost' married to Bianca, a woman he is consorting with, or that he is distracted from his soldierly duties because of his interest in women. Alternatively, both Othello and Cassio are damned by the presence of Desdemona, a fair and beautiful wife. Following the received wisdoms, this description underlines her innocence and purity as a character. From the beginning, virtue, innocence, and faithfulness are part of the emotional landscape realised in fair Desdemona. Later in the play, her demeanour takes a melancholic turn which also, according to Haydocke, could be represented by white (1598, 114–5). Fair, indicating light and white, underlines the importance her colour will have when contrasted with that of Othello.

Brabantio, calling for light to counteract the darkness of the moment, shouts '[l]ight, I say, light' (1.1.143), before introducing a chromatic reference to red, exclaiming '[o] treason of the blood' (1.1.167) which allows for, in this context, a reading of revenge and possibly martyrdom along with the literal betrayal of bloodlines, since, as his wife, Desdemona will be committed to bearing Othello's children. These potential responses to colour can be traced back to ideas in Haydocke's writings, which link 'blood' with sexual appetite and lasciviousness (1598, 117–8). Brabantio cannot understand how his 'maid' so 'fair and happy' (1.2.66) could '[r]un from her guardage to the sooty bosom/ Of such a thing as [Othello]' (1.2.70–1), using the colour dichotomies to augment previous slurs on Othello's character, and creating anxiety and fear amongst those listening to him.

In contrast to the black and white references punctuated with occasional red used thus far in reference to Othello, Senator I uses the epithet 'Moor' with the qualifier 'valiant' (1.3.49). As Othello enters, he is greeted by the Duke who reiterates the positive epithet. He also uses Othello's name thereby humanising him. However, Brabantio soon enters and changes the emotional register by stating that his daughter is dead to him as she has been 'corrupted [b]y spells' (1.3.61–2). It is interesting to note that Shakespeare used 'corrupted' in *Henry V* to describe the blood of corrupted or attainted persons, and this would resonate with Brabantio's earlier declaration discussed above (OED Online, 'corrupt'). Without knowledge of the person who has secured the affections of Desdemona, the Duke promises

> Whoe'er he be, that in this foul proceeding
> Hath thus beguiled your daughter of herself,
> And you of her, the bloody book of law
> You shall yourself read, in the bitter letter
>
> (1.3.66–9)

Of course, such a resolution becomes awkward when the Duke is faced with Othello in this capacity and the Duke is left asking Othello to explain himself. Notably absent in Othello's reply are any references to colour. It is a measured speech laying out facts as explanation rather than expressing an emotional plea for understanding. Brabantio, maintaining his heightened emotional state replies

> A maiden never bold,
> Of spirit so still and quiet that her motion
> Blushed at herself.
>
> (1.3.95–7)

Desdemona is described as a maiden of such sensibilities that even her own thoughts give her cause to blush. The ability to blush also points to the anxieties around blushing due to its potentially duplicitous emotional nature; it was variously attributed to love, shame, and modesty. In a mirroring act, the absence of blushing will be remarked upon again towards the end of the play as the arc of colour flows and ebbs. Again Brabantio mentions blood suggesting that Othello exerted some influence 'o'er the blood' (1.3.105), by means of a powerful potion. The red blood in question stands for Desdemona's passion and is related to her sexual appetite (Shakespeare [1603] 2004, n. line 105, 141).

The Duke attempts to finalise the marriage discussion with advice to Brabantio, saying

> If virtue no delighted beauty lack
> Your son-in-law is far more fair than black
>
> (1.3.290–1)

Although ending on a positive note of encouragement for Brabantio, the Duke reiterates the polemic of black versus white. To him, the emotional response triggered by Othello's colour should be tempered by looking to his virtuous good deeds which in moral terms allow him to be viewed as 'fair'. The Duke puns on 'fair' as meaning both 'beautiful' and 'of a light complexion'. In this case, suggesting the colour of Othello's skin is not an indicator of the expected negative connotations. However,

Brabantio, building on this, attempts to unsettle Othello's belief in the fair and steadfastness of Desdemona's love by asking him to '[l]ook to her, Moor, if thou has eyes to see: / She has deceived her father, and may thee' (1.3.293–4). Brabantio's exhortation underlines the sense of sight's deceptive nature. The return to physical colouring indicates the ongoing tensions around the cultural understandings of white and black.

Left alone with Roderigo, Iago uses the power of colour seated in humoral theory to convince Roderigo of his plan. He says '[i]f the balance of our lives had not one scale of reason to poise another of sensuality, the blood and baseness of our natures would conduct us to the most preposterous conclusions' (1.3.327–30). While pointing to the plans he has for Othello, he is actually inciting the same reaction in Roderigo that he professes they are avoiding. He is persuading Roderigo that Othello and Desdemona share a passion based only on lust – '[i]t is merely a lust of the blood' (1.3.335) – using references to blood to build the emotion. Alone, Iago closes the scene with reference to shades of black and white, saying, 'Hell and night / must bring this monstrous birth to the world's light' (1.3.402–3).

Continuing with this colour scheme, Iago engages Desdemona in witty conversation that plays on the relationship of white and black while also alerting the audience to the fact that Desdemona may not be as demure as Brabantio led us to believe. Iago begins '[i]f she be fair and wise, fairness and wit, / The one's for use, the other useth it' (2.1.129–30). He may be suggesting that a fair (white) complexioned woman may use her beauty for her own gain if she has the intelligence to do so. This is parried with a question from Desdemona, who asks '[h]ow if she be black and witty?' (2.1.131), where 'black' would normally mean 'dark-haired' but in this context will also suggest black skin. The answer descends to innuendo from Iago about sexual promiscuity and is tolerated by both Emilia and Desdemona. Throughout the exchange what is highlighted is Iago's sexual fascination and curiosity regarding the love union between Othello and Desdemona. It is only notable that Desdemona does not take offence nor even seem to realise what is at stake in the conversation. On Othello's arrival, he greets Desdemona as his 'fair warrior' (2.1.180), reinforcing the previous discussion between Desdemona and Iago and highlighting the importance of colour.

With colour references in mind, it is important to note how Iago describes Cassio. Cassio is 'handsome, young, and hath all those requisites in him that folly and green minds look after' (2.1.243–5). Within the play, this is the first reference to green, and through the wording, Iago aligns Cassio with Desdemona as unripe, inexperienced, and immature. There is also a naïve folly attached to both of them which, as we shall see, Iago is prepared to exploit. The colour green is associated with constancy, fertility, and marriage. It is also linked with youth, inexperience, rashness, and young maiden's greensickness. Cleopatra, in *Antony and Cleopatra*, uses green similarly, '[m]y salad days, when I was green in judgment, cold in blood' (1.5.77). Exploitable emotional inexperience resonates through this colour reference. The reference to green appears approximately one-third of the way through the play and foreshadows its later use.

The next colour reference in *Othello* features another description of Cassio by Iago who says 'he's rash and very sudden in choler, and haply with his truncheon may strike at you' (2.1.270–1), which is, of course, untrue. The humoral associations conjure up a character who is emotional and given to sudden anger. The reference may also lead to thoughts of yellow bile and the colour's associated emotions of joy, mirth, and jealousy. When next alone, Iago builds upon the slim notion of jealousy with a definite reference to his plan

> Or, failing so, yet that I put the Moor
> At least into a jealousy so strong
> That judgement cannot cure
>
> (2.1.298–300)

As Ania Loomba notes, 'male jealousy hinges upon racial difference as well as upon female infidelity' (2002, 99) which is exactly the understanding that Iago exploits. The play continues with some of Iago's intrigues coming to fruition. Roderigo sets upon Cassio, who has been plied with drink, and Montano enters the fray and is injured at the hands of Cassio. Othello and his attendants are aroused. Montano cries, '[z]ounds, [God's wounds] I bleed still; I am hurt to th'death' (2.3.160–1), bringing a figurative (and possibly a literal) splash of red onto the stage. Iago reinforces this colour saying the men began fighting '[i]n opposition bloody' (2.3.180). The rising emotional situation affects Othello, who now says

> My blood begins my safer guides to rule
> And passion, having my best judgment collied,
> Assays to lead the way.
>
> (2.3.201–3)

Othello has become the choleric man described by Iago, a slave to his passions and lacking rational control without the ability to regulate his emotions in ways demanded by his societal circumstances.

At this mid-way point in the play, the green-eyed monster appears (3.3.168) as the pinnacle of the colour arc. The arc is now about to descend back through the chromatic register in mirrored fashion. Iago, providing the ocular proof that is needed by Othello, mentions that

Cassio has used the handkerchief as a beard wipe. This stimulates a powerful response in Othello, who invokes a curse saying

> Arise, black vengeance, from the hollow hell,
> Yield up, O love, thy crown and hearted throne
> To tyrannous hate!
>
> (3.3.450–2)

Othello's embodiment of blackness has had an enigmatic quality until this point. In the Duke's conventional terms, his black exterior has belied a noble, brave, and valiant interior. Inexorably, his emotions become aligned with blackness of heart and deed, transforming him emotionally to a space of fear, doubt, and ultimately vengeful anger as he succumbs to the emotional machinations of Iago.

Likewise, the insistence on red references is also increasing. The visual images of blood-red passions increase and intensify with Othello crying, 'O, blood, blood, blood!' (3.3.454), followed shortly by

> Even so my bloody thoughts with violent pace
> Shall ne'er look back, ne'er ebb to humble love
> Till that a capable and wide revenge
> Swallow them up.
>
> (3.3.460–3)

The chromatic register is highlighted with red bursts of colour in the addition or *adiectio* of 'blood'. Othello is now the rhetorician persuading himself of his wife's guilt. Iago, building on this repetition finishes his rousing speech with: '[w]hat bloody business ever' (3.3.472). When parting, Othello refers to Desdemona as 'the fair devil' (3.3.481), counterpointing her outward fairness with a supposed inner blackness and evil which mirrors the chromatic switch that is happening in Othello.

Bianca enters as another character confounding the idea of black and white. Bianca is supposedly a courtesan, a trade which should mark her out as a sinner; yet her name translates as 'white'. Joyce Green MacDonald (2001, 195) proposes that white evokes notions of the distant and chaste Petrarchan model, which is at odds with her reputed sexuality, problematising our understanding of her. Added to this is the fact that Bianca herself consistently denies being a strumpet, we only have Iago's word to support this view of her. Again, this is an occasion amongst many where black and white are juxtaposed and serve to contrast each other's emotional potential. Cassio mentions her name four times in the space of 32 lines, emphasising both her presence and her contradictory character, which can be read in gendered terms to mean all women. The scene is comprised of a polarising black-and-white colour scheme which leaves Bianca portrayed as a model of established virtue or vice, unable to function in between.

Desdemona reintroduces the colour green when she is alone, preparing for what will be her death. She tells Emilia of her mother's maid called 'Barbary', whose name connotes a relationship to the Barbary Coast, suggesting a link both to Desdemona's present sorrow and also the source of that sorrow, Othello the Moor. Desdemona sings the mournful song first sung by Barbary, 'by a sycamore tree/ [s]ing all a green willow' (4.3.39–40). The sycamore tree, glossed as a pun on 'sick-amour' by Honigmann, (Shakespeare [1603] 2004, 291) is also mentioned in *Romeo and Juliet* as grove of trees in which the lovelorn Romeo wanders (1.1.119). Later in the song, Desdemona continues, '[s]ing all a green willow must be a garland' (4.3.50). Green, once the colour of lovers, mentioned in *Love's Labour's Lost* (1.2.83), develops a certain kind of *pathos*, in this context evoking feelings of sorrow and unrequited love rather than the jealousy described earlier.

Outside in a scene of darkness which mirrors the opening scene of the play, Iago and Roderigo are concocting a plan which, for Iago, is the culmination of all his scheming. In the ensuing furore, Cassio and Roderigo are wounded. Othello, witnessing the wounded Cassio, declares

> Minion, your dear lies dead,
> And your unblest fate hies; strumpet, I come.
> Forth of my heart those charms, thine eyes, are blotted,
> Thy bed, lust-stained, shall with lust's blood be spotted.
>
> (5.1.33–6)

The imagery of the wedding bed spotted red references Desdemona's virginal wedding-night blood and recalls the red-spotted handkerchief which provided ocular proof of Desdemona's supposed infidelity. The words echo Othello's previous repetition of the word 'blood' as his emotions are again stirred and roused to great heights. Within a couple of lines Roderigo, wounded by Cassio, reinforces the violent imagery saying 'then shall I bleed to death' (5.1.45). Roderigo is fatally stabbed by Iago who cries, '[k]ill men i'th' dark? Where be these bloody thieves?' (5.1.63). Again Iago says to Gratiano, '[t]hese bloody accidents must excuse my manners' (5.1.94), building up a persistent blood-red colouring in the imagination. The violence done, Iago turns to implicate Bianca suggesting that her paleness in some way suggests her involvement in fateful events. Despite earlier instances which suggest that the meaning behind a person's visage is malleable, Iago uses Bianca's paleness as an admission of guilt. The other feelings which could also be ascribed to her countenance such as fear, horror, and concern are denied to her. Dunne notes that since 'the character of Bianca has refused to blush with guilt, Iago must twist the meaning of her paleness – "the gastness of her eye" – from innocence to fear' (2016, 241).

Meanwhile, Othello, carrying a light, enters the bedchamber where Desdemona lies sleeping. Again there is a contrast between light and dark, black and white, which is the underlying chromatic movement of the play. Considering how he will commit his intended murder, Othello says

> Yet I'll not shed her blood
> Nor scar that whiter skin of hers than snow
> And smooth as monumental alabaster:
> Yet she must die, else she'll betray more men.
> Put out the light, and then put out the light!
> If I quench thee, thou flaming minister,
> I can again thy former light restore
> Should I repent me. But once put out thy light,
> Thou cunning'st pattern of excelling nature,
> I know not where is that Promethean heat
> That can thy light relume: when I have plucked the rose
> I cannot give it vital growth again,
> It needs must wither.
>
> (5.2.3–15)

In chromatic terms, Othello is putting away his rash nature and making efforts to find a rational justification for his murder of Desdemona. He will not have bloodshed, paradoxically underscoring violence which is about to occur, while suggesting that he is not in a fit emotional state as he carries out his crime. He notes the whiteness of Desdemona's skin which is confounding his imagined view of her character but in fact was foreshadowed by the previous mention of Patience (4.2.63–5). He will snuff out both her life and her whiteness just as he will put out the light. David Schalkwyk notes that monumentalising Desdemona raises her to a pale reified ideal, which is only achievable in death (2004, 6). By avoiding shedding her blood Othello is denying the Petrarchan ideal of red and white and offering her a cold, white pure death instead. When Desdemona awakes she is alarmed at Othello's talk of killing and she brings the red references back into focus saying, '[s]ome bloody passion shakes your very frame, / [t]hese are portents' (5.2.44–5). Othello follows this up by mentioning the handkerchief which also reminds the audience of splashes of red. The emotional tempo increases with the reintroduction of the colour red. The handkerchief becomes metonymic of truth as both Desdemona and Othello make genuine statements about it. Desdemona insists that she never gave it to Cassio while Othello insists that he saw it in Cassio's hand. Unfortunately, it is hard for both of these statements to be rationalised and Othello proceeds to smother Desdemona. After Desdemona's death, red disappears as an emotive, and there is a return to monochromatic black and white.

Conclusion

The play ends with Othello's character in tatters, destruction abounding. Othello laments his position as he stands over Desdemona crying

> Where should Othello go?
> Now: How dost thou look now? O ill-starred wench,
> Pale as thy smock. When we shall meet at compt
> This look of thine will hurl my soul from heaven
> And fiends will snatch at it.
> ...
> Whip me, ye devils,
>
> (5.2.269–73; 275)

At the final moment of Othello's acknowledgement of his utterly misplaced belief in Desdemona's deceit and her destruction at his hands comes his most personal insight in the face of his desecrated position in the white Venetian world. His question, 'Where should Othello go?' could, in my mind, apply equally to his wife. Where should they both go now? Desdemona is dead and gone, while Othello is lost forever. Desdemona's death has finally achieved Iago's insidious reformulation of attitudes around Othello's Moorish identity. After Othello calls Iago a devil and stabs him, Iago replies 'I bleed, sir, but not killed' (5.2.285), perhaps suggesting that although he has some human qualities like bleeding, since he outlives the injuries maybe he is the devil. Othello later refers to Iago as a 'demi-devil' (5.2.298). He describes himself, on the other hand, as

> An honourable murderer, if you will,
> For nought I did in hate, but all in honour.
>
> (5.2.291–2)

Othello denies acting 'in hate' but previous scenes have betrayed the emotional state which accompanied his actions. The play's pattern of affective colour shows the passions motivating his decision-making, and that considerations of 'honour' were not distinct but centrally involved in his aggressive emotional conclusions. Nevertheless, Othello impresses us with his shared humanity. Part of the discomfort felt by audiences is summed up by Skura who says, 'Othello's crime *is* monstrous, but Shakespeare does not allow his audience the comfort of thinking that he is capable of monstrosity *because* he is a Moor. He is one of us, not one of them' (2008, 325). We also understand his tragedy within a particular social context. Dadabhoy notes that 'Othello's transformation is not the result of a natural or cultural degeneracy but of a crisis in colonial subjectivity' (2014, 124).

While I have principally considered Othello with regard to the ways the colour register is explicitly and implicitly aligned with contemporary social and cultural commonplaces, I also wish to emphasise mobility in the chromatic register occurring across the entire play. As mentioned, the green-eyed monster appears at the very centre of the play, indicating the importance of this trope, while splashes of vivid red increase in frequency in areas that demonstrate strong emotions, aligning with Haydocke's recommendation for its use. The violent and emotion-filled conclusion to the play is punctuated with a few final flashes of red when Othello asks Cassio about the handkerchief, bringing its elusive red-spotted nature presence back to the fore. This red reference finishes upon Othello's suicide: Lodovico exclaims 'O bloody period!' (5.2.355). References to black and white appear throughout the play but these diminish in frequency when references to red and green appear.

In this final chapter, I have demonstrated the influential ways in which a burgeoning visual culture worked through colour to enhance affective patterns in *Othello*. I agree, however, with Dundas that although it is tempting 'to consider the use of a common symbolic language in the literature and art of the Renaissance as indicative of a common significance … the dangers of a reductive approach of this kind may well outweigh the interpretative gains' (1983, 51). I have, accordingly, tried to emphasise that many colour references contain nuanced and multivalenced meanings entirely dependent on context and audience reception. *Othello* is deeply engaged with the late Elizabethan language, race ideology and visual cultures of colour, including its strong commonplaces, but always actively, and in ways that create new possibilities of emotional insight and effect.

Notes

1. Bruce Smith makes a case for the importance attending to the sounds produced by the words in this quotation because of the power of assonance and alliteration (2004, 166).
2. Ania Loomba discusses the origins and use of the word 'race' in the early modern period. See Chapter 1, in *Shakespeare, Race, and Colonialism* (2002).
3. G. K. Hunter notes various media such as alabasters and manuscripts that show faces coloured black. See *Dramatic Identities and Cultural Tradition: Studies in Shakespeare and His Contemporaries* (1978, 34–9).
4. Habib notes the 'sizeability of the black presence in English life is particularly underlined by Queen Elizabeth's … deportation orders directed against blacks in 1596 and 1601 on the grounds that their numbers were aggravating an unemployment situation' (2000, 127).
5. Also Richard Hakluyt, *The Principal Navigations, Voyages, Traffiques and Discoveries of the English Nation: Made by Sea or Over-land to the Remote and Farthest Distant Quarters of the Earth at Any Time within the Compass of These 1600 Yeeres* ([1600] 1903).
6. Habib observes that the word race in Elizabethan times 'more often than not meant lineage rather than physical or cultural difference' (2000, 2).
7. Loomba also notes that although in this period the term 'Moor' became associated with blackness, originally it was used to describe those of Mahomet's sect.

8 Frank Kermode suggests that this scene is *charivari* which Iago is using for his own ends, in *Shakespeare's Language* (2001, 167).
9 See description of Aaron's hair in *Titus Andronicus*, 'My fleece of woolly hair now uncurls / even as an adder when she doth unroll / To do some fatal Execution?' (2.234–6). This also echoes the description by John Pory.
10 Loomba discusses the libidinous ideas discussed with regard to Moors and black people in general in *Shakespeare, Race, and Colonialism* (2002, 23).
11 Newman describes the link between blackness and the monstrous, in particular monstrous sexuality as described by early modern travel writers, in "'And Wash the Ethiop White': Femininity and the Monstrous in *Othello*" (2009, 45).
12 Farah Karim Cooper (2021) considers early modern constructions of black and white in her chapter "The Materials of Race: Staging the Black and White Binary in the Early Modern Theatre".
13 See Bath (1994, 85–9) for a discussion of the reception of Whitney in England; and Bath (1994, 28–53) for a discussion of the place of emblems within the wider English renaissance culture.
14 Wright says '[i]t seemeth a thing frequented in many Nations, to stir up beasts to fight by showing them some red colour, for thereby they imagine that the sight of blood inflameth them to the shedding of blood' ([1601] 1986, 2.2.145–71). See Chapter 3 above for the full quotation.
15 Ian Smith makes a strong case for the handkerchief itself being dark or black as Othello mentions that it is 'dyed in mummy' (2013, 15–21). However, the spoken lines and rhetorical echoes suggest that whatever colour the handkerchief itself is, there are definite red-strawberry coloured markings that can be seen. I am persuaded by Michael Neill's counterargument that the textile was not meant to remind the audience of the material nature of the stage actor's disguise as it were; it is more likely that as Othello describes Desdemona's skin as becoming 'begrimed', the actor was smeared with the stage makeup to indicate his colour, rather than clothed in black cloth which is reminiscent of courtly masques (2013, 26–31).
16 In *Shakespeare, Race, and Colonialism*, Loomba notes 'Burton writes that Jews and Africans "will not credit virginity without seeing the bloody napkin."' A concept which Loomba indicates originates in the writings of Leo Africanus (2002, 101).
17 Lynda E. Boose notes the association that strawberries had with the Virgin Mary and by association with virginity itself in "Othello's Handkerchief: 'The Recognizance and Pledge of Love'" (1975, 362).
18 For a further discussion on considerations of the face in *Othello* see Sean Lawrence "The Two Faces of Othello" (2015).
19 Stanton notes 'the word "whore" functions in hegemonic use in a roughly similar way as the word "nigger" does for blacks and the word "queer" does for homosexuals: to keep troubling individuals grouped in their marginalised place and to insist that the place is a vulgar, degraded one from which they can never escape' (2001, 81).
20 Honigmann discusses the complexities of this line in his long notes in Shakespeare, *Othello*, ([1603] 2004, 335).

References

Ahmed, Sara. 2010. "Happy Objects." In *The Affect Theory Reader*, edited by Melissa Gregg and Gregory J. Seigworth, 29–51. Durham, NC: Duke University Press.
Aristotle. (c350BCE) 1984. "Rhetoric." In *The Complete Works of Aristotle The Revised Oxford Translation*, edited by Jonathan Barnes, translated by W. Rhys Roberts, 2152–69. Princeton, NJ: Princeton University Press.

Bartels, Emily C. 1990. "Making More of the Moor: Aaron, Othello, and Renaissance Refashioning." *Shakespeare Quarterly* 41, no. 4: 433–54.
Barthelemy, Anthony Gerard. 1994. "Ethiops Washed White: Moors of the Nonvillainous Type." In *Critical Essays on Shakespeare's Othello*, edited by Anthony Gerard Barthelemy, 91–103. New York: G. K. Hall & Co.
Bath, Michael. 1994. *Speaking Pictures: English Emblem Books and Renaissance Culture*. London; New York: Longman Group UK.
Baumbach, Sibylle. 2008. *Shakespeare and the Art of Physiognomy*. Leicester: Troubador Publishing.
Boose, Lynda E. 1975. "Othello's Handkerchief: 'The Recognizance and Pledge of Love'." *English Literary Renaissance* 5, no. 3: 360–74.
Corredera, Vanessa. 2016a. "Complex Complexions: The Facial Signification of the Black Other in *Lust's Dominion*." In *Shakespeare and the Power of the Face*, edited by James A. Knapp, 93–112. London and New York: Routledge.
Corredera, Vanessa. 2016b. "'Not a Moor Exactly': Shakespeare, Serial, and Modern Constructions of Race." *Shakespeare Quarterly* 67, no. 1: 30–50.
Dadabhoy, Ambereen. 2014. "Two Faced: The Problem of Othello's Visage." In *Othello: The State of Play*, edited by Lena Cowen Orlin, 121–48. London; New York: Bloomsbury Arden Shakespeare.
Dadabhoy, Ambereen. 2021. "Barbarian Moors: Documenting Racial Formation in Early Modern England." In *The Cambridge Companion to Shakespeare and Race*, edited by Ayanna Thompson, 30–46. Cambridge: Cambridge University Press.
Daly, Peter M. 1998. *Literature in the Light of the Emblem: Structural Parallels between the Emblem and Literature in the Sixteenth and Seventeenth Centuries*. Toronto: University of Toronto Press.
Dundas, Judith. 1983. "Shakespeare's Imagery: Emblem and the Imitation of Nature." *Shakespeare Studies* 16: 45–56.
Dunne, Derek. 2016. "Blushing on Cue: The Forensics of the Blush in Early Modern Drama." *Shakespeare Bulletin* 34, no. 2: 233–52.
Elam, Keir. 2019. *Shakespeare's Pictures: Visual Objects in the Drama*. London; New York: Bloomsbury Arden Shakespeare.
Erickson, Peter and Clark Hulse. 2000. "Introduction." In *Early Modern Visual Culture*, edited by Peter Erickson and Clark Hulse, 1–14. Philadelphia: University of Pennsylvania Press.
Floyd-Wilson, Mary. 2004. "English Mettle." In *Reading the Early Modern Passions: Essays in the Cultural History of Emotions*, edited by Gail Kern Paster, Katherine Rowe, and Mary Floyd-Wilson, 130–46. Philadelphia: University of Pennsylvania Press.
Frye, Susan. 2000. "Staging Women's Relations to Textiles in Shakespeare's Othello and Cymbeline." In *Early Modern Visual Culture: Representation, Race, and Empire in Renaissance England*, edited by Peter Erickson and Clark Hulse, 215–50. Philadelphia: University of Pennsylvania Press.
Habib, Imtiaz. 2000. *Shakespeare and Race: Postcolonial Praxis in the Early Modern Period*. Lanham; New York; Oxford: University Press of America.
Habib, Imtiaz. 2008. *Black Lives in the English Archives, 1500–1677: Imprints of the Invisible*. Aldershot, Hampshire: Ashgate Publishing Ltd.
Hakluyt, Richard. (1600) 1903. *The Principal Navigations, Voyages, Traffiques and Discoveries of the English Nation*. Glasgow: MacLehose.

Haydocke, Richard, trans. 1598. *A Tracte Containing the Artes of Curious Paintinge, Caruinge & Buildinge*. By Io. Paul Lomatius. Oxford: Joseph Barnes.
Hunt, John Dixon. 1989. "Pictura, Scriptura, and Theatrum: Shakespeare and the Emblem." *Poetics Today* 10, no. 1: 155–71.
Hunter, G. K. 1978. *Dramatic Identities and Cultural Tradition: Studies in Shakespeare and His Contemporaries*. Liverpool: Liverpool University Press.
Keller, Stefan D. 2010. "Combining Rhetoric and Pragmatics to Read *Othello*." *English Studies* 94, no. 4: 398–411.
Kermode, Frank. 2001. *Shakespeare's Language*. London: Penguin Books.
Lawrence, Sean. 2015. "The Two Faces of Othello." In *Shakespeare and the Power of the Face*, edited by James A. Knapp, 61–74. Farnham, Surrey: Ashgate Publishing Ltd.
Loomba, Ania. 2002. *Shakespeare, Race, and Colonialism*. Oxford: Oxford University Press.
MacDonald, Joyce Green. 2001. "Black Ram, White Ewe: Shakespeare, Race, and Women." In *A Feminist Companion to Shakespeare*, edited by Dympna Callaghan, 188–207. Malden and Oxford: Blackwell Publishing.
Meek, Richard. 2009. *Narrating the Visual in Shakespeare*. Farnham, Surrey: Ashgate Publishing Ltd.
Neill, Michael 2013. "Othello's Black Handkerchief: Response to Ian Smith." *Shakespeare Quarterly* 64, no. 1: 26–31.
Newman, Karen. 2009. "'And Wash the Ethiop White': Femininity and the Monstrous in Othello." In *Essaying Shakespeare*, edited by Karen Newman, 39–58. Minneapolis; London: University of Minnesota Press.
Oxford University Press. n.d. "Oxford English Dictionary Online." Accessed August, 2021. https://www.oed.com/
Plett, Heinrich F. 2004. *Rhetoric and Renaissance Culture*. Berlin: Walter de Gruyter.
Porter, Chloe. 2011. "Shakespeare and Early Modern Visual Culture." *Literature Compass* 8, no. 8: 543–53.
Porter, Chloe. 2013. *Making and Unmaking in Early Modern English Drama: Spectators, Aesthetics and Incompletion*. Manchester: Manchester University Press.
Pory, John. 1600. *A Geographical Historie of Africa, Written in Arabicke and Italian by Iohn Leo a More*. Londini: Eliot's Court Press. Impensis Georg. Bishop.
Richardson, Catherine. 2011. *Shakespeare and Material Culture*. Oxford: Oxford University Press.
Schalkwyk, David. 2004. "Race, Body, and Language in Shakespeare's Sonnets and Plays." *English Studies in Africa* 47, no. 2: 5–23.
Scheer, Monique. 2012. "Are Emotions a Kind of Practice (And Is That What Makes Them Have a History)?: A Bourdieuian Approach to Understanding History." *History and Theory* 51, no. 2: 193–220.
Scot, Reginald. 1584. *The Discovery of Witchcraft*. London: Andrew Clarke.
Shakespeare, William. (1597) 2012. *Romeo and Juliet*. Edited by Rene Weis. London: Bloomsbury Arden Shakespeare.
Shakespeare, William. (1603) 2004. *Othello*. Edited by E. A. J. Honigmann. London; New York: Bloomsbury Arden Shakespeare.

Shakespeare, William. (1607) 2014. *Antony and Cleopatra*. Edited by John Wilders. London; New York: Bloomsbury Arden Shakespeare.

Skura, Meredith Anne. 2008. "Reading Othello's Skin: Contexts and Pretexts." *Philological Quarterly* 87, no. 3/4: 299–334.

Smith, Bruce. 2004. "Hearing Green." In *Reading the Early Modern Passions: Essays in the Cultural History of Emotions*, edited by Gail Kern Paster, Katherine Rowe, and Mary Floyd-Wilson, 147–66. Philadelphia: University of Pennsylvania Press.

Smith, Ian. 1998. "Barbarian Errors: Performing Race in Early Modern England." *Shakespeare Quarterly* 49, no. 2: 168–86.

Smith, Ian. 2013. "Othello's Black Handkerchief." *Shakespeare Quarterly* 64, no. 1: 1–25.

Sofer, Andrew. 1997. "Felt Absences: The Stage Properties of 'Othello's' Handkerchief." *Comparative Drama* 31, no. 3: 367–94.

Stanton, Kay. 2001. "'Made to Write "Whore" Upon?': Make and Female Use of the Word 'Whore' in Shakespeare's Canon." In *A Feminist Companion to Shakespeare*, edited by Dympna Callaghan, 80–102. Oxford: Blackwell Publishers Ltd.

Stubbes, Phillip. 1583. *The Anatomie of Abuses*. London: Richard Jones.

Tassi, Marguerite A. 2005. *The Scandal of Images: Iconoclasm, Eroticism, and Painting*. Selinsgrove: Susquehanna University Press.

Thompson, Ayanna. 2016. "Introduction." In *Othello*, by William Shakespeare, edited by E. A. J. Honigmann, 1–116. London; New York: Bloomsbury Arden Shakespeare.

University of Michigan. n.d. "The Middle English Dictionary Online." Accessed August 2021. http://quod.lib.umich.edu/cgi/m/mec/med-idx?type=id&id=MED51203

Vaughan, Virginia Mason. 1997. "The Construction of Barbarism in *Titus Andronicus*." In *Race, Ethnicity, and Power in the Renaissance*, edited by Joyce Green MacDonald, 165–80. Cranbury, New Jersey: Associated University Presses.

Vaughan, Virginia Mason. 2005. *Performing Blackness on English Stages, 1500–1800*. Cambridge: Cambridge University Press.

Whitney, Geoffrey. 1586. *A Choice of Emblemes and Other Devises*. Leyden: Christopher Plantyn.

Wright, Thomas. (1601) 1986. *The Passions of the Mind in General*. Edited by William Webster Newbold. New York: Garland.

Yachnin, Paul. 1996. "Magical Properties: Vision, Possession, and Wonder in 'Othello'." *Theatre Journal* 48, no. 2: 197–209.

Afterword

In this book, I set out to explore the expressive possibilities of colour in the text and performance of several of William Shakespeare's works. In the course of the enquiry, I analysed the cultural specificity of early modern emotions, using references to colour as an aid to understanding emotional registers. Contemporary ideas and cultural norms were shown to use colour as a means to move emotions. It has been necessary in this book to avoid supposing that a common symbolic language linking colour and emotion existed in the early modern period; such a reductive belief would deny the rich and individual nature of emotion and its expression. Rather, the detailed analysis of the five plays treated in this monograph offers original ways of reading Shakespeare and early modern literature, through a completely new look at his colour use and its emotional effects.

Though each chapter of the book stands alone, together they provide a coherent reassessment of early modern emotions in relation to such contemporary ideas as rhetoric, science, physiognomy, and visual culture. My analysis investigated both the cognitive and the physiological emotional responses flagged, referenced, or promoted by the use of normative colour terms and their specific employments. An understanding of the normative function and relevance of colour terms and images in their early modern English cultural and social contexts allows the possibility of understanding in more detail how the contemporary audience and readership of Shakespeare linked colour to emotional response in their reading of his plays. I do not suggest that the plays cannot be understood and enjoyed in modern productions and with modern mindsets, rather that the experience of them can be more accessible and richer through new insights into the early modern emotional register.

My research has focused on colour as a term that can receive many different emotional inflections whilst remaining firmly rooted in its own cultural context. To do so redresses a gap in the critical canon which has previously treated colour terms as static in meaning, or more recently surveyed the use of colour terms in literature without noting the qualifying cultural structures surrounding their meaning. This research acknowledges that there are various aids that can be used to form an emotional connection with an audience or readership, and that, in drama, colour has been proved to be one of them. For dramatic works to provoke a powerful audience response they must connect to the emotional codes and patterns that are understood and shared by the audience. Uncovering how those shared codes work emotionally leads to a greater understanding of the early modern emotional codes in general. One such emotional code that I discuss is related to the powerful influence of humanist education on speech and writing in Shakespeare's time. Moving the passions through speech was a central tenet of humanist teaching on rhetoric, and, as an embellishment of speech, colour was thought to heighten affect in an audience. Previous studies of early modern rhetoric and the passions have often failed to acknowledge that moving the passions by speech was bound up integrally with both the mind and the body. My book respects that connection by paying particular attention to the embodied nature of emotions in Shakespeare's work, for instance, through an examination of the movements of colour in the face, and how these relate to the passions of the mind. An examination of conventional interpretations of facial colouring and its changes, combined with the influence of humanist rhetorical education and contemporary concerns about artificial embellishment of the face, has uncovered subtleties of emotional expression in Shakespeare which both subvert or collude with early modern English orthodoxies of gender and morality.

Many studies examining early modern emotions focus on humoral theory. As it is a large part of the medical canon of the period it provides many opportunities for analysing the colour register within an emotions framework. My book includes vision and imagination in that analysis to allow for a fuller appreciation of the use of colour within these theories. Reference to colour in early modern ideas of the body and of clothing has generated a fuller understanding of the balance and complexity of feelings in the emotional relationships Shakespeare represents. Within the emotional paradigm of the body and its coverings, colour sometimes offers a subversive insight which is not always immediately apparent. Colour also augments and inflects the force of emotional transactions in the malleable relationship between the body and the environment. Clothing forms part of that environment in a unique way because of its close proximity to the body, and the mind, and by its association with the emotions of a person. My final chapter demonstrates the influential ways in which early modern visual and cultural chromatic commonplaces shaped and enhanced emotional patterns in the plays. Understanding the contextual import of changes in contemporary terminology, social context, and the visual culture for analysing the relation of colours to the passions offers new possibilities of emotional insight and affect in reading and viewing Shakespeare. Within this discussion, I considered the chromatic register deployed in relation to race since this is an influencing factor in emotional responses to black people in the early modern context.

My work has focused on plays that offer diverse features to aid the cultural analysis which I was undertaking. However, further work in this field could uncover similar depths of emotional registers in other Shakespearean works. I explain in my introduction how the colour red could be associated with blood. This association, and the emotional range of meanings it brings, invites further investigation in Shakespearean works. For example, in *Macbeth*, 'blood' and 'bloody' are mentioned 40 times. The reference gains weight and force once Macbeth, realising his situation, conflates literal and metaphorical 'blood': 'No, this my hand will rather/ The multitudinous seas incarnadine, / Making the green, one red' (2.2.62–4). An investigation into context and emotional weight of colour used in the play would thus be likely to yield a deeper understanding of the emotional resonances that play. Examining the work of other early modern playwrights might offer further research questions, such as why Shakespeare concentrated colour terms within his emotional register, when not all early modern playwrights were similarly inclined. For example, Ben Jonson, even in moments of heightened emotionality, does not employ many colour terms in his work, despite producing works that create emotional connections, albeit through other means ([1596–1637] 1981).

It has been necessary in my work to avoid supposing that a common symbolic language linking colour and emotion existed in the early modern period; such a reductive belief would deny the rich and individual nature of emotion and its expression. Rather, my detailed analysis of the five plays in this book offers original ways of reading Shakespeare and early modern literature, through a completely new look at his colour symbolism and its emotional effects. My approach also allows for the possibility of opening up new interpretations of his works, and those of other playwrights, on a broad scale. Likewise, the approach could also be used to examine other vectors of emotional influences, which might contribute to our understanding of disparate emotional communities, drawing as it does on a variety vof intellectual and cultural frameworks. Although colour has always remained mutable in meaning, I hope that by paying particular attention to its multivalent role in Shakespeare's time, this book has uncovered emotional significances that both allows for a deeper understanding of early modern modes of feeling and heightens the experience of Shakespeare's drama for the modern audience. By linking colour and emotion, I hope both readers and playgoers may appreciate the subtle ways we can enrich our understanding of both the detail and the broader experience of early modern plays. In the words of Richard Haydocke, '[b]ut to conclude these significations of colours, blacke and all other colours signifie good or euill, as they are rightly applyed' (1598, 114).

References

Haydocke, Richard, trans. 1598. *A Tracte Containing the Artes of Curious Paintinge, Caruinge & Buildinge*. By Io. Paul Lomatius. Oxford: Joseph Barnes.

Jonson, Ben. (1596–1637) 1981. *The Complete Works of Ben Jonson*. Edited by G. A. Wilkes. Oxford: Oxford University Press.

Shakespeare, William. (1606) 2015. *Macbeth*. Edited by Sandra Clark and Pamela Mason. London: Bloomsbury Arden Shakespeare.

Index

Note: Page numbers followed by "n" refer to end notes.

affection 6, 7, 10, 11, 20, 46, 47, 52, 82, 86, 91, 99, 109, 117, 124, 125, 126, 132, 157
anger 3, 9, 56, 83, 92, 104, 118, 119, 132, 159, 160
Anglicus, Bartholomaeus 9, 49–51, 53, 80, 87, 128
Anglin, Emily 84, 96
anxiety 40, 57, 73, 119, 141, 150, 151, 153, 156, 157
apparel *see* clothing
Arikha, Noga 81, 101, 106n3
Aristotle 10, 11, 19, 27, 151
Ascham, Roger 39
azure 92

Bartels, Emily C. 144
Baumbach, Sibylle 64, 68, 74, 74n3, 142
black 9, 11, 17, 25–26, 31–33, 35–37, 39, 49, 57, 62, 64–66, 80–82, 84, 87, 92–93, 95–97, 101, 105, 109, 119, 130, 131, 141–143, 144, 146, 148, 154, 157, 158, 160, 162
blood 8–9, 11, 17–18, 23, 25, 26, 29, 30, 32, 37, 45, 51, 54, 68, 70, 82–84, 86, 91–93, 101, 102, 105, 130, 145, 152, 155–162, 171
blue 87, 92
body 2, 5–7, 13, 30, 38, 40, 49–50, 54, 56, 80–81, 87–90, 101, 106, 109–135, 150, 170; imprinting of 120–122; porous 57–58, 123; vulnerable 122, 124
Bourdieu, Pierre 4–5
Bright, Timothy 80, 101
brown 54, 59

Chaucer, Geoffrey 56, 114
choler 11, 51, 54, 80–84, 91–94, 102, 104, 105, 129, 130, 159
Cicero 19–22, 25
cloth 106n4, 109, 112, 134n11; branched velvet 118, 127, 134n9; linen 154; taffeta 112; ingrain 113
clothes *see* clothing
clothing 13, 26, 55, 70, 83, 96, 109–135, 142, 170; stocking 97, 119, 124–132; veil 113, 117, 134n6
Coeffeteau, Nicholas 45–47, 131
colour: arc 14, 140–141, 155–162; associations 7–8, 24, 29, 127, 130, 139–140, 145, 149; cultural phenomenon 7–12, 127, 129, 130, 140, 141; Humours (*see* humoral theory); memory 8, 83, 85, 87, 91, 121, 131, 151; scientific theories 80–85
concealment 71, 109–110
conscience 84–85, 89–90, 102
Corredera, Vanessa 143
cosmetics 9, 46, 53, 55–58, 66, 68, 74, 99, 113, 147; paint 35, 55–56, 58, 61–62, 68, 113, 147
crimson 30, 56, 90
Crooke, Helkiah 80, 86–87
cross-dressing 111, 115, 116, 117
cultural commonplaces 2, 13, 139–168

Dadabhoy, Ambereen 142, 143, 152, 163
Dawson, Lesel 62, 69
desire 7, 11, 20, 31, 47, 49, 51, 59, 60, 62, 113, 117–120, 122, 127, 128, 129, 130, 132, 139, 151

Index

devil 35, 37, 56, 66, 81, 98, 102, 114, 120, 145, 146–147, 152, 160, 163
Dickson, Vernon Guy 28
dread 9, 22, 51, 54, 80, 92
Drew-Bear, Annette 52, 60

Elam, Keir 92, 117, 119, 148
embarrassment 61, 113, 130
emblem 12, 130, 133, 140, 150, 153–155
emotion: counterfeit 96, 103, 113; embodied 6, 170; emotional communities 4, 5, 171; emotional control 4, 20, 48, 71, 83, 87–91, 94, 95, 104, 159; emotional register 4, 12, 21, 23, 24, 30, 34, 40, 52, 68, 93, 106, 110, 117, 140, 145, 156, 169, 171; emotive 1, 2, 4, 6, 92, 149, 150, 162; genuine 1, 8, 94; methodology 2–7; mobilising 6, 27, 95; naming 6, 23, 38, 48, 63, 139; practice 5, 48, 139; performance 48, 71, 88, 90, 91–95, 96, 99, 103, 104, reason 20, 23, 56, 58, 60, 70, 83, 85, 86, 87–91, 100, 102, 104, 105, 116, 126, 155; regulation 20, 48, 71, 85, 95, 147, 159; senses 25, 60, 79–108, 129, 152; transactions 2–5, 8, 12, 18, 48, 79, 110, 117, 129, 133, 170
Enterline, Lynn 3, 18, 20
Escolme, Bridget 111
eye 46–48, 58, 60–64, 66–67, 73, 79–80, 85–88, 91, 94–95, 100–102, 125, 126, 129, 132, 139, 145, 158, 161; duplicity 37; sight 7, 9, 13, 23, 58, 60, 79, 85–86, 102, 125, 139; vision 10, 48–49, 59–61, 73, 79, 81, 85–87, 91, 96, 100, 106, 125, 139, 170

face 1–3, 9, 12, 30, 33, 37, 45–78, 82, 99, 100, 103, 113, 117, 121, 129, 153–54, 163, 170; blushing 3–4, 26, 30, 36–37, 39, 45–46, 53, 66, 69, 70, 100, 116, 157, 162; complexion 3, 32, 36, 39, 46, 49–58, 60–62, 64–69, 70–71, 74, 82, 84, 91–94, 100, 104, 118, 124, 126, 149, 153–54, 157; duplicity 24, 37, 50, 53, 55, 58, 61, 64, 70–72, 89, 97, 157; perfection 54–58, 61, 63, 71, 124, 162; visage 51, 58, 59–62, 94, 95, 98, 152–53, 161

fashion 66, 99, 110, 112, 119, 121, 123–125, 129, 133
fear 4, 9, 17, 20, 23, 53, 62, 66, 72, 79, 82, 89, 99, 112, 119, 123, 132, 150, 151, 156, 160, 161
Fernie, Ewan 130, 132, 133
flame 10, 92, 101, 124–25

Galen 81; galenic theory 1, 81
gender mutability 57, 73, 115, 116, 117, 121, 122
gold 10, 24, 29, 32, 36, 39, 70, 117–18, 122, 128, 129
Golding, Arthur 19, 28
Gosson, Stephen 56
green 11, 17, 22–24, 26, 28–29, 46, 48, 51–52, 63–64, 82–83, 97, 109, 110, 118, 119, 127, 139–140, 154, 158–59, 161, 164
grey 30, 95
grief 1, 6, 23, 26, 27, 38, 63, 69, 72, 73, 82, 83, 86, 87, 88, 93, 95–97, 100, 101, 103, 104, 109, 110, 151
gules 92

Habib, Imtiaz 141
habitus 4–6, 13, 38, 142
Hamet, Muly 142
hand(s) 27, 28, 29, 32, 33, 34, 38, 40, 70, 72, 84, 98, 104, 113, 150, 152, 162, 171
handkerchief 150–152, 160, 161, 162, 164
happiness 99, 115, 121, 127, 131, 150, 156
Harington, Sir John 81, 84, 100, 103
hate 7, 86, 114, 160, 163
Haydocke, Richard 9–12, 57, 127, 128, 149, 156, 171
Hilliard, Nicholas 10
Hobgood, Allison P. 131, 132
hope 11, 12, 63, 117, 127, 128, 139
hose *see* clothing
humanism 38, 39, 40, 170; and education 18–21; and morality 31–38
humoral theory 1, 2, 7, 53, 54, 57, 79, 80–84, 85, 86, 90–93, 96, 97, 99–102, 104–106, 118, 154, 158, 159, 170
Hunter, G. K. 133, 143
Huxtable, Michael J. 9

Index 175

imagination 13, 30, 83, 85, 90–92, 106, 125, 127, 129, 161, 170

jealousy 29, 73, 102, 119, 128–129, 139–140, 159, 161
Jones, Ann Rosalind and Peter Stallybrass 110, 115, 122
Jonson, Ben 128, 171
joy 11, 31, 35, 71, 118, 128, 129, 139, 159

Karim-Cooper, Farah 35, 48, 57, 61, 63, 89
Knecht, Ross 96, 98

Lemnius, Levinus 50, 52, 54, 82
Leo, John 142
Linthicum, M. Channing 128, 129
Loomba, Ania 39, 64, 142, 143, 159
love 3, 4, 11, 29, 37, 47, 51–53, 59–65, 67, 68–73, 83, 86, 97–100, 103, 104, 109, 113, 116–18, 120, 122–24, 126–132, 145, 150, 157, 158, 160, 161

make-up *see* cosmetics
Manningham, John 131
masks 46, 53, 59, 60, 70, 71, 73, 74; visor 72
material objects 150, 151
Matt, Susan 3, 4
Maund, Barry 8
McNamer, Sarah 2, 4
Meek, Richard 6, 93, 148
melancholy 10, 11, 29, 49, 51, 54, 59, 62, 67–8, 80–84, 88, 91, 93, 95–99, 100–105, 109, 110, 112, 119, 124, 129, 130, 156
Moor 8, 31, 33, 36–39, 81, 100, 141–148, 151, 152, 156, 158, 159, 161, 163
morality 1, 11, 14, 27, 28, 31–38, 39, 57, 91, 100, 111, 112, 149, 150, 157, 170
motley 119, 123, 125
Munday, Anthony 87, 112, 114, 125

Neely, Carol Thomas 98

Ovid 23, 28–30, 32, 33, 34, 38, 40, 116, 128

pale 3, 9, 18, 30, 32, 34, 35, 37, 50–52, 54, 56, 69, 72, 74, 79–80, 90, 97, 99, 101, 105, 124, 154, 161, 163
painting 1, 9–10, 11, 55–58, 65–66, 74, 99, 103, 113, 141, 147–148
Parker, Patricia 81, 100
passions 2, 3, 7, 10, 12, 40, 46, 47, 49, 53–54, 58, 60, 64, 79, 80, 82, 85–88, 90, 95–97, 101, 103–105, 115, 118, 122, 124, 128, 130, 140, 147, 152, 154, 159, 160, 163, 170
Paster, Gail Kern 12, 57, 83, 92
Pearson, Meg F. 28, 39, 40
Petrarchan 54, 65, 70, 72, 124, 145, 160, 162; courtly lover 110
phlegmatic 51, 54, 80–83, 101, 103, 104
physiognomy 2, 13, 53, 62, 64, 142, 154, 169
pitch: as colour 32, 60–62, 146
Plett, Heinrich 32, 60–62, 146
Poitevin, Kimberley 56, 57
Pollard, Tanya 55, 58, 93
Pory, John 142
Potter, Ursula 51
pride 3, 29, 32, 36, 39, 56, 60, 82, 105, 114, 117–120, 124–26, 129, 132
Prynne, William 112
purple 10, 11, 104, 120

Quintilian 19, 22, 23, 27, 28, 55

race 14, 35, 46, 57, 58, 140, 142, 143–148, 159, 170; racism 35, 66
rage 83, 93, 101, 102, 103
Rainolde, Richard 23, 25
Rainolds, John 111, 114, 116
reason *see* emotion
red 3, 8–11, 17, 18, 23, 25, 26, 28–32, 34, 35, 37, 46, 52–54, 56, 58, 66, 68, 73, 74, 80, 82–84, 87, 92, 93, 101–103, 105, 110, 113, 124, 125, 145, 150, 152, 156, 157, 159–162, 164, 171
Reddy, William 3, 4, 7
revenge 11, 23, 28, 29, 31, 34, 37, 40, 83, 85, 93, 156, 160
rhetoric 6, 14, 17–44, 58, 61, 64, 74, 144, 151, 169, 170; *Imitatio* 26–31, 40, 145, oratory 17–19, 21–23, 26–31, 40
rhetorical device 21–26, 28, 139; argument 19, 25, 34; *chria* 24; *destruccion* 23–24, embellishment

18, 21–22, 30, 40, 55, 74, 89, 147, 170; *enargeia* 23, 30; narracion 25; trope 26, 89, 97, 117, 124, 145, 147, 164
Rosenwein, Barbara 3, 4, 5
russet 72, 125

sable 92, 102, 103
sadness 11, 67, 68, 80, 91, 98, 109
Sandys, George 70
sanguine 10, 35, 80, 81, 83, 100, 105
Scheer, Monique 5, 6, 18, 20, 40, 139, 147
self-control 4, 20, 48, 49, 71, 83, 87, 88, 90, 94, 95, 104, 159
self-fashioning 19, 20, 33, 73, 74, 110; identity 9, 20, 27, 33, 40, 71, 73, 109, 111, 112, 118, 121, 122, 143, 144, 163; individual 5, 7, 20, 31, 61, 80, 82, 83, 88, 89, 92; inwardness 9, 49, 50, 51, 53, 54, 60, 80, 82, 97, 101, 105, 131, 143
Shakespeare, William, works: *As You Like It* 3; *Comedy of Errors* 50; *Coriolanus* 105; *Hamlet* 2, 13, 56, 79–108, 110; *King Henry IV, Part 1* 50, 81; *Henry V* 156; *Julius Caesar* 91; *King Lear* 85; *Love's Labour's Lost* 13, 45—78, 128, 161; *Macbeth* 105, 111, 171; *The Merchant of Venice* 1, 6, 116; *Much Ado About Nothing* 45, 69; *Othello* 11, 13, 139–168; *Rape of Lucrece* 3; *Romeo and Juliet* 52, 161; *Timon of Athens* 11; *Titus Andronicus* 13, 17–44, 50, 143, 144; *Twelfth Night* 109–138
shame 4, 9, 26, 30, 36, 37, 39, 45, 47–49, 56, 59, 62–66, 68–73, 100, 103–104, 113, 118–120, 129–133, 157
Sidney, Sir Philip 129
Simmons, Davis R. 8
social position 89, 111, 112, 118, 122, 130, 132, 141, 143, 145, 163
sorrow 26, 29, 30, 31, 35, 37, 62, 73, 82, 86, 87, 103, 123, 161
Stubbes, Philip 55, 56, 115, 125, 126, 154
sumptuary laws 110–112, 118, 122, 133

tawny 36, 54, 66, 125
textiles 110, 150, 151

unheard voice 17, 27

Vaughan, Virginia Mason 141, 143
vengeful 37, 103, 132, 160
visual culture 13, 140, 141, 148–150, 164, 169, 170

white 9, 11–12, 17, 23, 28, 31, 35–37, 46, 49, 51–54, 56, 58, 64, 68, 72, 74, 80–82, 84, 86–87, 100, 102, 103, 109, 113, 114, 119, 124, 125, 142–145, 148, 149, 154, 156–158, 160, 162–164
Whitney, Geoffrey 12, 149, 153–155
will 85, 86, 88–89, 91, 93, 97, 105
Wilson, Thomas 6, 21
Wright, Thomas 45, 83, 85–86, 88, 90–91, 123, 140, 148

yellow 10, 11, 29, 54, 73, 80, 82, 83, 87, 92, 109, 110, 119, 124, 126–132, 159